BIBLE-BASED
PRAYER
POWER

OTHER BOOKS BY KEN ANDERSON

WHERE TO FIND IT IN THE BIBLE

BOLD AS A LAMB

HIMALAYAN HEARTBEAT

GAMES FOR ALL OCCASIONS

BIBLE-BASED PRAYER POWER

Using Relevant
Scripture to Pray
with Confidence
for All Your
Needs

KEN ANDERSON

THOMAS NELSON PUBLISHERS®
Nashville

Published in Nashville, Tennessee, by Thomas Nelson, Inc.

Unless otherwise noted, Scripture quotations are from THE NEW KING JAMES VERSION. Copyright © 1979, 1980, 1982, Thomas Nelson, Inc., Publishers.

Scripture quotations noted KJV are from THE KING JAMES VERSION of the Bible.

Library of Congress Cataloging-in-Publication Data

Anderson, Ken.
    Bible-based prayer power : using relevant scripture to pray with confidence for all your needs / Ken Anderson.
      p. cm.
    Includes bibliographical references and index.
    ISBN 0-7852-6869-3 (pbk.)
    1. Prayer—Christianity. 2. Bible—Devotional use. 3. Bible—Indexes. I. Title.

BV215 .A53 2000
248.3'2—dc21

00—022510
CIP

Printed in the United States of America.
1 2 3 4 5 6 QPV 05 04 03 02 01 00

To
our daughter
Margaret,
for whom
God has
remarkably
answered
prayer

Contents

1. Introducing STEPS   3

2. The Origin of STEPS   11

3. Prototypes to Get You Started   19

Topics   43

Appendix A: Proof Positive   287

Appendix B: STEPS Spin-Offs   289

Topics Index   291

STEPS Nuggets Index   294

About the Author   295

The chief purpose of
prayer is that God may be
glorified in the answer.

—R. A. Torrey

1

Introducing STEPS

Welcome to STEPS, new ideas about prayer that are as old as the Bible.

STEPS is an acronym formed from the identifying statement that Scripture Teaches Effective Prayer Strategies. Through investigation and implementation, this new approach has enriched for me the meaning and function of prayer beyond anything I could have anticipated or imagined.

> More things are wrought by prayer than this world dreams of.
>
> —ALFRED, LORD TENNYSON

As I shall more fully explain, STEPS involves reinforcing your prayers with precepts and promises from the Bible. In the discovery, development, and use of this new method, I have learned two important truths.

I have learned what prayer is not. It is not dialing Heaven 911 in times of emergency, imploring God to come to our rescue, solve all our problems, heal, and fortify. Nor is prayer like a letter to Santa, listing our wants, which God is to promptly provide, plus making known our wishes for His priority attention.

Instead, I am learning that when I pray, I become like a lamb in the arms of its shepherd, which is a relationship more intimate than the most endearing of human involvements. It is the kind of fellowship Jesus indicated when in John 15:4, He said to His disciples, "Abide in Me, and I in you." This abiding involves basic trust in which my supreme desire is to please Him, even in the requests I make to Him. I desire more to please Him than to seek favors from Him. If my prayers are not answered as I would wish them to be, I can say, "In everything give thanks; for this is the will of God in Christ Jesus for you" (1 Thess. 5:18).

> Prayer opens the heart to God.
>
> —JOHN BUNYAN

For many years, I struggled with prayer. I knelt by my bed at night as if that formality might have virtue of some sort. In later years, I paced back and forth in my room or went for long walks during which I tried to pray. I never felt at ease, no matter what position or procedure I used.

Time seemed to drag, I often became bored while in prayer. Once I even wondered if my watch had stopped. Most difficult of all was group prayer. I have never felt comfortable talking to God in the presence of others.

Developing a prayer notebook helped me a bit. I was even commissioned to produce a prayer notebook for the small denomination of which I was a member. It was impressively published, and I experienced a moment of pride when I first held it in my hands and thumbed through it. I tried to use it, but the old boredom syndrome prevailed and I soon set it aside.

At a conference I attended, an all-night prayer meeting was announced, beginning at ten-thirty. I estimated some fifty people were there. I participated—once—but words seemed to knot up on my tongue. We were all kneeling in the conference chapel, and by eleven, my knees began to ache. Around midnight, a few people arose to leave. The leader rebuked them kindly, urging them to stay. Two or three remained another half hour or so.

One man fell asleep and snored loudly.

In spite of the leader's admonition, people continued to leave, and by two o'clock, intervals between prayers had grown longer and longer. After an abrupt benediction, we were dismissed

The memory of that extended prayer time lingered long. It troubled me.

Years later, passing through London on my way to a European film assignment, I was invited to give a midnight report to the all-night prayer meeting of a large mission. When I arrived, people were having a coffee break. They seemed happy, relaxed, purposeful.

"One seldom hears of all-night prayer meetings anymore," I said to the director of the mission.

"We do it every month," he replied. "We begin at nine o'clock, and it takes us at least until four in the morning to pray for all the people, all the families, remembering everyone individually by name, plus all the activities in which these people are involved. There are more than two thousand of them."

I think this group's experience was the exception, not the rule. I'm not speaking against lengthy times of prayer. I'm simply document-ing the problem I had for many years.

But then the Lord brought STEPS into my life. By its very format, it vitalized my times of prayer.

1. STEPS is an easily understood and applied procedure.

2. Related promises from the Bible reinforce people, circumstances, and needs in my prayers.

3. I pray reverently but informally, enjoying warm rapport with the Lord.

You, too, can benefit from using the STEPS method.

Here is an example of STEPS in action.

Let's suppose you are under much stress. Your job gets you down. Money is scarce. You may also be the victim of demeaning gossip. Having checked the topics section of this book, you proceed alphabetically to *Stress.* There you find several selections for your consideration. Realizing that your Lord has a whimsical as well as a solemn nature, and that He wishes to relate to you in your humanness rather than any kind of stuffy piety, you consider initially reinforcing your prayer with the listing "In up to your neck, Psalm 69:1": "Save me, O God! For the waters have come up to my neck."

> Effective prayers are God's promises breathed out of human hearts.
>
> —CHARLES SPURGEON

You could then pray in this way: "That says it for me, Lord—up to my neck and then some. You know what kind of day I've had. Please help me to settle down. Help me to get a better grip on myself."

Next, you could turn to another item under *Stress:* "Your Lord can handle your load, Psalm 55:22": "Cast your burden on the LORD, and He shall sustain you."

"That's a new one," you perhaps pray. "You mean, I actually transfer these tensions and pressures onto You? It's like learning a new language. Okay, I'll give it a try."

Here is where you begin a new approach to prayer. Checking the *Deliverance* references, you find Psalm 57:2: "I will cry out to God . . . who performs all things for me." Your prayer may continue like this: "Just the way it says in the Bible here, Lord, I throw these problems onto You. I don't know how it happens, but by faith, I do it because the Bible tells me to do it. Your Word assures me that it is You who performs all things for me."

In the exercise of your faith, you take the Bible at face value. You name your tension points as you cast your burden on the Lord. In this brief example of prayer concerning stress, your procedure would be to quietly wait. Let the Lord calm you with His gentleness and diminish your stress until it is gone.

You will develop expertise as you become familiar with and practiced in the STEPS method. In another chapter, I offer a series of prototypes to help you develop your prayers.

Heavy stuff? Not necessarily. Just because something is new doesn't make it complicated.

STEPS is not a gimmick or an attempt to be clever. It is a new approach for talking to God that lies at the heart of the Bible.

CORRECT USE OF BIBLE PROMISES

Here are simple guidelines to assist you, especially when you face urgent circumstances.

Need Help?

If you question your faith, the dependability of the Bible, and the value of prayer, turn to Appendix A: Proof Positive (page 287).

1. Spend several moments with John 16:13, inviting the Holy Spirit to guide you into the correct understanding and use of Scripture.

2. As you pray, quote the promise you consider using, and ask the Lord to help you.

3. Consult one of the standard Bible commentaries, such as *Matthew Henry's Commentary on the Whole Bible* or *Jamieson, Fausset and Brown's Commentary,* for clearer understanding. You may find them at Christian bookstores, your church library, or most public libraries.

4. Avoid hurrying. In quiet meditation, wait upon the Lord to guide you.

5. Rest your case with James 1:5–6.

> Prayer is the key that opens the storehouse of God's infinite grace and power.
>
> —R. A. TORREY

There is no need for apprehension. As you experience the vitality of 2 Peter 3:18 and "grow in the grace and knowledge of our Lord and Savior Jesus Christ," your motivations will become increasingly positive. You will be comfortable with both the Old Testament and the New Testament, developing expertise in "rightly dividing the word of truth."

May these be holy moments as you contemplate the new spiritual agenda discussed in *Bible-Based Prayer Power.* Let your foremost desire be an ever-intensifying personal relationship with your Lord. In Colossians 1:9–10, Paul prayed for his friends "that you may be filled with the knowledge of His will in all wisdom and spiritual understanding; that you may walk worthy of the Lord, fully pleasing Him, being fruitful in every good work and increasing in the knowledge of God."

You dare not miss what the Lord is telling you in these quotations! You can be "fully pleasing Him."

It will happen when—through prayer and widened understanding of the Bible—you are increasing in the knowledge of God.

Have a great walk!

Here's What Can Happen to You

Your Bible can become the *central force* in your life when you pray.

Your Bible can give you *intimacy with your Lord* as you pray.

Your Bible can inspire *boldness and confidence* while you pray.

Your Bible can assure *answers and understanding* after you pray.

Your Bible can *increase your faith* because you pray.

2

The Origin of STEPS

It may be helpful for you to know the events that caused the STEPS method to become such a vital part of my Christian experience.

For several summers, I served as one of the chaplains in the Baseball Chapel ministry, which touches the lives of many professional athletes with the influence of the Bible. My first chapel assignment was with the Chicago Cubs. We met in their conditioning room at Wrigley Field where I used as my pulpit the seat of an exercise bicycle.

With no thought of selecting a theme significant to myself, but searching for something catchy out of pro baseball jargon, I chose as my subject "The Bible Is God's Contract."

It was contract time for several of the Cubbies, and they listened intently. Using Proverbs 3:5–6, I showed the men what God expects of us and what we can expect of Him when we ask for guidance.

Your Part	*God's Part*
Trust in the LORD with all your heart, and lean not on your own understanding; in all your ways acknowledge Him,	And He shall direct your paths.

On a hunch, I had made extra copies of my notes in case any of the players wished to have the Bible references for review. To my delight, nearly every man took one, then headed out to the field for pregame warm-ups. A member of the pitching staff lingered.

"My wife and I have a neighborhood Bible study," he told me. He kept glancing at the notes.

A half dozen copies remained, and I gave them to him.

A year later, I received a chapel assignment with the Oakland A's. Entering the dressing room, I was startled to hear someone call my name. It was the same ballplayer who, during the winter months, had been traded to the Athletics by the Cubs.

"My wife and I are still working on that thought of the Bible being God's contract," he told me. "You've got something there. Are you planning to do anything with it?"

I don't remember the thought ever crossing my mind until then. I had just completed my book *Where to Find It in the Bible,* and as I browsed its pages, I realized there were troves of contractual statements in the Bible. I began seeking them out and using them in my prayers. I found the procedure most pleasant and, in many instances, productive.

If you'd like to experiment, consider Philippians 4:6–7, one of the most prominent prayer promises in the Bible, especially for use during troubled times. The following example shows how you might pray as you allow the Bible to reinforce what you say to your heavenly Father. (In the example, the Scripture phrase is in italics, followed by the suggested prayer.)

> *Be anxious for nothing,*
>
> But I am anxious, Lord. Tied up in knots. I can't get rid of my anxiety. Not in my own strength. I've got to have help . . . Your help.

but in everything by prayer and supplication, with thanksgiving, let your requests be made known to God;

I don't understand the supplication part, Lord. Please teach me. You know my biggest problem. I'm terrified that the boss is coming down any day now to evaluate my department. But You tell me not to worry. The only way that can happen is for You to take the worry away. With thanksgiving, the Bible says. Okay, by faith I thank You for the help You are going to give me. You promise, Lord. Help me to believe Your promise.

and the peace of God, which surpasses all understanding, will guard your hearts and minds through Christ Jesus.

You said it, Lord. It's in the terms of Your contract with me. I'm promised peace instead of anxiety. I trust You to do what You say You will do.

This example is from one of the Bible's most familiar passages, Psalm 23 (the Scripture phrase is in italics, followed by the suggested prayer):

The LORD is my shepherd;

My Shepherd. I like the sound of it, Lord, but I admit I've never really understood it before, much less experienced it. But I want it now. I want You for my Shepherd, and I want to be one of Your lambs. Please take control of my thinking. Please make it happen.

I shall not want.

I know it's true. You will take care of me anywhere, under any circumstances. Help me to get it into my head, to be able to believe fully.

He makes me to lie down in green pastures; He leads me beside the still waters.

What's this all about? Life's no flower garden. I don't expect it to be. But as in that planning meeting where they put the scissors to my proposal, You helped me hang in there. I was really shocked. But thank You, Lord, for helping me enough that I didn't shout any more than I did.

He restores my soul;

I stray and come back, O Lord. That's where I so often miss it. Show me what You mean when You say You restore my soul. You promise restoration, right here in Your Word. Help me to believe it and receive it.

He leads me in the paths of righteousness for His name's sake.

Lord, I'm sinful to the core. It's for "His name's sake," Your righteousness in me, that makes the difference.

Yea, though I walk through the valley of the shadow of death, I will fear no evil; for You are with me; Your rod and Your staff, they comfort me.

I've always had this thing about death. But here it isn't the valley of death. It's the valley of the *shadow* of death. I want to live a long time, but I realize now that when death comes, it's through the shadow into Your presence.

You prepare a table before me in the presence of my enemies; You anoint my head with oil; my cup runs over.

I live in this secular world, Lord. I can't possibly make it on my own. I didn't realize how available You are. I'm so grateful for all of Your blessings.

Surely goodness and mercy shall follow me all the days of my life; and I will dwell in the house of the LORD forever.

It's not just what You did for me yesterday, Lord, or the plans You have for today. There's tomorrow's blessing. I thank and praise You. All this and heaven too. What a deal!

The following selection from Psalm 139 (vv. 23–24) further demonstrates how you can blend scripture in your prayer. It's one of the best selections in the Bible for searching your heart, examining your motives, and shaping up your thought life.

The prayer is illustrative only. I suggest you have your own STEPS experience with this excellent example. Personalize your prayer vocabulary. Express your feelings. Make it your prayer.

Search me, O God,

When I get down to the reality of what the Bible says here, it scares me. With Your help, I can handle it.

and know my heart;

I mean it, Lord. Know me.

try me, and know my anxieties;

So much pressure. Never sure of myself. I miss half the sermon, wondering—mostly worrying—about Monday. Isn't the Christian life supposed to be better than this?

and see if there is any wicked way in me,

See if I have sins? I have them, Lord. Please make me clean. Being really clean is where it's at. I know that, Lord.

and lead me in the way everlasting.

As Your Word says, You lead me. I will fall flat on my face if I try to make it on my own. Be my Shepherd, my Lord.

This casual approach to God may be awkward for you at first, especially if you're accustomed to the "Thee and Thou" kind of formality. There is nothing wrong with the formal approach as long as it occurs in the intimate spirit I mentioned earlier.

Yes, you are praying to the King of kings and Lord of lords. He understands you in whatever manner you approach Him. The point is that God understands you best when you speak to Him as a child to his father, in this case his heavenly Father!

Words of the Bible, especially verbs, have become stimulating gems of exploration.

On a motion picture assignment in Honduras, for example, I flew one day with a missionary pilot on an hour's jaunt. Reaching for a Bible alongside his flight log, he shouted to me above the din of the single-engine Piper, "When I have good weather and clear passage, I often use flying to fit in some time with the Book."

"Finding any new things?" I asked.

"Sure am," he replied. He handed the Bible to me. "Look up the Thirty-seventh Psalm."

I found the psalm and gestured for the pilot to proceed.

"Read the fourth verse," he said.

Almost shouting, I read, "Delight yourself also in the LORD, and He shall give you the desires of your heart."

At that moment, we hit one of those precarious downdrafts common to Honduran mountain terrain. It was as though the maneuver caused the verse to leap up from the page before my eyes.

"What do you think it means?" the pilot shouted.

"I'm not sure," I replied. "I sometimes have desires that don't really qualify for answers."

"The Bible isn't talking about *our* desires," he said. He checked his instrument panel and made a brief course correction. "It hit me between the eyes a few weeks ago. I had a weather delay at Minas de Oro. It came to me as clear as the sky is today. What God is talking about here involves the desires He wants to give us."

"You've got my attention," I called to him.

"You see," he continued, "when we delight in the Lord, He can give us our desires. When our prayers are based on the desires He gives us, we always pray in His will."

I began sensing the glimmer of a helpful concept, tangible assistance for my chronic hang-ups with prayer.

Soon after, I told my wife, "What we need is an anchor verse."

"Something from the Bible that shows us how to make our prayers more effective," she added.

She with her Bible, I with mine, we began an extended search. Both of us came up empty. With assistance from several of our children, especially a daughter-in-law, we developed the acronym STEPS for Scripture Teaches Effective Prayer Strategies.

But we needed a basic text, something as distinct as the Ten Commandments, yet as simple as John 3:16.

"Why don't you call John Davis?" my wife suggested.

A friend of many years, Dr. John Davis was formerly president of Grace College and Seminary. He now teaches Hebrew and Old Testament. His humility camouflages the intellectual disparity between us and enables us to enjoy long-lasting camaraderie.

I explained STEPS and told him of our need for an anchor verse.

"What you're looking for," he questioned, "either Old Testament or New, is where we are told to link our prayers with related quotes from the Bible?"

"Exactly," I responded.

He thought a moment. Then he said, "How about what Jesus said in John 15:7?" He quoted it from memory: "If you abide in Me, and My words abide in you, you will ask what you desire, and it shall be done for you."

So there it was! STEPS—Scripture Teaches Effective Prayer Strategies. A sunburst of newness warmed my heart!

3

Prototypes to Get You Started

The following prototypes were developed to help you more clearly understand the STEPS method and effectively put it to use. You may want to test a couple of them in times of personal prayer. They are, of necessity, abbreviated.

However, the sooner you launch out on your own, using the topics to construct personal prayers, the more meaningful STEPS will be for you. That is especially true when from personal reading of the Bible, you catalog prayer references for yourself.

"The word of the LORD is right," the Bible tells us in Psalm 33:4, "and all His work is done in truth." Move a few pages ahead to Psalm 119:133, and make the prayer your own: "Direct my steps by Your word."

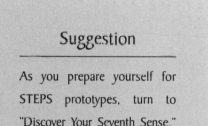

Suggestion

As you prepare yourself for STEPS prototypes, turn to "Discover Your Seventh Sense," page 91, and "To Whom Am I Speaking?" page 243.

Mystical? No. Unfamiliar? Initially yes.

Be patient. Be assured that, as you become increasingly familiar and thus more comfortable with STEPS, you will experience life in provocative dimensions. You will become a new and improved human being.

You may need to schedule time for prayer. Even an alarm clock loses some of its dissonance when it summons one of God's children to the joy of intercession.

PROTOTYPE I: MORNING PRAYER

Topics in this section were chosen for illustration and instruction from the selections listed under *Intro, Praise, Asking,* and *Attitude.* Browse the Topics Index (pages 293–96) to note the numerous other areas you could have used if you were building the prayer for yourself. In this case I chose the Psalm selection.

INTRO

Good morning, Lord

PSALM 5:1–3—"Give ear to my words, O LORD . . . Give heed to the voice of my cry, . . . for to You I will pray. My voice You shall hear in the morning, O LORD; . . . and I will look up."

When you use the STEPS method, morning prayer can become a refreshing, inspiring way to start every day. Your prayer could begin, "Good morning, Lord. I'm grateful for the good night's sleep. I thank You for it. Such a wonderful body You have given me. 'My voice You

---

Prayer brings us to the holy Throne Room of God, where we join all those who are there to worship and adore Him.
—FLOSSIE MCNEILL

shall hear in the morning,' I realize, is Your invitation for me to pray."

Do you feel uncomfortable speaking in such familiar terms with your Lord? Approach Him in awe if you prefer. That is your option. But the closer you come to Him in relationship, the more casual your prayers are likely to become. I like to note what James, the brother of Jesus, wrote in his New Testament letter: "Abraham . . . was called the friend of God" (2:23).

Isn't that what you want in your relationship with the Lord—neither frivolous nor formal but friend speaking to Friend?

Morning prayer lends itself especially to praise, so we turn again to the topics and find an entry for *Praise*.

PRAISE

Thinking about God's greatness

PSALM 86:10–12—"You are great, and do wondrous things; You alone are God. Teach me Your way, O LORD; I will walk in Your truth . . . I will praise You, O LORD my God, with all my heart, and I will glorify Your name forevermore."

Perhaps look out your window as the beauty of the morning spreads before you, then pray in this manner: "That sunrise, Lord, is always on schedule. If You bring the sun above the horizon at exactly the right moment, I know You will do great things in my life. I praise You for the wonders of Your creation as I see them now. Be the Creator of the corrections and improvements I need in my lifestyle.

"Lord, be the Creator of my day. Let me walk in Your truth. I've got the meaning straight. 'Your truth' simply means what the Bible tells me. I can't do it without Your help. As I go to work, and all through the day, please bring to my mind the assurances from the Bible that will be my sure guidance for this day."

Unless you have memorized scriptures about guidance, you will need promises with you. Even as part of your prayer, turn to the section of *Guidance* topics, and jot down thoughts from the Bible to help you.

ASKING

The Lord invites you to ask

1 KINGS 3:5—"God said, 'Ask! What shall I give you?'"

Do just that. Remembering Psalm 37:4, in which you invite the Lord to give you desires that please Him, open your heart fully.

Tell the Lord exactly what you want. Remember your family. Friends. Tasks of the day. Anticipated or potential difficulties. When you pray in God's will, He wishes to grant your requests. He wants to bless and enrich you.

Select from the topics special needs for the day. Let's say, for instance, you want to have a good attitude at your workplace.

> ## STEPS—Scripture Teaches Effective Prayer Strategies
>
> My words abide in you—your Bible.
> Ask what you desire—your prayers.
> It shall be done for you—God's promise.

When you develop your own STEPS prayers, you may, of course, use as many topics as you need.

ATTITUDE

Renewed spirit

PSALM 51:10—"Create in me a clean heart, O God, and renew a steadfast spirit within me."

Try to begin the day with a positive outlook—on yourself, your activities, your encounters, your challenges, everyone and everything. Itemize aspects of the day and relate Psalm 51:10 to them.

Will your prayer be heard? Will it be answered? In proper STEPS procedure, you again consult the topics. You find an *Answer* listing, also *Assurance*. You select Psalm 27:13–14 and proceed.

Be patient when you pray, Psalm 27:13–14: "I would have lost heart, unless I had believed that I would see the goodness of the LORD in the land of the living. Wait on the LORD; be of good courage, and He shall strengthen your heart. Wait, I say, on the LORD!"

Likewise, in the topics section you would find under *Assurance*, Psalm 84:11:

No good thing will He withhold from those who walk uprightly.

Your prayer could be, "Forgive me, Lord. Right now I can't see it, but this is what the Bible says, and I'm depending on You to please give me the confidence I need to rest on it. Amen."

> When I face a very busy day, I pray three hours instead of two.
> —MARTIN LUTHER

PROTOTYPE 2: EVENING PRAYER

Only four topics entries appear in this prototype. If you use this example for a time of prayer, consider browsing the Topics Index for other Bible reinforcement you may choose to use. STEPS is motivational. The more you utilize your own ideas and choices, the sooner STEPS will become your personal prayer procedure.

Always remember the acronym:

Scripture Teaches Effective Prayer Strategies

May God bless you with the realization of the progress you are making:

1. You are using the Bible as your Prayer Book.

2. You are blending Bible promises into your prayers.

3. You are learning to recognize the Lord as your Shepherd.

4. In your prayers, you are speaking to the Lord as to your closest Friend.

Selected for beginning your prayer is another entry from the *Intro* section:

God knows those who trust Him

> NAHUM 1:7—"The LORD is good, a stronghold in the day of trouble; and He knows those who trust in Him."

You could pray: "I surely am one of those who trusts You, Lord. Thanks for seeing me through another day. Teach me how to express my gratitude the way I feel it. Show me how to praise You. Please give me the spirit of a true Christian. Help me get into what the Bible says in 2 Peter 3:18, 'Grow in the grace and knowledge of our Lord and Savior Jesus Christ.'"

Spend a moment in quiet meditation. Think about how you have sensed your Lord's presence through this day. Remember that the most important part of prayer is praise, and let spontaneous praise lift heavenward from your heart.

You could pray in this manner: "I had increased confidence today and I praise You for that. You really were a stronghold when the boss came to my department. You gave me peace and even an opportunity to witness to him. There was some pressure at that staff meeting, but with Your help, as I prayed, I kept my cool. I praise You!"

EVALUATION

Work for the Lord has value

> 1 CORINTHIANS 15:58—"Be steadfast, immovable, always abounding in the work of the Lord, knowing that your labor is not in vain in the Lord."

Day's end brings time for inventory and evaluation. Perhaps you itemized the requests you made in the morning. How did you do during the day? Were there victories, lessons learned, for which you give your Lord praise and gratitude? How about mistakes, failures?

Your Lord understands an expression such as, "I blew it on that one," and responds to, "I'm just not making it in that category. Please help me."

Have your spiritual roots deepened? Be thankful for specific times you sensed the Lord's presence and help.

A quick browse into the topics takes you to *Growth* and 1 Samuel 2:26: "Samuel grew in stature, and in favor both with the LORD and men."

Have you seen growth in your life today? Thank God for it. Have you recognized any areas of weakness where you need help? Lay it on the line!

GRATITUDE

Morning and evening gratefulness

> PSALM 92:1–2—"It is good to give thanks to the LORD, and to sing praises to Your name, O Most High; to declare Your lovingkindness in the morning, and Your faithfulness every night."

STEPS Nugget

GETTING SERIOUS ABOUT PRAYER

Think about developing a STEPS notebook.

Using the topics resource, prepare an outline to follow while you pray. As thoughts come to your mind during prayer, jot them down for later consideration.

You may want to list people and situations for prayer.

As you read your Bible, apart from times of prayer, begin gathering your additional reinforcements. A residual blessing from the STEPS method will be your widening knowledge of the Bible as God's Word impacts and enriches your character and personality.

I like the way Jeremiah put it in his prophetic book when he told the Lord, "Your word was to me the joy and rejoicing of my heart" (15:16).

So may it be for you!

Continue to review the day. Have you remembered to "give thanks to the LORD" for all you have accomplished this day? Especially note His "faithfulness" in specific details. Praise Him for all that has happened from "morning" until "night." You may even find this time of praise conducive to sleep.

SLEEP
Have a sweet sleep

PROVERBS 3:24—"When you lie down, you will not be afraid; yes, you will lie down and your sleep will be sweet. Amen!"

PROTOTYPE 3: ANXIETY

There are eleven Bible quotations under the *Anxiety* entry in the top-ics section. Routinely, you would turn to that resource as you con-struct a STEPS prayer. For the sake of experience, however, let us return again to *Intro,* which has several openers for you to consider.

For instance: "Hear, O LORD, when I cry with my voice! Have mercy also upon me, and answer me. When You said, 'Seek My face,' my heart said to You, 'Your face, LORD, I will seek'" (Ps. 27:7–8).

Face-to-face indicates close fellowship, spiritual intimacy. As Proverbs 18:24 puts it, "There is a friend who sticks closer than a brother." Recognize this intimacy as the bedrock of your prayer. Ask for clear understanding of what such intimacy can mean to prayer.

> The true prayer of faith is hammered out on the anvil of experience.
>
> —PAUL MARTIN

You could pray, "Here I go again, Lord, loaded with anxiety. Here's pretty much the full list." So you tell the Lord your cares and concerns, just as you would share with a close friend. Then turning to the topics, you take a look at the entries for *Trust,* where you find Isaiah 41:10: "Fear not, for I am with you; be not dis-mayed, for I am your God. I will strengthen you, yes, I will help you, I will uphold you with My righteous right hand."

Your prayer could be something like this: "I have wrestled with anxiety so long, Lord. I just can't get on top of it. Please show me how to seek Your face, how to put my complete dependence upon You. I must learn how to trust You, have You strengthen and uphold me, and I can do it only as You teach me."

You turn now to the *Anxiety* section and find John 14:27, the words of Jesus Himself saying: "Peace I leave with you, My peace I give to you; not as the world gives do I give to you. Let not your heart be troubled, neither let it be afraid."

You could pray, "How many times have I heard that verse? Please understand my naïveté, Lord, but I sort of thought of it as something you heard mostly at funerals, not for everyday needs such as I'm bringing to You now. As I understand it, Your peace is available to take the sting out of all this tension. Show me how to let You do it."

Tell your Friend about your anxiety. Share your deepest thoughts with Him. Tell Him all your cares and concerns. He is for real!

> Prayer is the one mission to the world all Christians can share.
> —DAVID BENSON

Let's consider the role played by emotion in prayer. You could become emotional at this point in your prayer concerning anxiety—perhaps with tears. Don't reprimand yourself. Turn to the *Emotions* entries.

For now, let's go with this: mind and heart, Job 38:36: "Who has put wisdom in the mind? Or who has given understanding to the heart?"

Job had it right: the mind—left hemisphere of the brain, intellect; the heart—right hemisphere of the brain, emotions. Both—mind (intellect) and heart (emotions)—are strategic in effective prayer. In my experience, emotions refer to fervent prayer (James 5:16) and prayer and supplication (Phil. 4:6).

You could pray, "I realize I was born with certain traits and characteristics. I appreciate the drive You gave me when You made me, Lord. I don't want to lose that. Please touch me and help me get on top of the tendency for being so anxious. You not only know I have anxiety, but You know what causes it. I trust You to take care of me. Give me patience as I learn."

You may wish to reinforce other subjects in a prayer similar to this prototype; refer to the Topics Index on pages 293–96. *Praise* and *Gratitude* surely apply in all prayers, but especially this one. Also look at listings under *Answer.*

Prayer is serious business. It's you, a mortal human being, in conference with your Creator—risen Savior, King of all kings, Lord of lords. Prestigious earth appointments become trivial by comparison. These kinds of prayers, involving mind and heart and the Bible, are prayers your heavenly Father hears and answers. Amen.

And always remember: it's God's responsibility, not yours, to make His promises work!

PROTOTYPE 4: GUIDANCE

In a world of sophisticated guidance systems, let us always remember that our Lord is ever alert to our need for guidance. As you proceed on your own with the STEPS prayer method, you need to be thoroughly aware of the prayer preludes available in the *Intro* section. For example:

You can be sure God listens

PSALM 116:1–2—"I love the LORD, because He has heard my voice and my supplications. Because He has inclined His ear to me, therefore I will call upon Him as long as I live."

You can be sure of it. God says what He means and means what He says. Take a moment to reconsider the STEPS anchor verse, John 15:7: "If you abide in Me, and My words abide in you, you will ask what you desire, and it shall be done for you." These are the words of the Lord Jesus, spoken directly to you. Take them at face value. They are absolutely trustworthy.

Your prayer based on Psalm 116:1–2 could be: "Lord, I'm just going by what You say. You hear me when I pray. You incline Your ear, missing nothing. I've been pretty much a secular Christian with more confidence in material guidance systems than in Your promises. Psalm 90:2 says of You, 'From everlasting to everlasting, You are God.' And about Jesus, John 1:1 tells me, 'In the beginning was the Word, and the Word was with God, and the Word was God.' I've believed that with my head but don't really get it down into my heart. Please help me to realize You are older than the skies and everything around me was designed by Your Son, my Lord Jesus. You can cross our galaxy in an instant. O Lord, help me get a measure of who You really are!"

If you are a strictly modern Christian, you could continue: "Forgive me, Lord, for being more at ease with a computer than with a Bible, for having been more compatible with E-mail than with prayer. I was like a toddling infant who knows nothing about a broadband Internet connection that once functioned at 14.4 or 56K but now at megabytes per second. I was a child equally ignorant of audio packets and data bytes. But I'm catching on, Lord. I've been victimized by a secular world. I've had a secular faith, prayed secular prayers, tried to acclimate my feeble churchianity to the views of pragmatic rationalists. Thanks for Your patience, Lord. I'm beginning to realize that the Bible allows me to interface with the real You better than any modem could do."

If you are not familiar with the electronic world around you, perhaps you want to pray in this manner: "I am a worldly Christian, Lord. I think more about earthly things than I do about heavenly things. I am more interested in cars and clothes and television sets than I am in my need for You and Your willingness to meet my need."

Your prayer for guidance could begin in this manner: "You not only made the universe, Lord, but You placed within that universe laws and forces to guide it. Stars, billions of light-years from earth, are in Your perfect control. So are the tiny atoms that surround me. If I can depend on anyone for guidance, surely it is Someone who has such control. O Lord, I want to be Master controlled. Please give me confidence to believe that the Creator of the universe will make this a reality for me."

With widening awareness of prayer potential, we move once more to the topics and check out *Guidance,* where we find: Sure formula for guidance, Proverbs 3:5–6: (1) "Trust in the LORD with all your heart," (2) "Lean not on your own understanding," (3) "In all your ways acknowledge Him," and (4) "He shall direct your paths."

Going to the topics, you check out *Obedience* and find in 1 Corinthians 4:2: "It is required in stewards that one be found faithful."

You could pray: "I want to be a faithful steward of the intelligence You have given me, especially things I'm learning about prayer. I praise You for the confidence You are giving me. I want to inventory my life, especially how I stand on this crucial matter of obedience. Please give me joy in obeying You, Lord. Help me to see that, in many ways, *obedience* and *guidance* are the same word."

You may also want to check out *Cleansing* and *Purity* in the topics.

Avoid mere structure and formula, aiming at all times for spontaneity. You are not servant to Master, underling to Overlord. You are friend to Friend with your Lord, child to Parent, seeker to Counselor.

Since these prototypes are learning instruments, let's look at other topics to consider in continuing and concluding such a prayer as this.

ASSURANCE

Your Lord has unlimited capability

JOB 42:2—"I know that You can do everything, and that no purpose of Yours can be withheld from You."

You are likely in awe of God but, I trust, also moving from respect to rapport. And as you have progressed this far into the STEPS experience, I hope you sense expanding confidence in your heavenly Father. If so, tell Him. Be specific. Watch your faith and fulfillment increase!

> Prayer is not to change God but to change us.
>
> —CHARLES FINNEY

TRUST

Upheld by God's strength

ISAIAH 41:10—"Fear not, for I am with you; be not dismayed, for I am your God. I will strengthen you, yes, I will help you, I will uphold you with My righteous right hand."

Take a personal inventory of weaknesses that hinder you from following the Lord's guidance. Ask Him to help you see how those weaknesses relate to some of the Bible promises you are involving in your prayers. One aspect of the Bible's involvement in your search for guidance surely involves discipline. Check it out in the topics.

DISCIPLINE

Disciplined lifestyle

COLOSSIANS 2:6–7—"As you therefore have received Christ Jesus the LORD, so walk in Him, rooted and built up in Him and established in the faith, as you have been taught, abounding in it with thanksgiving."

You could pray, "I am going to think of spiritual discipline as related to good physical conditioning. I want to be in good shape with my body, Lord, so help me to also be in good shape with my soul."

Again, as an example for you to observe, conclude the prayer with praise. Praise is to your prayer what breath is to your body.

PRAISE

Worthy of praise

2 SAMUEL 22:4—"I will call upon the LORD, who is worthy to be praised."

Your prayer could be: "I praise You, Lord, for the growth I see in my faith. I praise You for all of Your promises and how You will make them apply to my life."

If you wanted to use this prototype as an outline for intercession, you would likely make other choices, especially as you become more familiar with the topics. STEPS is meant to be an aid to spontaneity. As I mentioned previously, in your personal Bible reading, you will find additional reinforcement for prayer.

You're in for an enriching adventure! Amen.

PROTOTYPE 5: SORROW

In times of sorrow, you may take a different approach to prayer. In the case of our prototype, I suggest selecting a scripture from the topics entries for *Sorrow,* such as: heart stricken, Psalm 102:4: "My heart is stricken and withered like grass, so that I forget to eat my bread."

It's human nature to feel sorry for oneself at times of grief, loss, and sadness. Isaiah 53:3 speaks of Jesus as "a Man of sorrows and acquainted with grief."

You could also select a related listing for *Sorrow:* Jesus knows your sorrow, Isaiah 53:4: "Surely He has borne our griefs and carried our sorrows." What a resource in time of sorrow—just for the asking!

Let's say that you have been laid off. Your prayer could begin: "Just as the Bible says, Lord, I am 'stricken and withered like grass.' I know I can't lose my job outside Your will, which means that You have permitted this to happen for my good, thus for gain. Also, Lord, You tell me that You 'carried our sorrows.' Please show me how to put that into practice. Please show me how to make this add up in the way I think, in my attitude when I'm going through tough times."

Try to think of sorrow as an earth dimension, meant to prepare you for an eternity of joy and fulfillment. Prayer in the STEPS manner views life as a dual entity—both mortal and immortal, temporal and eternal.

If you find difficulty coping with such statements, be patient. Romans 10:17 teaches that "faith comes by hearing, and hearing by the word of God." It assures you that as you integrate the Bible into your prayers, your understanding and use of faith increase.

Browse through the topics to find other scriptures supportive of prayer in times of sorrow. Build them into your prayers as demonstrated in other prototypes.

TESTING

God knows those who trust Him

NAHUM 1:7—"The LORD is good, a stronghold in the day of trouble; and He knows those who trust in Him."

Your prayer could be: "Show me how You can become my 'stronghold,' Lord. The Bible assures me You know those who trust in You. If my trust doesn't have the depth it needs for Your recognition, then please help me because I can't depend on myself. I can trust You only in the measure that You give me trust."

Jesus says you are so well known to your heavenly Father that "the very hairs of your head are all numbered" (Matt. 10:30). Such assured identity permits you to speak to your Lord as friend to Friend. And always remember, one of the evidences of maturing prayer lies in a natural urge to praise God, not just petition Him, when you talk to Him. Never force praise, however, but cultivate it.

COMFORT

The God of all comfort

2 CORINTHIANS 1:3–4—"Blessed be the God and Father of our Lord Jesus Christ, the Father of mercies and God of all comfort, who comforts us in all our tribulation, that we may be able to comfort those who are in any trouble, with the comfort with which we ourselves are comforted by God."

You are comforted to be able to comfort others. Pray through this scripture several times; experience promised comfort; envision helping others now and in the future.

HOPE

Courage, strength, and hope

PSALM 31:24—"Be of good courage, and He shall strengthen your heart, all you who hope in the LORD."

You could pray, "You are very wise, Lord. You permit me to experience sorrow so that the comfort You give me helps me share with others. Please help me become the quality person for whom this really can happen. My sorrow now is very deep. You tell me to 'be of good courage.' But here's how it is, Lord. Unless You give me the courage, I am a hopeless coward. Please teach me. Make me teachable."

If you are truly teachable, looking for growth in your life, and if you lack courage, then one of your problems may be a hesitancy to witness.

WITNESS

Tell God's wonders

PSALM 9:1—"I will praise You, O LORD, with my whole heart; I will tell of all Your marvelous works."

The Lord's grace and mercy, through times of sorrow, can provide opportunity for outreach to others, particularly those involved with you in grieving. Amen.

So you pray, "People are watching me. They want me to wipe out so I can't praise You in a tough time like this. I want to praise You 'with my whole heart.' I want to 'tell of all Your marvelous works.' But I need You to help me. Help me not to want victory so I will look good. I want to relate to people who need to see how You meet my needs and could meet theirs."

PROTOTYPE 6: FAMILY

You not only grow a family; you build one. And prayer, reinforced by scripture, can make the difference between success and disappointment.

In these days, rewarding fulfillment awaits the man and woman who will establish a home and, with the use of Bible principles, cause that home and its family to endure as a testimony to other parents and families.

INTRO

Praise God for His greatness

PSALM 145:3—"Great is the LORD, and greatly to be praised; and His greatness is unsearchable."

Think of prayer on behalf of your family not as comradeship with your heavenly Father, where you are on a par with Him, but as a relationship in which you sense His presence and counsel. Stay close to the Scriptures, infusing the Bible into your prayers, and such relationship becomes spontaneous.

When we pray for families, we need to pray especially for fathers. It is God's plan for the father to be both the spiritual and the secular leader of his home.

FAMILY

Like father, like family

PROVERBS 20:7—"The righteous man walks in his integrity; his children are blessed after him."

Note the profile of a good father—righteous, honest, with his children following his example. With so few good fathers in many areas of society, it will be your option to structure a prayer for a father you select. If he is a man of faith but negligent as a father, your prayer could be: "Help him to see it, Lord. More than supporting his family, more than providing for their future, he must be the best example they know of what a Christian father is and does."

HOME

Elements of a good home

PROVERBS 24:3–4—"Through wisdom a house is built, and by understanding it is established; by knowledge the rooms are filled with all precious and pleasant riches."

Prayer could go in one of two directions here: thanking God for children who are following the example of exemplary parents, or praying that this might occur.

An inclusive prayer could be: "You tell me that I need wisdom and understanding, Lord. With them I will gain knowledge. But where do I get wisdom and understanding except from You? Guide me as I search my Bible for these gifts from Your mind to mine. And what about those 'precious and pleasant riches,' Lord? I want my home filled with Your glory! Show me what I must do to make it happen."

> Prayer is not overcoming God's reluctance. It is laying hold on His willingness.
>
> —ARCHBISHOP TRENCH

PARENTS

Parents teach children

JOEL 1:3—"Tell your children about it, let your children tell their children, and their children another generation."

You could pray, "I know it is Your will, Lord, for my family to have an enduring Christian heritage. Show me what part of that is my responsibility and how I can find the guidance You have for me in Your Word."

Your prayers are important for the children in your immediate and collective family and the parents responsible for them. By nature, every child asks questions that, when answered properly, will guide that child toward faith. Pray for specifics in this regard: "Show me how I can be the best possible influence to my family. I must be careful, Lord. Please don't let me be an intrusion. Show me how to be positive, not negative."

LOVE

Love is the greatest

1 Corinthians 13:13—"Now abide faith, hope, love, these three; but the greatest of these is love."

> Prayer should not be our last resort but our first. Prayer is the highest use of human speech.
>
> —P. T. FORSYTH

Here is the crux of it all, the central intent of your prayer. What is the present state between family members? Are there reasons for gratitude and praise? What elements of love need improvement? What can you do about it?

You could pray, "So many times I quote those three words: *faith, hope, love.* Sometimes it's as though I'm quoting them for the first time because I seem to understand little of what they mean. I know You want me to experience those three words, Lord, or they wouldn't be in Your Book. Please help me, Lord. Illuminate my mind. Show me what *faith* means in this context for me and my family. Teach me about *hope*, Lord, and above all, help me understand the role that love can play in our family. Please show me how I can be a channel of Your *love*."

COMMITMENT

Long-term commitment

2 TIMOTHY 1:12—"He is able to keep what I have committed to Him."

Many wayward children, committed to God's care by their parents, have found their way back to faith. Review the texts in this prototype, and relate family needs to them. Put your prayers into action. Call on Bible-based prayer power. If applicable, admit wrong. Ask forgiveness.

Continually familiarize yourself with relevant topics, and always keep a treasure hunter's alert eye whenever you read your Bible. Amen.

Your prayer could be: "I have committed everyone in my family to You, Lord. I recommit all of them, and I now commit myself anew. In hope, by faith, Lord, I put my family into Your eternal trust!"

PROTOTYPE 7: RENEWAL

Old-fashioned revivalists launched out in eloquent denunciation of backsliders. In today's more laid-back styles of preaching, such spiritual maladies are frequently described as the need for renewal. Often when spiritual well-being wanes, one of the first casualties is prayer.

If you sense such a problem in your life, give special attention to the elements of renewal in the Christian life. If you are a growing Christian, you're not likely to experience backsliding and the need for renewal. But let's suppose you sense such a need in your Christian experience.

Again, using selections from the topics, take a look at some elements of prayer for renewal.

CORRECTION

Some wise, others stupid

PROVERBS 12:1—"Whoever loves instruction loves knowledge, but he who hates correction is stupid."

Your opening prayer could be: "I love instruction and knowledge, though I can't say I enjoy correction, but I know my spiritual condition has slipped a little. I am open to Your help, Lord, even if it hurts a bit."

Renewal invariably involves repentance. The revivalists of whom I spoke a moment ago would call it "getting right with God."

REPENTANCE

Restored hearts

LAMENTATIONS 5:21—"Turn us back to You, O LORD, and we will be restored."

You could pray, "Wherever I may have strayed, Lord, I ask You to lead me back. If there is sin in my life, please remove it. I ask You not only to make right the past, but also to give me renewed impetus for the future."

RENEWAL

Renewal lifestyle, the fruit of the spirit

GALATIANS 5:22–23—"The fruit of the Spirit is love, joy, peace, longsuffering, kindness, goodness, faithfulness, gentleness, self-control."

Prayer: "That's for me, Lord! Whatever I have to get rid of in my thinking, habits, or attitudes, help me get rid of it that I may experience these magnificent attributes in my life."

By this time in your prayer, you will sense the reality of renewal taking place within you.

Your next emphasis in prayer should be *praise*. In the topics we find 2 Samuel 22:4:

I will call upon the LORD, who is worthy to be praised.

And you do just that. Conclude your prayer with praise, especially praising the Lord in advance for victories you anticipate because of the renewal you know He will give you.

Topics

Here is an assortment of Bible verses, arranged by relevant topics for you to consider using when you pray. As you have seen in the pro- totypes, the scriptures you select can become the very pulse of your prayers. Invest some time browsing through the topics that especially relate to your needs. Ask the Lord for guidance. Biblical reinforce- ment—STEPS— will make a tangible difference in your prayers.

Many topics list Bible selections for meditation. They are intended to offer specific prayer guidance. For example, under the topic *Authority* you find the entry: "*Meditation:* Unlimited range of author- ity, Romans 8:35–39."

First, read verses 35 through 39 for content. Next, slowly ponder your way, phrase by phrase and word by word, inviting the Holy Spirit to make what the Bible teaches meaningful to you. Quietly concentrate as the teaching penetrates your mind and heart. Most important, relate the scripture to you as a person, your activities, and your concerns.

Note the specific points of this meditation:

- "Who shall separate us?" Nothing. No one. Think about it, and thank God for the security you have in Him.

- "Sheep for the slaughter." We are prime targets of Satan's wiles, but see the next verse.

- "More than conquerors." You have authority in the name of your Lord Jesus. What are the problems you face? Name each one as you pray. Thank God for His power and the victory made possible for you through your exercise—by faith—of that power.

- "I am persuaded." The ultimate confidence can be yours as you pray your way into the Bible's storehouse, treasury, and arsenal.

It is not good for a man to pray cream and live skim milk.

—HENRY WARD BEECHER

Pray and praise your way through the concluding verses. They are yours to own and enjoy!

You will also find STEPS Nuggets within this section, with inspirational and informational content relating to the experience of prayer. (The STEPS Nuggets Index is on page 295.)

ABILITY

Do you think that others have more ability than you? Listen up, friend. You have exactly the abilities you need to fulfill God's plan for each day of your life.

"Observe to do" translates "find it in the Bible, live it, and succeed"

JOSHUA 1:8—"This Book of the Law shall not depart from your mouth, but you shall meditate in it day and night, that you may observe to do according to all that is written in it. For then you will make your way prosperous, and then you will have good success."

Beyond your ability

ZECHARIAH 4:6—"'Not by might nor by power, but by My Spirit,' says the LORD of hosts."

Ability is a synonym for faith

ACTS 6:8—"Stephen, full of faith and power, did great wonders and signs among the people."

Don't complain about your limitations

2 CORINTHIANS 11:5–6—"I consider that I am not at all inferior to the most eminent apostles. Even though I am untrained in speech, yet I am not in knowledge. But we have been thoroughly manifested among you in all things."

Take the im out of impossible

PHILIPPIANS 4:13—"I can do all things through Christ who strengthens me."

ABORTION

When you are contemplating abortion or praying for those who do, these Bible verses offer principles and guidance.

The sixth commandment

EXODUS 20:13—"You shall not murder."

Children, a heritage from the Lord

PSALM 127:3–5—"Children are a heritage from the LORD, the fruit of the womb is a reward. Like arrows in the hand of a warrior, so are the children of one's youth. Happy is the man who has his quiver full of them; they shall not be ashamed, but shall speak with their enemies in the gate."

Child known to God in womb

JEREMIAH 1:4–5—"Then the word of the LORD came to me, saying: 'Before I formed you in the womb I knew you; before you were born I sanctified you; I ordained you a prophet to the nations.'"

Meditation: **Jesus identified with children,** Matthew 18:3–5: "Assuredly, I say to you, unless you are converted and become as little children, you will by no means enter the kingdom of heaven. Therefore whoever humbles himself as this little child is the greatest in the kingdom

---

STEPS Nugget

SIMPLICITY IS THE KEY

Prayer is a profound experience, but it is not complicated. Turn to the Twenty-third Psalm if you need to be reminded that God speaks to us as a Father to His children, not as a professor to his students.

The seven notes of the musical scale illustrate the Creator's methodology. Using those seven sounds, a mother sings a lullaby and puts her child to sleep. With those same seven notes, Beethoven wrote his nine symphonies.

In John 16:29, the disciples told Jesus, "You are speaking plainly," and in Romans 6:19, the apostle Paul declared, "I speak in human terms."

of heaven. Whoever receives one little child like this in My name receives Me."

Kingdom citizens

LUKE 18:16—"Jesus called them to Him and said, 'Let the little children come to Me, and do not forbid them; for of such is the kingdom of God.'"

ABUNDANCE

Help yourself to a spiritual cornucopia when you undergird your prayers with the promises and precepts of the Bible.

Abundant goodness

PSALM 31:19—"Oh, how great is Your goodness, which You have laid up for those who fear You, which You have prepared for those who trust in You!"

See for yourself what a difference Jesus makes

JOHN 10:10—"The thief does not come except to steal, and to kill, and to destroy. I have come that they may have life, and that they may have it more abundantly."

God wants to fill you with joy and peace

ROMANS 15:13—"May the God of hope fill you with all joy and peace in believing, that you may abound in hope by the power of the Holy Spirit."

Experience abundant wisdom and grace

EPHESIANS 1:7–8—"In Him we have redemption through His blood, the forgiveness of sins, according to the riches of His grace which He made to abound toward us in all wisdom and prudence."

Vast abundance

EPHESIANS 3:20–21—"Now to Him who is able to do exceedingly abundantly above all that we ask or think, according to the power that works in us, to Him be glory in the church by Christ Jesus to all generations, forever and ever. Amen."

ACCESS

As a Christian, you have a right to request God's help at any time and in any circumstance. His door is open. Enter!

Jesus is your entry door

JOHN 10:9—"I am the door. If anyone enters by Me, he will be saved, and will go in and out and find pasture."

Find the Way, believe the truth, live the life

JOHN 14:6—"Jesus said to him, 'I am the way, the truth, and the life. No one comes to the Father except through Me.'"

Discover the rights your faith gives you

ROMANS 5:1–2—"Having been justified by faith, we have peace with God through our Lord Jesus Christ, through whom also we have access by faith into this grace in which we stand, and rejoice in hope of the glory of God."

Christ is your Lobbyist in heaven

1 TIMOTHY 2:5—"There is one God and one Mediator between God and men, the Man Christ Jesus."

You have an in with the Lord

HEBREWS 4:14–16—"Seeing then that we have a great High Priest who has passed through the heavens, Jesus the Son of God, let us hold fast our confession. For we do not have a High Priest who cannot sympathize with our weaknesses, but was in all points tempted as we are, yet without sin. Let us therefore come boldly to the throne of grace, that we may obtain mercy and find grace to help in time of need."

ACCOMPLISHMENT

Give thanks to God, and give Him the credit when you are blessed with accomplishments. Also see Success.

True measure of success

PSALM 37:16—"A little that a righteous man has is better than the riches of many wicked."

Always give God the credit

JEREMIAH 9:23–24—"Thus says the LORD: 'Let not the wise man glory in his wisdom, let not the mighty man glory in his might, nor let the rich man glory in his riches; but let him who glories glory in this, that he understands and knows Me, that I am the LORD, exercising lovingkindness, judgment, and righteousness in the earth. For in these I delight.'"

The Lord leads and rewards

JEREMIAH 32:19—"You are great in counsel and mighty in work, for your eyes are open to all the ways of the sons of men, to give everyone according to his ways and according to the fruit of his doings."

All glory to God

1 CORINTHIANS 3:6–7—"I planted, Apollos watered, but God gave the increase. So then neither he who plants is anything, nor he who waters, but God who gives the increase."

To God be the glory

1 CORINTHIANS 10:31—"Whether you eat or drink, or whatever you do, do all to the glory of God."

No need to blow your own horn

2 CORINTHIANS 10:17–18—"But 'he who glories, let him glory in the LORD.' For not he who commends himself is approved, but whom the Lord commends."

ACCUSATION

Do others accuse you? Thank God for the privilege of honoring His name in all of life's circumstances.

When you feel speechless

MATTHEW 10:19–20—"When they deliver you up, do not worry about how or what you should speak. For it will be given to you in that hour what you should speak; for it is not you who speak, but the Spirit of your Father who speaks in you."

The Holy Spirit is in your corner

LUKE 12:11–12—"When they bring you to the synagogues and magistrates and authorities, do not worry about how or what you should answer, or what you should say. For the Holy Spirit will teach you in that very hour what you ought to say."

Example of Jesus

JOHN 8:12–14—"Then Jesus spoke to them again, saying, 'I am the light of the world. He who follows Me shall not walk in darkness, but have the light of life.' The Pharisees therefore said to Him, 'You bear witness of Yourself; Your witness is not true.' Jesus answered and said to them, 'Even if I bear witness of Myself, My witness is true, for I know where I came from and where I am going; but you do not know where I come from and where I am going.'"

Unproved accusations

ACTS 25:7—"When he had come, the Jews who had come down from Jerusalem stood about and laid many serious complaints against Paul, which they could not prove."

AGREEMENT

Making and keeping agreements can be integral to Christian character and witness.

Congregational agreement

JOSHUA 24:22—"Joshua said to the people, 'You are witnesses against yourselves that you have chosen the LORD for yourselves, to serve Him.' And they said, 'We are witnesses!'"

Put it in writing

NEHEMIAH 9:38—"Because of all this, we make a sure covenant and write it; our leaders, our Levites, and our priests seal it."

Fellow Christians in agreement

1 CORINTHIANS 1:10—"Now I plead with you, brethren, by the name of our Lord Jesus Christ, that you all speak the same thing, and that there be no divisions among you, but that you be perfectly joined together in the same mind and in the same judgment."

Yes or no? Be specific

2 CORINTHIANS 1:17—"When I was planning this, did I do it lightly? Or the things I plan, do I plan according to the flesh, that with me there should be Yes, Yes, and No, No?"

Being of the same mind

PHILIPPIANS 4:2—"I implore Euodia and I implore Syntyche to be of the same mind in the Lord."

ALCOHOL

Christians who imbibe in social drinking should be aware of what the Bible says about alcohol.

Getting "high" with the Lord

PSALM 4:7—"You have put gladness in my heart, more than in the season that their grain and wine increased."

Led astray by wine and liquor

PROVERBS 20:1—"Wine is a mocker, strong drink is a brawler, and whoever is led astray by it is not wise."

Poor judgment caused by alcohol

ISAIAH 28:7; 56:12—"They also have erred through wine, and through intoxicating drink are out of the way; the priest and the prophet have erred through intoxicating drink, they are swallowed up by wine, they are out of the way through intoxicating drink; they err in vision, they stumble in judgment . . . 'Come,' one says, 'I will bring wine, and we will fill ourselves with intoxicating drink; tomorrow will be as today, and much more abundant.'"

Consider your influence over others

ROMANS 14:21—"It is good neither to eat meat nor drink wine nor do anything by which your brother stumbles or is offended or is made weak."

Not drunk with wine

EPHESIANS 5:18—"Do not be drunk with wine, in which is dissipation; but be filled with the Spirit."

ANGELS

Bible-alert Christians realize the role of angels in their lives.

Angel of the Lord nearby

PSALM 34:7—"The angel of the LORD encamps all around those who fear Him, and delivers them."

Protected by angels

PSALM 91:11–12—"He shall give His angels charge over you, to keep you in all your ways. In their hands they shall bear you up, lest you dash your foot against a stone."

Angel in lions' den

DANIEL 6:22—"My God sent His angel and shut the lions' mouths, so that they have not hurt me, because I was found innocent before Him; and also, O king, I have done no wrong before you."

Children's angels

MATTHEW 18:10—"Take heed that you do not despise one of these little ones, for I say to you that in heaven their angels always see the face of My Father who is in heaven."

Angels with Jesus in the wilderness

MARK 1:13—"He was there in the wilderness forty days, tempted by Satan, and was with the wild beasts; and the angels ministered to Him."

Angels knocking at your door

HEBREWS 13:2—"Do not forget to entertain strangers, for by so doing some have unwittingly entertained angels."

ANGER

Troubled by a quick, hot temper? Find help in the Bible.

Soft words calm bad tempers

PROVERBS 15:1—"A soft answer turns away wrath, but a harsh word stirs up anger."

Turn your temper into a controlled asset

PROVERBS 16:32—"He who is slow to anger is better than the mighty, and he who rules his spirit than he who takes a city."

Don't advertise your frustrations

PROVERBS 29:11—"A fool vents all his feelings, but a wise man holds them back."

Never twist an angry man's nose

PROVERBS 30:33—"For as the churning of milk produces butter, and wringing the nose produces blood, so the forcing of wrath produces strife."

Go easy with anger

ECCLESIASTES 7:9—"Do not hasten in your spirit to be angry, for anger rests in the bosom of fools."

Righteous indignation and dangerous sunsets

EPHESIANS 4:26—"'Be angry, and do not sin': do not let the sun go down on your wrath."

Anger and its evil associates

COLOSSIANS 3:8—"Now you yourselves are to put off all these: anger, wrath, malice, blasphemy, filthy language out of your mouth."

Put the brakes on anger

JAMES 1:19–20—"So then, my beloved brethren, let every man be swift to hear, slow to speak, slow to wrath; for the wrath of man does not produce the righteousness of God."

ANSWER

Anchor your confidence in what the Bible teaches about answers to prayer.

God's people didn't give up

1 SAMUEL 7:8—"The children of Israel said to Samuel, 'Do not cease to cry out to the LORD our God for us, that He may save us from the hand of the Philistines.'"

King Solomon asked God to hear his prayer

2 CHRONICLES 6:19—"Yet regard the prayer of Your servant and his supplication, O LORD my God, and listen to the cry and the prayer which Your servant is praying before You."

Be grateful for the answer

PSALM 28:6–7—"Blessed be the LORD, because He has heard the voice of my supplications! The LORD is my strength and my shield; my heart trusted in Him, and I am helped; therefore my heart greatly rejoices, and with my song I will praise Him."

Sins confessed and forgiven

PSALM 32:5—"I acknowledged my sin to You, and my iniquity I have not hidden. I said, 'I will confess my transgressions to the LORD,' and You forgave the iniquity of my sin."

When desires are granted

PSALM 37:4—"Delight yourself also in the LORD, and He shall give you the desires of your heart."

No good thing withheld

PSALM 84:11—"The LORD God is a sun and shield; the LORD will give grace and glory; no good thing will He withhold from those who walk uprightly."

Hear my prayer, Lord

PSALM 102:1–2—"Hear my prayer, O LORD, and let my cry come to You. Do not hide Your face from me in the day of my trouble; incline Your ear to me; in the day that I call, answer me speedily."

Be assured the Lord has heard

PSALM 116:1–2—"I love the LORD, because He has heard my voice and my supplications. Because He has inclined His ear to me, therefore I will call upon Him as long as I live."

Answers worth waiting for

PROVERBS 13:12—"Hope deferred makes the heart sick, but when the desire comes, it is a tree of life."

Ask, seek, knock

LUKE 11:9–10—"I say to you, ask, and it will be given to you; seek, and you will find; knock, and it will be opened to you. For everyone who asks receives, and he who seeks finds, and to him who knocks it will be opened."

How to cause your own problem

JAMES 4:3—"You ask and do not receive, because you ask amiss, that you may spend it on your pleasures."

Meditation: **Asking in God's will,** 1 John 5:14–15: "This is the confidence that we have in Him, that if we ask anything according to His will, He hears us. And if we know that He hears us, whatever we ask, we know that we have the petitions that we have asked of Him."

ANXIETY

When anxious thoughts hinder you from experiencing peace and confidence, spend some time centering your prayers around these promises and premises. Also see Stress.

Strength and courage overcome fear and discouragement

JOSHUA 1:9—"Have I not commanded you? Be strong and of good courage; do not be afraid, nor be dismayed, for the LORD your God is with you wherever you go."

Give your burden to the Lord

PSALM 55:22—"Cast your burden on the LORD, and He shall sustain you; He shall never permit the righteous to be moved."

Troubles? Tell the Lord; He will answer

PSALM 86:7—"In the day of my trouble I will call upon You, for You will answer me."

Ask God to diagnose your anxiety

PSALM 139:23—"Search me, O God, and know my heart; try me, and know my anxieties."

Cornucopia of promise

ISAIAH 41:10—"Fear not, for I am with you; be not dismayed, for I am your God. I will strengthen you, yes, I will help you, I will uphold you with My righteous right hand."

Through fire and water

ISAIAH 43:2—"When you pass through the waters, I will be with you; and through the rivers, they shall not overflow you. When you walk through the fire, you shall not be burned, nor shall the flame scorch you."

Peace beyond human experience

JOHN 14:27—"Peace I leave with you, My peace I give to you; not as the world gives do I give to you. Let not your heart be troubled, neither let it be afraid."

Overcoming peace, yours for the asking

JOHN 16:33—"These things I have spoken to you, that in Me you may have peace. In the world you will have tribulation; but be of good cheer, I have overcome the world."

The Lord is on your side

PHILIPPIANS 4:6–7—"Be anxious for nothing, but in everything by prayer and supplication, with thanksgiving, let your requests be made known to God; and the peace of God, which surpasses all understanding, will guard your hearts and minds through Christ Jesus."

Learn how to handle things

PHILIPPIANS 4:11–13—"Not that I speak in regard to need, for I have learned in whatever state I am, to be content: I know how to be abased, and I know how to abound. Everywhere and in all things I have learned both to be full and to be hungry, both to abound and to suffer need. I can do all things through Christ who strengthens me."

Give your anxiety to the Lord

1 PETER 5:7—"Casting all your care upon Him, for He cares for you."

ARGUMENT

The Bible offers practical guidance for handling arguments and disputes.

Solving conflict over property

GENESIS 13:6–11—"The land was not able to support them, that they might dwell together, for their possessions were so great that they could not dwell together. And there was strife between the herdsmen of Abram's livestock and the herdsmen of Lot's livestock. The Canaanites and the Perizzites then dwelt in the land. So Abram said to Lot, 'Please let there be no strife between you and me, and between my herdsmen and your herdsmen; for we are brethren. Is not the whole land before you? Please separate from me. If you take the left, then I will go to the right; or, if you go to the right, then I will go to the left.' And Lot lifted his eyes and saw all the plain of Jordan, that it was well watered everywhere (before the LORD destroyed Sodom and Gomorrah) like the garden of the LORD, like the land of Egypt as you go toward Zoar. Then Lot chose for himself all the plain of Jordan, and Lot journeyed east. And they separated from each other."

Counseled to use tact

GENESIS 31:24—"God had come to Laban the Syrian in a dream by night, and said to him, 'Be careful that you speak to Jacob neither good nor bad.'"

Assurance when your cause is right

PSALM 37:6—"He shall bring forth your righteousness as the light, and your justice as the noonday."

Fine art of gentle speech

PROVERBS 15:1—"A soft answer turns away wrath, but a harsh word stirs up anger."

Nip argument in the bud

PROVERBS 17:14—"The beginning of strife is like releasing water; therefore stop contention before a quarrel starts."

Try to find early agreement

MATTHEW 5:25—"Agree with your adversary quickly, while you are on the way with him, lest your adversary deliver you to the judge, the judge hand you over to the officer, and you be thrown into prison."

Danger! Avoid arguing with the Lord

ROMANS 9:20—"O man, who are you to reply against God? Will the thing formed say to him who formed it, 'Why have you made me like this?'"

Avoid a negative attitude

PHILIPPIANS 2:14–15—"Do all things without complaining and disputing, that you may become blameless and harmless, children of God without fault in the midst of a crooked and perverse generation, among whom you shine as lights in the world."

Harness the power of good thinking

2 TIMOTHY 1:7—"God has not given us a spirit of fear, but of power and of love and of a sound mind."

How to handle arguments

2 TIMOTHY 2:23–26—"Avoid foolish and ignorant disputes, knowing that they generate strife. And a servant of the Lord must not quarrel but be gentle to all, able to teach, patient, in humility correcting those who are in opposition, if God perhaps will grant them repentance, so that they may know the truth, and that they may come to their senses and escape the snare of the devil, having been taken captive by him to do his will."

Allow no time for foolish arguments

TITUS 3:9—"Avoid foolish disputes, genealogies, contentions, and strivings about the law; for they are unprofitable and useless."

ASKING

The defining moment of prayer comes when you tell the Lord what you want Him to do for you.

The Lord invites you to ask

1 KINGS 3:5—"At Gibeon the LORD appeared to Solomon in a dream by night; and God said, 'Ask! What shall I give you?'"

Request the Lord's attention

1 KINGS 8:28—"Yet regard the prayer of Your servant and his supplication, O LORD my God, and listen to the cry and the prayer which Your servant is praying before You today."

Ask God to give you desires

PSALM 37:4—"Delight yourself also in the LORD, and He shall give you the desires of your heart."

Jesus invites you to ask

MATTHEW 7:8—"For everyone who asks receives, and he who seeks finds, and to him who knocks it will be opened."

Put your faith to work

MATTHEW 21:22—"Whatever things you ask in prayer, believing, you will receive."

Need wisdom? Ask for it

JAMES 1:5—"If any of you lacks wisdom, let him ask of God, who gives to all liberally and without reproach, and it will be given to him."

You can ask with confidence

1 JOHN 5:14—"This is the confidence that we have in Him, that if we ask anything according to His will, He hears us."

ASSURANCE

Full assurance in prayer comes from trusting what the Bible says. Also see Promise.

Dial 911 prayer

2 SAMUEL 22:7—"In my distress I called upon the LORD, and cried out to my God; He heard my voice from His temple, and my cry entered His ears."

Your Lord has unlimited capability

JOB 42:2—"I know that You can do everything, and that no purpose of Yours can be withheld from You."

Be assured that your Lord hears

PSALM 6:9—"The LORD has heard my supplication; the LORD will receive my prayer."

You are the apple of His eye

PSALM 17:7–8—"Show Your marvelous lovingkindness by Your right hand, O You who save those who trust in You from those who rise up against them. Keep me as the apple of Your eye; hide me under the shadow of Your wings."

Be patient when you pray

PSALM 27:13–14—"I would have lost heart, unless I had believed that I would see the goodness of the LORD in the land of the living. Wait on the LORD; be of good courage, and He shall strengthen your heart; wait, I say, on the LORD!"

Something good is going to happen

PSALM 84:11—"The LORD God is a sun and shield; the LORD will give grace and glory; no good thing will He withhold from those who walk uprightly."

Assured of your Lord's guidance

ISAIAH 48:17—"Thus says the LORD, your Redeemer, the Holy One of Israel: 'I am the LORD your God, who teaches you to profit, who leads you by the way you should go.'"

Walking in darkness? Your Lord offers you light

ISAIAH 50:10—"Who among you fears the LORD? Who obeys the voice of His Servant? Who walks in darkness and has no light? Let him trust in the name of the LORD and rely upon his God."

Nothing too hard for the Lord

JEREMIAH 32:27—"I am the LORD, the God of all flesh. Is there anything too hard for Me?"

Quorum for small group prayer

MATTHEW 18:20—"Where two or three are gathered together in My name, I am there in the midst of them."

It pays to pray

JAMES 5:16—"Confess your trespasses to one another, and pray for one another, that you may be healed. The effective, fervent prayer of a righteous man avails much."

ATTITUDE

Ask the Lord to help you handle your attitude problems. He will!

Positive attitude in negative experience

JOB 1:20–21—"Job arose, tore his robe, and shaved his head; and he fell to the ground and worshiped. And he said: 'Naked I came from my mother's womb, and naked shall I return there. The LORD gave, and the LORD has taken away; blessed be the name of the LORD.'"

Renewed spirit

PSALM 51:10—"Create in me a clean heart, O God, and renew a steadfast spirit within me."

Bad attitude check urgently needed

PROVERBS 16:18—"Pride goes before destruction, and a haughty spirit before a fall."

Let pride give way to humility

JEREMIAH 9:23–24—"Thus says the LORD: 'Let not the wise man glory in his wisdom, let not the mighty man glory in his might, nor let the rich man glory in his riches; but let him who glories glory in this, that he understands and knows Me, that I am the LORD, exercising lovingkindness, judgment, and righteousness in the earth. For in these I delight.'"

Having people trouble? You can react positively

MATTHEW 5:11–12—"Blessed are you when they revile and persecute you, and say all kinds of evil against you falsely for My sake. Rejoice and be exceedingly glad, for great is your reward in heaven, for so they persecuted the prophets who were before you."

Attitude blueprint, the example of Jesus

PHILIPPIANS 2:5–8—"Let this mind be in you which was also in Christ Jesus, who, being in the form of God, did not consider it robbery to be equal with God, but made Himself of no reputation, taking the form of a bondservant, and coming in the likeness of men. And being found in appearance as a man, He humbled Himself and became obedient to the point of death, even the death of the cross."

STEPS Nugget

FRAGRANT INTERCESSION

After leaving the ark, Noah built an altar, his tactical means of special communion with God. As the sacrifice burned, Genesis 8:21 records, "the LORD smelled a soothing aroma." Numerous other references, such as Numbers 28:24, speak of sacrifices as "a sweet aroma to the LORD."

Old Testament believers thought of the sacrifice as rising to the very nostrils of the Lord. In Amos 5:21, God said He will ignore the burnt offerings of wayward people. The King James Version renders it, "I will not smell in your solemn assemblies."

Take a look at the first two verses of Romans 12, which we think of as an altar, with verses 3 through 21 being the smoke rising from the altar as what was "conformed to this world" becomes "transformed by" the Holy Spirit's fire.

Ephesians 5:2 tells us we can be identified with Christ as "an offering and a sacrifice to God for a sweet-smelling aroma."

Meditation: **Positive prayer attitude,** Philippians 4:4-8: "Rejoice in the Lord always. Again I will say, rejoice! Let your gentleness be known to all men. The Lord is at hand. Be anxious for nothing, but in everything by prayer and supplication, with thanksgiving, let your requests be made known to God; and the peace of God, which surpasses all understanding, will guard your hearts and minds through Christ Jesus. Finally, brethren, whatever things are true, whatever things are noble, whatever things are just, whatever things are pure, whatever things are lovely, whatever things are of good report, if there is any virtue and if there is anything praiseworthy—meditate on these things."

Keep your cool

JAMES 1:19–20—"Let every man be swift to hear, slow to speak, slow to wrath; for the wrath of man does not produce the righteousness of God."

Give yourself a mirror checkup

JAMES 1:22–25—"Be doers of the word, and not hearers only, deceiving yourselves. For if anyone is a hearer of the word and not a doer, he is like a man observing his natural face in a mirror; for he observes himself, goes away, and immediately forgets what kind of man he was. But he who looks into the perfect law of liberty and continues in it, and is not a forgetful hearer but a doer of the work, this one will be blessed in what he does."

AUTHENTICITY

You can believe your Bible, by faith and in fact. Also see Truth.

Give your word

MATTHEW 5:37—"Let your 'Yes' be 'Yes,' and your 'No,' 'No.' For whatever is more than these is from the evil one."

Birth of the Savior

LUKE 2:11—"There is born to you this day in the city of David a Savior, who is Christ the Lord."

Authentic Messiah

LUKE 24:27—"Beginning at Moses and all the Prophets, He expounded to them in all the Scriptures the things concerning Himself."

Authenticated faith

JOHN 20:30–31—"Truly Jesus did many other signs in the presence of His disciples, which are not written in this book; but these are written that you may believe that Jesus is the Christ, the Son of God, and that believing you may have life in His name."

AUTHORITY

Not who you are—but whose—gives you authority over Satan himself.

True measure of success

PSALM 37:16—"A little that a righteous man has is better than the riches of many wicked."

God's name gives you authority

PSALM 54:1—"Save me, O God, by Your name, and vindicate me by Your strength."

Utilize your Lord's authority

MATTHEW 28:18–20—"Jesus came and spoke to them, saying, 'All authority has been given to Me in heaven and on earth. Go therefore and make disciples of all the nations, baptizing them in the name of the Father and of the Son and of the Holy Spirit, teaching them to observe all things that I have commanded you; and lo, I am with you always, even to the end of the age.' Amen."

Meditation: **Unlimited range of authority,** Romans 8:35–39: "Who shall separate us from the love of Christ? Shall tribulation, or distress, or persecution, or famine, or nakedness, or peril, or sword? As it is written: 'For Your sake we are killed all day long; we are accounted as sheep for the slaughter.' Yet in all these things we are more than conquerors through Him who loved us. For I am persuaded that neither death nor life, nor angels nor principalities nor powers, nor things present nor things to come, nor height nor depth, nor any other created thing, shall be able to separate us from the love of God which is in Christ Jesus our Lord."

Mighty weapons for you to use

2 CORINTHIANS 10:3–4—"For though we walk in the flesh, we do not war according to the flesh. For the weapons of our warfare are not carnal but mighty in God for pulling down strongholds."

Your Bible, the sword of the Spirit

EPHESIANS 6:17—"Take the helmet of salvation, and the sword of the Spirit, which is the word of God."

Resist Satan by faith

1 PETER 5:8–9—"Be sober, be vigilant; because your adversary the devil walks about like a roaring lion, seeking whom he may devour. Resist him, steadfast in the faith, knowing that the same sufferings are experienced by your brotherhood in the world."

Your enemy's work destroyed

1 JOHN 3:8—"He who sins is of the devil, for the devil has sinned from the beginning. For this purpose the Son of God was manifested, that He might destroy the works of the devil."

BACKSLIDING

The Hebrew root word indicates "apostate, turning away from the Lord" and urgently needing the counsel of the Bible. Also see Carnality, Renewal.

Ask your Lord for an urgently needed paradigm shift

PSALM 37:27—"Depart from evil, and do good; and dwell forevermore."

Pray for personal revival

PSALM 85:6—"Will You not revive us again, that Your people may rejoice in You?"

If you have fallen, the Lord will lift you up

PSALM 145:14—"The LORD upholds all who fall, and raises up all who are bowed down."

No sin is beyond forgiveness

ISAIAH 1:18—"'Come now, and let us reason together,' says the LORD, 'though your sins are like scarlet, they shall be as white as snow; though they are red like crimson, they shall be as wool.'"

Backsliding! Call it by name

JEREMIAH 14:7—"O LORD, though our iniquities testify against us, do it for Your name's sake; for our backslidings are many, we have sinned against You."

Looking unto Jesus

HEBREWS 12:1–2—"Therefore we also, since we are surrounded by so great a cloud of witnesses, let us lay aside every weight, and the sin which so easily ensnares us, and let us run with endurance the race that is set before us, looking unto Jesus, the author and finisher of our faith, who for the joy that was set before Him endured the cross, despising the shame, and has sat down at the right hand of the throne of God."

BANKRUPTCY

Always remember you are in partnership with your Lord. Also see Debt, Provision.

Family member's financial problem

DEUTERONOMY 15:3—"Of a foreigner you may require it; but you shall give up your claim to what is owed by your brother."

Your Lord's great wealth

PSALM 50:10—"Every beast of the forest is Mine, and the cattle on a thousand hills."

Promised guidance

PROVERBS 3:5–6—"Trust in the LORD with all your heart, and lean not on your own understanding; in all your ways acknowledge Him, and He shall direct your paths."

Loss of dishonest wealth

JEREMIAH 17:11—"As a partridge that broods but does not hatch, so is he who gets riches, but not by right; it will leave him in the midst of his days, and at his end he will be a fool."

Forgotten prosperity

LAMENTATIONS 3:17—"You have moved my soul far from peace; I have forgotten prosperity."

In the hands of creditors

HABAKKUK 2:7—"Will not your creditors rise up suddenly? Will they not awaken who oppress you? And you will become their booty."

Your heavenly Father knows

MATTHEW 6:31–32—"Do not worry, saying, 'What shall we eat?' or 'What shall we drink?' or 'What shall we wear?' For after all these things the Gentiles seek. For your heavenly Father knows that you need all these things."

Hard-nosed creditor

MATTHEW 18:23–27—"The kingdom of heaven is like a certain king who wanted to settle accounts with his servants. And when he had begun to settle accounts, one was brought to him who owed him ten thousand talents. But as he was not able to pay, his master commanded that he be sold, with his wife and children and all that he had, and that payment be made. The servant therefore fell down before him, saying, 'Master, have patience with me, and I will pay you all.' Then the master of that servant was moved with compassion, released him, and forgave him the debt."

BEHAVIOR

Much of the Bible deals with God's children and their behavioral problems; it offers guidelines on how to make amends.

Ignorance and blinding darkness

PROVERBS 4:19—"The way of the wicked is like darkness; they do not know what makes them stumble."

Losing spiritual perspective

1 CORINTHIANS 3:3—"You are still carnal. For where there are envy, strife, and divisions among you, are you not carnal and behaving like mere men?"

How to correct another's misbehavior

GALATIANS 6:1—"If a man is overtaken in any trespass, you who are spiritual restore such a one in a spirit of gentleness, considering yourself lest you also be tempted."

Meditation: **Goal for exemplary conduct,** Philippians 1:8–11: "For God is my witness, how greatly I long for you all with the affection of Jesus Christ. And this I pray, that your love may abound still more and more in knowledge and all discernment, that you may approve the things that are excellent, that you may be sincere and without offense till the day of Christ, being filled with the fruits of righteousness which are by Jesus Christ, to the glory and praise of God."

Behavior of church leader

1 TIMOTHY 3:2–7—"A bishop then must be blameless, the husband

of one wife, temperate, sober-minded, of good behavior, hospitable, able to teach; not given to wine, not violent, not greedy for money, but gentle, not quarrelsome, not covetous; one who rules his own house well, having his children in submission with all reverence (for if a man does not know how to rule his own house, how will he take care of the church of God?); not a novice, lest being puffed up with pride he fall into the same condemnation as the devil. Moreover he must have a good testimony among those who are outside, lest he fall into reproach and the snare of the devil."

Maintain good works

TITUS 3:8—"This is a faithful saying, and these things I want you to affirm constantly, that those who have believed in God should be careful to maintain good works. These things are good and profitable to men."

Looking unto Jesus

HEBREWS 12:1–2—"We also, since we are surrounded by so great a cloud of witnesses, let us lay aside every weight, and the sin which so easily ensnares us, and let us run with endurance the race that is set before us, looking unto Jesus, the author and finisher of our faith, who for the joy that was set before Him endured the cross, despising the shame, and has sat down at the right hand of the throne of God."

At peace with all

HEBREWS 12:14–15—"Pursue peace with all people, and holiness, without which no one will see the Lord: looking carefully lest anyone fall short of the grace of God; lest any root of bitterness springing up cause trouble, and by this many become defiled."

Brotherly love

HEBREWS 13:1—"Let brotherly love continue."

BIBLE

Resource above all resources, the Bible is your Guidebook to a productive life.

Key to all of life

JOSHUA 1:8—"This Book of the Law shall not depart from your mouth, but you shall meditate in it day and night, that you may observe to do according to all that is written in it. For then you will make your way prosperous, and then you will have good success."

Meditation: **Contemplating Scripture,** Psalm 19:1–14: "The heavens declare the glory of God; and the firmament shows His handiwork. Day unto day utters speech, and night unto night reveals knowledge. There is no speech nor language where their voice is not heard. Their line has gone out through all the earth, and their words to the end of the world. In them He has set a tabernacle for the sun, which is like a bridegroom coming out of his chamber, and rejoices like a strong man to run its race. Its rising is from one end of heaven, and its circuit to the other end; and there is nothing hidden from its heat. The law of the LORD is perfect, converting the soul; the testimony of the LORD is sure, making wise the simple; the statutes of the LORD are right, rejoicing the heart; the commandment of the LORD is pure, enlightening the eyes; the fear of the LORD is clean, enduring forever; the judgments of the LORD are true and righteous altogether. More to be desired are they than gold, yea, than much fine gold; sweeter also than honey and the honeycomb. Moreover by them Your servant is warned, and in keeping them there is great reward. Who can understand his errors? Cleanse me from secret faults. Keep back Your servant also from presumptuous sins; let them not have dominion over me. Then I shall be blameless, and I shall be innocent of great transgression. Let the words of my mouth and the meditation of my heart be acceptable in Your sight, O LORD, my strength and my Redeemer."

Ask for your eyes to be opened

PSALM 119:18—"Open my eyes, that I may see wondrous things from Your law."

The Bible, your Guiding Light

PSALM 119:105—"Your word is a lamp to my feet and a light to my path."

Understandable teaching

PSALM 119:130—"The entrance of Your words gives light; it gives understanding to the simple."

The Bible, your Guidebook

PSALM 119:133—"Direct my steps by Your word."

The Word accomplishes its purpose

ISAIAH 55:10–11—"For as the rain comes down, and the snow from heaven, and do not return there, but water the earth, and make it bring forth and bud, that it may give seed to the sower and bread to the eater, so shall My word be that goes forth from My mouth; it shall not return to Me void, but it shall accomplish what I please, and it shall prosper in the thing for which I sent it."

Your source of faith

ROMANS 10:17—"Faith comes by hearing, and hearing by the word of God."

Effective Word of God

1 THESSALONIANS 2:13—"For this reason we also thank God without ceasing, because when you received the word of God which you heard from us, you welcomed it not as the word of men, but as it is in truth, the word of God, which also effectively works in you who believe."

Use your two-edged sword

HEBREWS 4:12—"The word of God is living and powerful, and sharper than any two-edged sword, piercing even to the division of soul and spirit, and of joints and marrow, and is a discerner of the thoughts and intents of the heart."

Meditation: **Put your Bible into action,** James 1:22–25: "Be doers of the word, and not hearers only, deceiving yourselves. For if anyone is a hearer of the word and not a doer, he is like a man observing his natural face in a mirror; for he observes himself, goes away, and immediately forgets what kind of man he was. But he who looks into the perfect law of liberty and continues in it, and is not a forgetful hearer but a doer of the work, this one will be blessed in what he does."

BIRTHDAY

The older you get, the greater the need to inventory your life, clean up past mistakes, and seek guidance for the future.

So quickly life is over

JOB 16:22—"When a few years are finished, I shall go the way of no return."

Evaluate your life

PSALM 39:4–5—"LORD, make me to know my end, and what is the measure of my days, that I may know how frail I am. Indeed, You have made my days as handbreadths, and my age is as nothing before You; certainly every man at his best state is but vapor."

Wisely consider your days

PSALM 90:12—"Teach us to number our days, that we may gain a heart of wisdom."

Thoughtful look at good old days

ECCLESIASTES 7:10—"Do not say, 'Why were the former days better than these?' For you do not inquire wisely concerning this."

Learn not to worry about the future

MATTHEW 6:34—"Do not worry about tomorrow, for tomorrow

will worry about its own things. Sufficient for the day is its own trouble."

Make the most of your time

EPHESIANS 5:15–16—"See then that you walk circumspectly, not as fools but as wise, redeeming the time, because the days are evil."

Life is like a passing fog

JAMES 4:14—"Whereas you do not know what will happen tomorrow. For what is your life? It is even a vapor that appears for a little time and then vanishes away."

> If we cannot go to the house of the Lord, we can go by faith to the Lord of the house.
>
> —MATTHEW HENRY

BLESSING

One of prayer's primary functions involves requesting and bestowing blessing. These Bible portions will help you in this quest.

Wonders and blessings received

PSALM 40:5—"Many, O LORD my God, are Your wonderful works which You have done; and Your thoughts toward us cannot be recounted to You in order; if I would declare and speak of them, they are more than can be numbered."

Those eligible for blessing

PROVERBS 28:20—"A faithful man will abound with blessings, but he who hastens to be rich will not go unpunished."

Blessing promised for trusting

JEREMIAH 17:7—"Blessed is the man who trusts in the LORD, and whose hope is the LORD."

STEPS Nugget

UNANSWERED PRAYER

When we pray in our Lord's will, there is no such thing as an unanswered prayer. "Now this is the confidence that we have in Him," 1 John 5:14 states, "that if we ask anything according to His will, He hears us." Further, 1 Peter 3:12 assures us that "His ears are open" when we pray. To the cry of the man with leprosy, He responded, "I am willing; be cleansed" (Matt. 8:3).

The answer could be, "No." It could be, "Wait." Whatever it is, the Lord's response is always for our good. John 15:7, our STEPS anchor verse, holds the key: "If you abide in Me, and My words abide in you, you will ask what you desire, and it shall be done for you."

Showers of blessing

EZEKIEL 34:26—"I will make them and the places all around My hill a blessing; and I will cause showers to come down in their season; there shall be showers of blessing."

First things first, then blessing

MATTHEW 6:33—"Seek first the kingdom of God and His righteousness, and all these things shall be added to you."

Every spiritual blessing

EPHESIANS 1:3—"Blessed be the God and Father of our Lord Jesus Christ, who has blessed us with every spiritual blessing in the heavenly places in Christ."

Tough times bring blessing

JAMES 1:2–4—"Count it all joy when you fall into various trials, knowing that the testing of your faith produces patience. But let patience have its perfect work, that you may be perfect and complete, lacking nothing."

Your source of blessing

JAMES 1:17—"Every good gift and every perfect gift is from above, and comes down from the Father of lights, with whom there is no variation or shadow of turning."

BOLDNESS

Quiet type? Slow to assert yourself? You can pray with boldness! Also see Courage.

Bold witness and prayer

DANIEL 6:10—"When Daniel knew that the writing was signed, he went home. And in his upper room, with his windows open toward Jerusalem, he knelt down on his knees three times that day, and prayed and gave thanks before his God, as was his custom since early days."

Prayer is God, the Holy Spirit, talking to God, the Father, in the name of God, the Son, and the believer's heart is the prayer room.

—SAMUEL M. ZWEMMER

It's whom you know

ACTS 4:13—"When they saw the boldness of Peter and John, and perceived that they were uneducated and untrained men, they marveled. And they realized that they had been with Jesus."

Not ashamed of the gospel

ROMANS 1:16—"I am not ashamed of the gospel of Christ, for it is the power of God to salvation for everyone who believes, for the Jew first and also for the Greek."

Leadership with authority

TITUS 2:15—"Speak these things, exhort, and rebuke with all authority. Let no one despise you."

Boldness in prayer

HEBREWS 4:14–16—"Seeing then that we have a great High Priest who has passed through the heavens, Jesus the Son of God, let us hold fast our confession. For we do not have a High Priest who cannot sympathize with our weaknesses, but was in all points tempted as we are, yet without sin. Let us therefore come boldly to the throne of grace, that we may obtain mercy and find grace to help in time of need."

BUILDING

Aspects of construction, enlarging and remodeling your church premises, deserve prominence in your prayers.

Abundant building fund

EXODUS 36:6–7—"Moses gave a commandment, and they caused it to be proclaimed throughout the camp, saying, 'Let neither man nor woman do any more work for the offering of the sanctuary.' And the people were restrained from bringing, for the material they had was sufficient for all the work to be done—indeed too much."

Laying the foundation with praise

EZRA 3:10—"When the builders laid the foundation of the temple of the LORD, the priests stood in their apparel with trumpets, and the Levites, the sons of Asaph, with cymbals, to praise the LORD, according to the ordinance of David king of Israel."

The Master Builder

PSALM 127:1—"Unless the LORD builds the house, they labor in vain who build it."

Carefully budgeted financing

LUKE 14:28–29—"Which of you, intending to build a tower, does not sit down first and count the cost, whether he has enough to finish it—lest, after he has laid the foundation, and is not able to finish, all who see it begin to mock him."

The Chief Cornerstone

ACTS 4:11—"This is the 'stone which was rejected by you builders, which has become the chief cornerstone.'"

BURDEN

Bearing a burden can become a blessing.

Daily benefits and lifted burdens

PSALM 68:19—"Blessed be the Lord, who daily loads us with benefits, the God of our salvation!"

Someone to bear your burdens

MATTHEW 11:28–30—"Come to Me, all you who labor and are heavy laden, and I will give you rest. Take My yoke upon you and learn from Me, for I am gentle and lowly in heart, and you will find rest for your souls. For My yoke is easy and My burden is light."

Care and concern for others

GALATIANS 6:2—"Bear one another's burdens, and so fulfill the law of Christ."

A pastor's burden

COLOSSIANS 1:28—"Him we preach, warning every man and teaching every man in all wisdom, that we may present every man perfect in Christ Jesus."

BUSINESS

Take the Lord into partnership, or better yet, give Him full ownership.

With the Lord's blessing, business is good

PSALM 13:6—"I will sing to the LORD, because He has dealt bountifully with me."

Money in the bank isn't everything

PSALM 37:16—"A little that a righteous man has is better than the riches of many wicked."

Righteousness is good for business

PSALM 112:5—"A good man deals graciously and lends; he will guide his affairs with discretion."

Sixteen ounces to the pound

PROVERBS 11:1—"Dishonest scales are an abomination to the LORD, but a just weight is His delight."

Successful businesswoman

ACTS 16:14—"A certain woman named Lydia heard us. She was a seller of purple from the city of Thyatira, who worshiped God. The Lord opened her heart to heed the things spoken by Paul."

CARNALITY

Must a materialistic world cause you to become a secularized Christian? Not if you maintain alertness against the wiles of the devil.

Boasting about sin

PSALM 52:1—"Why do you boast in evil, O mighty man? The goodness of God endures continually."

When wrong seems right

PROVERBS 14:12—"There is a way that seems right to a man, but its end is the way of death."

Big battle, odds against you, but you can win

ROMANS 7:24–25—"O wretched man that I am! Who will deliver me from this body of death? I thank God—through Jesus Christ our Lord!

So then, with the mind I myself serve the law of God, but with the flesh the law of sin."

By God's help, you can control carnal nature

GALATIANS 5:16—"I say then: Walk in the Spirit, and you shall not fulfill the lust of the flesh."

Total guilt

JAMES 2:10—"Whoever shall keep the whole law, and yet stumble in one point, he is guilty of all."

The guilt of intentional sin

JAMES 4:17—"To him who knows to do good and does not do it, to him it is sin."

Confession brings cleanliness

1 JOHN 1:9—"If we confess our sins, He is faithful and just to forgive us our sins and to cleanse us from all unrighteousness."

Carnality in three dimensions

1 JOHN 2:15–17—"Do not love the world or the things in the world. If anyone loves the world, the love of the Father is not in him. For all that is in the world—the lust of the flesh, the lust of the eyes, and the pride of life—is not of the Father but is of the world. And the world is passing away, and the lust of it; but he who does the will of God abides forever."

CHARACTER

Your Bible is the top-of-the-line resource for character building.

Blameless and upright person

JOB 1:8—"The LORD said to Satan, 'Have you considered My servant Job, that there is none like him on the earth, a blameless and upright man, one who fears God and shuns evil?'"

Consistent conduct

PSALM 106:3—"Blessed are those who keep justice, and he who does righteousness at all times!"

Meditation: **State-of-the-art character development,** Psalm 139:23–24: "Search me, O God, and know my heart; try me, and know my anxieties; and see if there is any wicked way in me, and lead me in the way everlasting."

Reflected inner values

PROVERBS 27:19—"As in water face reflects face, so a man's heart reveals the man."

Recognized traits of a good mother

PROVERBS 31:28—"Her children rise up and call her blessed; her husband also, and he praises her."

Reputation for generosity

ISAIAH 32:8—"A generous man devises generous things, and by generosity he shall stand."

Mind and heart determine character

JEREMIAH 17:10—"I, the LORD, search the heart, I test the mind, even to give every man according to his ways, according to the fruit of his doings."

The Lord's standard of character

MICAH 6:8—"He has shown you, O man, what is good; and what does the LORD require of you but to do justly, to love mercy, and to walk humbly with your God?"

Balanced life of Jesus

LUKE 2:52—"Jesus increased in wisdom and stature, and in favor with God and men."

Good character overcomes evil

ROMANS 12:21—"Do not be overcome by evil, but overcome evil with good."

CHILDREN

Parents who pray for, and properly teach, their children enhance the potential of those children's lives. Also see Family.

Child's duty to parents

DEUTERONOMY 5:16—"Honor your father and your mother, as the LORD your God has commanded you, that your days may be long, and that it may be well with you in the land which the LORD your God is giving you."

Ignorant generation

JUDGES 2:10—"When all that generation had been gathered to their fathers, another generation arose after them who did not know the LORD nor the work which He had done for Israel."

A child prior to conversion

1 SAMUEL 3:7—"Samuel did not yet know the LORD, nor was the word of the LORD yet revealed to him."

Children are from the Lord

PSALM 127:3—"Children are a heritage from the LORD, the fruit of the womb is a reward."

Exemplary sons and daughters

PSALM 144:12—"That our sons may be as plants grown up in their youth; that our daughters may be as pillars, sculptured in palace style."

Solemn promise to parents

PROVERBS 22:6—"Train up a child in the way he should go, and when he is old he will not depart from it."

Disciplining children

PROVERBS 29:17—"Correct your son, and he will give you rest; yes, he will give delight to your soul."

Jesus' love for little children

MATTHEW 19:14—"Jesus said, 'Let the little children come to Me, and do not forbid them; for of such is the kingdom of heaven.'"

Scriptures known from childhood

2 TIMOTHY 3:14–15—"You must continue in the things which you have learned and been assured of, knowing from whom you have learned them, and that from childhood you have known the Holy Scriptures, which are able to make you wise for salvation through faith which is in Christ Jesus."

CHOICE

In His love and wisdom, a sovereign God gives you freedom of choice by which you determine your own destiny. Also see Decision.

Choosing truth

PSALM 119:30—"I have chosen the way of truth; Your judgments I have laid before me."

Your choice, the Lord's guidance

PROVERBS 16:9—"A man's heart plans his way, but the LORD directs his steps."

The Lord chose you

JOHN 15:16—"You did not choose Me, but I chose you and appointed you that you should go and bear fruit, and that your fruit should remain, that whatever you ask the Father in My name He may give you."

Choosing reproof or love

1 CORINTHIANS 4:21—"What do you want? Shall I come to you with a rod, or in love and a spirit of gentleness?"

Making a tough decision

HEBREWS 11:25—"Choosing rather to suffer affliction with the people of God than to enjoy the passing pleasures of sin."

CHRISTMAS

Take the X out of Xmas; with Bible-based holiday prayers, put the Christ *back in Christmas.*

Star of wonder

NUMBERS 24:17—"I see Him, but not now; I behold Him, but not near; a Star shall come out of Jacob; a Scepter shall rise out of Israel, and batter the brow of Moab, and destroy all the sons of tumult."

The Light of the World dispels darkness

ISAIAH 9:2—"The people who walked in darkness have seen a great light; those who dwelt in the land of the shadow of death, upon them a light has shined."

Messiah's dimensions of authority and wonder

ISAIAH 9:6—"For unto us a Child is born, unto us a Son is given; and the government will be upon His shoulder. And His name will be called Wonderful, Counselor, Mighty God, Everlasting Father, Prince of Peace."

Bethlehem prophecy

MICAH 5:2—"You, Bethlehem Ephrathah, though you are little among the thousands of Judah, yet out of you shall come forth to Me the One to be Ruler in Israel, whose goings forth are from of old, from everlasting."

Awe-inspiring impact of Christmas reality

LUKE 2:9–11—"An angel of the Lord stood before them, and the glory of the Lord shone around them, and they were greatly afraid. Then the angel said to them, 'Do not be afraid, for behold, I bring you good tidings of great joy which will be to all people. For there is born to you this day in the city of David a Savior, who is Christ the Lord.'"

All-inclusive meaning of Christmas

JOHN 3:16–17—"For God so loved the world that He gave His only begotten Son, that whoever believes in Him should not perish but have everlasting life. For God did not send His Son into the world to condemn the world, but that the world through Him might be saved."

CHURCH

Your church, where you worship and enjoy Christian fellowship, deserves priority consideration in your prayers.

United together in Christ

JOHN 15:4–5—"Abide in Me, and I in you. As the branch cannot bear fruit of itself, unless it abides in the vine, neither can you, unless you abide in Me. I am the vine, you are the branches. He who abides in Me, and I in him, bears much fruit; for without Me you can do nothing."

Do not pray for easy lives. Pray to be stronger men.

—JOHN F. KENNEDY

Congregational unity

ROMANS 15:5–6—"May the God of patience and comfort grant you to be like-minded toward one another, according to Christ Jesus, that you may with one mind and one mouth glorify the God and Father of our Lord Jesus Christ."

Bear another's burden

GALATIANS 6:2—"Bear one another's burdens, and so fulfill the law of Christ."

Varied talents in congregation

EPHESIANS 4:11–13—"He Himself gave some to be apostles, some prophets, some evangelists, and some pastors and teachers, for the equipping of the saints for the work of ministry, for the edifying of the body of Christ, till we all come to the unity of the faith and of the knowledge of the Son of God, to a perfect man, to the measure of the stature of the fullness of Christ."

Attitude toward church officers

1 THESSALONIANS 5:12–13—"We urge you, brethren, to recognize those who labor among you, and are over you in the Lord and admonish you, and to esteem them very highly in love for their work's sake. Be at peace among yourselves."

Consistent message

2 TIMOTHY 4:1–4—"I charge you therefore before God and the Lord Jesus Christ, who will judge the living and the dead at His appearing and His kingdom: Preach the word! Be ready in season and out of season. Convince, rebuke, exhort, with all longsuffering and teaching. For the time will come when they will not endure sound doctrine, but according to their own desires, because they have itching ears, they will heap up for themselves teachers; and they will turn their ears away from the truth, and be turned aside to fables."

Best seats in the house

JAMES 2:1–4—"My brethren, do not hold the faith of our Lord Jesus Christ, the Lord of glory, with partiality. For if there should come into your assembly a man with gold rings, in fine apparel, and there should also come in a poor man in filthy clothes, and you pay attention to the one wearing the fine clothes and say to him, 'You sit here in a good place,' and say to the poor man, 'You stand there,' or, 'Sit here at my footstool,' have you not shown partiality among yourselves, and become judges with evil thoughts?"

Fellowship of people with forgiven sin

1 JOHN 1:7—"If we walk in the light as He is in the light, we have

fellowship with one another, and the blood of Jesus Christ His Son cleanses us from all sin."

CITIZENSHIP

Be a good citizen on earth by being a good citizen of heaven.

Change of leadership

JOSHUA 1:16–17—"They answered Joshua, saying, 'All that you command us we will do, and wherever you send us we will go. Just as we heeded Moses in all things, so we will heed you. Only the LORD your God be with you, as He was with Moses.'"

Pay your taxes

LUKE 20:21–25—"They asked Him, saying, 'Teacher, we know that You say and teach rightly, and You do not show personal favoritism, but teach the way of God in truth: Is it lawful for us to pay taxes to Caesar or not?' But He perceived their craftiness, and said to them, 'Why do you test Me? Show Me a denarius. Whose image and inscription does it have?' They answered and said, 'Caesar's.' And He said to them, 'Render therefore to Caesar the things that are Caesar's, and to God the things that are God's.'"

Obey your government

ROMANS 13:1—"Let every soul be subject to the governing authorities. For there is no authority except from God, and the authorities that exist are appointed by God."

Pray for your leaders in government

1 TIMOTHY 2:1–3—"I exhort first of all that supplications, prayers, intercessions, and giving of thanks be made for all men, for kings and all who are in authority, that we may lead a quiet and peaceable life in all godliness and reverence. For this is good and acceptable in the sight of God our Savior."

CLEANSING

To be spiritually clean is the highest level of freedom. Also see Carnality, Purity.

Prayer for cleansing

PSALM 51:2—"Wash me thoroughly from my iniquity, and cleanse me from my sin."

Whiter than snow

PSALM 51:7—"Purge me with hyssop, and I shall be clean; wash me, and I shall be whiter than snow."

Cleansed by the Lord

ISAIAH 1:18—"'Come now, and let us reason together,' says the LORD, 'though your sins are like scarlet, they shall be as white as snow; though they are red like crimson, they shall be as wool.'"

Cleansing congregation

1 CORINTHIANS 5:12–13—"For what have I to do with judging those also who are outside? Do you not judge those who are inside? But those who are outside God judges. Therefore 'put away from yourselves the evil person.'"

Set free from cancerous negatives

1 PETER 2:1–2—"Laying aside all malice, all deceit, hypocrisy, envy, and all evil speaking, as newborn babes, desire the pure milk of the word, that you may grow thereby."

COMFORT

The Bible provides the finest therapy for distressed spirits, disturbed emotions, and diseased bodies.

Good Shepherd in action

ISAIAH 40:11—"He will feed His flock like a shepherd; He will gather the lambs with His arm, and carry them in His bosom, and gently lead those who are with young."

Meditation: **Faithfulness new every morning,** Lamentations 3:22–24: "Through the LORD's mercies we are not consumed, because

His compassions fail not. They are new every morning; great is Your faithfulness. 'The LORD is my portion,' says my soul, 'therefore I hope in Him!'"

Those facing discouragement and death

JOHN 14:1–2—"Let not your heart be troubled; you believe in God, believe also in Me. In My Father's house are many mansions; if it were not so, I would have told you. I go to prepare a place for you."

The God of all comfort

2 CORINTHIANS 1:3–4—"Blessed be the God and Father of our Lord Jesus Christ, the Father of mercies and God of all comfort, who comforts us in all our tribulation, that we may be able to comfort those who are in any trouble, with the comfort with which we ourselves are comforted by God."

Consistent resource

2 THESSALONIANS 2:16–17—"May our Lord Jesus Christ Himself, and our God and Father, who has loved us and given us everlasting consolation and good hope by grace, comfort your hearts and establish you in every good word and work."

Assured peace

2 THESSALONIANS 3:16—"May the Lord of peace Himself give you peace always in every way. The Lord be with you all."

Our Lord understands from experience

HEBREWS 4:15–16—"We do not have a High Priest who cannot sympathize with our weaknesses, but was in all points tempted as we are, yet without sin. Let us therefore come boldly to the throne of grace, that we may obtain mercy and find grace to help in time of need."

COMMENDATION

Learn the art of receiving compliments to the glory of God.

Dangerous flattery

JOB 32:21–22—"Let me not, I pray, show partiality to anyone; nor let me flatter any man. For I do not know how to flatter, else my Maker would soon take me away."

Well-timed words

PROVERBS 15:23—"A word spoken in due season, how good it is!"

What others say about you

PROVERBS 27:21—"The refining pot is for silver and the furnace for gold, and a man is valued by what others say of him."

When rebuke is better than flattery

PROVERBS 28:23—"He who rebukes a man will find more favor afterward than he who flatters with the tongue."

Overt commendation

2 CORINTHIANS 7:4—"Great is my boldness of speech toward you, great is my boasting on your behalf. I am filled with comfort. I am exceedingly joyful in all our tribulation."

Let the Lord commend you

2 CORINTHIANS 10:17–18—"'He who glories, let him glory in the LORD.' For not he who commends himself is approved, but whom the Lord commends."

COMMITMENT

The Bible offers counsel and assurance as you commit yourself and your concerns into the care of your Lord.

Clear thinking through commitment

PROVERBS 16:3—"Commit your works to the LORD, and your thoughts will be established."

To die is to live

JOHN 12:24–25—"Most assuredly, I say to you, unless a grain of wheat falls into the ground and dies, it remains alone; but if it dies, it produces much grain. He who loves his life will lose it, and he who hates his life in this world will keep it for eternal life."

STEPS Nugget

DISCOVER YOUR SEVENTH SENSE

Beyond your senses of taste, touch, sight, smell, and hearing lie two additional and oft-ignored senses.

The first of these, the sixth, is the sense of a Divine Being greater than ourselves. Every person on earth has this sense. Note Ecclesiastes 3:11: "He has put eternity in their hearts."

The seventh and most important sense exists solely for Christian believers but is overlooked by multitudes of them. This sense is documented in Ephesians 3:14–19, with the key facet stated in verse 19, "To know the love of Christ which passes knowledge; that you may be filled with all the fullness of God." This involves experiencing fellowship with God in a reality deeper than mere human emotion. It is to realize and practice that the primary purpose of mortality is to prepare us for immortality.

By definition, then, the seventh sense is the sense of discipleship. Earth and heaven become interrelated rather than disjointed. Thus, the seventh sense is integral to STEPS intercession.

Put yourself on the altar

ROMANS 12:1–2—"I beseech you therefore, brethren, by the mercies of God, that you present your bodies a living sacrifice, holy, acceptable to God, which is your reasonable service. And do not be conformed to this world, but be transformed by the renewing of your mind, that you may prove what is that good and acceptable and perfect will of God."

Faithfulness, your first priority

1 CORINTHIANS 4:2—"It is required in stewards that one be found faithful."

Meditation: **Self versus resurrection power,** Philippians 3:7–10: "What things were gain to me, these I have counted loss for Christ. Yet indeed I also count all things loss for the excellence of the knowledge of Christ Jesus my Lord, for whom I have suffered the loss of all things, and count them as rubbish, that I may gain Christ and be found in Him, not having my own righteousness, which is from the law, but that which is through faith in Christ, the righteousness which is from God by faith; that I may know Him and the power of His resurrection, and the fellowship of His sufferings, being conformed to His death."

Relentless pursuit of God's best

PHILIPPIANS 3:13–14—"I do not count myself to have apprehended; but one thing I do, forgetting those things which are behind and reaching forward to those things which are ahead, I press toward the goal for the prize of the upward call of God in Christ Jesus."

Long-term commitment

2 TIMOTHY 1:12—"For this reason I also suffer these things; nevertheless I am not ashamed, for I know whom I have believed and am persuaded that He is able to keep what I have committed to Him until that Day."

Meditation: **Commitment of good soldier and athlete,** 2 Timothy 2:1–5: "You therefore, my son, be strong in the grace that is in Christ Jesus. And the things that you have heard from me among many witnesses, commit these to faithful men who will be able to teach others also. You therefore must endure hardship as a good soldier of Jesus Christ. No one engaged in warfare entangles himself with the affairs of this life, that he may please him who enlisted him as a soldier. And also if anyone competes in athletics, he is not crowned unless he competes according to the rules."

COMMUNICATION

God understands when you have communication problems. He has been having them since the Garden of Eden!

Asking to communicate with the Lord

PSALM 19:14—"Let the words of my mouth and the meditation of my heart be acceptable in Your sight, O LORD, my strength and my Redeemer."

Finding the right words

ECCLESIASTES 12:10—"The Preacher sought to find acceptable words; and what was written was upright—words of truth."

Why some cannot understand

JOHN 8:47—"He who is of God hears God's words; therefore you do not hear, because you are not of God."

Father communicating with children

EPHESIANS 6:4—"You, fathers, do not provoke your children to wrath, but bring them up in the training and admonition of the Lord."

Confusing vocabulary

2 TIMOTHY 2:14—"Remind them of these things, charging them before the Lord not to strive about words to no profit, to the ruin of the hearers."

COMPASSION

These Bible principles and promises, integrated into your prayers, will help you experience and implement compassion.

Showing compassion to prisoners

2 CHRONICLES 28:15—"The men who were designated by name rose up and took the captives, and from the spoil they clothed all who were naked among them, dressed them and gave them sandals, gave them food and drink, and anointed them; and they let all the feeble ones ride on donkeys. So they brought them to their brethren at Jericho, the city of palm trees. Then they returned to Samaria."

Reciprocated compassion

PSALM 41:1—"Blessed is he who considers the poor; the LORD will deliver him in time of trouble."

God's abundant compassion

PSALM 86:15—"But You, O Lord, are a God full of compassion, and gracious, longsuffering and abundant in mercy and truth."

Divine compassion

PSALM 145:8—"The LORD is gracious and full of compassion, slow to anger and great in mercy."

Compassion toward your enemy

PROVERBS 24:17—"Do not rejoice when your enemy falls, and do not let your heart be glad when he stumbles."

New every morning

LAMENTATIONS 3:22–23—"Through the LORD's mercies we are not consumed, because His compassions fail not. They are new every morning; great is Your faithfulness."

Given compassion

EZEKIEL 36:26—"I will give you a new heart and put a new spirit within you; I will take the heart of stone out of your flesh and give you a heart of flesh."

Unprecedented compassion

ROMANS 9:1–4—"I tell the truth in Christ, I am not lying, my conscience also bearing me witness in the Holy Spirit, that I have great sorrow and continual grief in my heart. For I could wish that I myself were accursed from Christ for my brethren, my countrymen according to the flesh, who are Israelites, to whom pertain the adoption, the glory, the covenants, the giving of the law, the service of God, and the promises."

COMPLACENCY

The Bible cautions you to shun this common human weakness.

The complacency of fools

PROVERBS 1:32—"The turning away of the simple will slay them, and the complacency of fools will destroy them."

All my discoveries have been made in answer to prayer.

—SIR ISAAC NEWTON

Avoid a dangerous "who cares?" attitude

ISAIAH 51:7—"Listen to Me, you who know righteousness, you people in whose heart is My law: Do not fear the reproach of men, nor be afraid of their insults."

Casually passing by one in need

LAMENTATIONS 1:12—"Is it nothing to you, all you who pass by? Behold and see if there is any sorrow like my sorrow, which has been brought on me, which the LORD has inflicted in the day of His fierce anger."

Materialism causes complacency toward God

HOSEA 13:6—"When they had pasture, they were filled; they were filled and their heart was exalted; therefore they forgot Me."

Sleeping disciples

MATTHEW 26:40–41—"Then He came to the disciples and found them sleeping, and said to Peter, 'What? Could you not watch with Me one hour? Watch and pray, lest you enter into temptation. The spirit indeed is willing, but the flesh is weak.'"

Sinful complacency

JAMES 4:17—"To him who knows to do good and does not do it, to him it is sin."

Be alert to the cause of complacency

1 PETER 5:8–9—"Be sober, be vigilant; because your adversary the devil walks about like a roaring lion, seeking whom he may devour. Resist him, steadfast in the faith, knowing that the same sufferings are experienced by your brotherhood in the world."

COMPREHENSION

The Bible is your first resource to help you comprehend God's will and way.

Minute perception, magnificent potential

JOB 26:14—"These are the mere edges of His ways, and how small a whisper we hear of Him! But the thunder of His power who can understand?"

Receiving light from God's light

PSALM 36:9—"With You is the fountain of life; in Your light we see light."

A humble servant's request

PSALM 119:125—"I am Your servant; give me understanding, that I may know Your testimonies."

Searching and finding

PROVERBS 2:1–6—"My son, if you receive my words, and treasure my commands within you, so that you incline your ear to wisdom, and apply your heart to understanding; yes, if you cry out for discernment, and lift up your voice for understanding, if you seek her as silver, and search for her as for hidden treasures; then you will understand the fear of the LORD, and find the knowledge of God. For the LORD gives wisdom; from His mouth come knowledge and understanding."

Given wisdom and understanding

DANIEL 12:10—"Many shall be purified, made white, and refined, but the wicked shall do wickedly; and none of the wicked shall understand, but the wise shall understand."

Childhood comprehension

MATTHEW 11:25—"At that time Jesus answered and said, 'I thank You, Father, Lord of heaven and earth, that You have hidden these things from the wise and prudent and have revealed them to babes.'"

Privileged comprehension

LUKE 10:23–24—"He turned to His disciples and said privately, 'Blessed are the eyes which see the things you see; for I tell you that many prophets and kings have desired to see what you see, and have not seen it, and to hear what you hear, and have not heard it.'"

Taught by the Holy Spirit

JOHN 16:13—"When He, the Spirit of truth, has come, He will guide you into all truth; for He will not speak on His own authority, but whatever He hears He will speak; and He will tell you things to come."

Beyond human comprehension

1 CORINTHIANS 2:9—"Eye has not seen, nor ear heard, nor have entered into the heart of man the things which God has prepared for those who love Him."

COMPROMISE

You need the Bible's intervention and guidance to deal with the human tactic of compromise.

King Solomon's spiritual compromise

1 KINGS 3:3—"Solomon loved the LORD, walking in the statutes of his father David, except that he sacrificed and burned incense at the high places."

Secret compromise

2 KINGS 17:9—"The children of Israel secretly did against the LORD their God things that were not right, and they built for themselves high places in all their cities, from watchtower to fortified city."

You cannot serve two masters

MATTHEW 6:24—"No one can serve two masters; for either he will hate the one and love the other, or else he will be loyal to the one and despise the other. You cannot serve God and mammon."

Avoid compromised lifestyle

ROMANS 8:5–6—"Those who live according to the flesh set their minds on the things of the flesh, but those who live according to the Spirit, the things of the Spirit. For to be carnally minded is death, but to be spiritually minded is life and peace."

Sure cure for compromising

ROMANS 12:1–2—"I beseech you therefore, brethren, by the mercies of God, that you present your bodies a living sacrifice, holy, acceptable to God, which is your reasonable service. And do not be conformed to this world, but be transformed by the renewing of your mind, that you may prove what is that good and acceptable and perfect will of God."

Cure for compromise

GALATIANS 5:16—"Walk in the Spirit, and you shall not fulfill the lust of the flesh."

Do not grieve the Holy Spirit

EPHESIANS 4:30—"Do not grieve the Holy Spirit of God, by whom you were sealed for the day of redemption."

Anticipating Christ's return

TITUS 2:11–14—"The grace of God that brings salvation has appeared to all men, teaching us that, denying ungodliness and worldly lusts, we should live soberly, righteously, and godly in the present age, looking for the blessed hope and glorious appearing of our great God and Savior Jesus Christ, who gave Himself for us, that He might redeem us from every lawless deed and purify for Himself His own special people, zealous for good works."

CONFESSION

Putting things right between yourself and God and others can be a fulfilling occurrence.

Meditation: **Prayer of confession and restoration,** Judges 10:15: "The children of Israel said to the LORD, 'We have sinned! Do to us whatever seems best to You; only deliver us this day, we pray.'"

Nehemiah's prologue

NEHEMIAH 1:4–11—"So it was, when I heard these words, that I sat down and wept, and mourned for many days; I was fasting and praying before the God of heaven. And I said: 'I pray, LORD God of heaven, O great and awesome God, You who keep Your covenant and mercy with those who love You and observe Your commandments, please let Your ear be attentive and Your eyes open, that You may hear the prayer of Your servant which I pray before You now, day and night, for the children of Israel Your servants, and confess the sins of the children of Israel which we have sinned against You. Both my father's house and I have sinned. We have acted very corruptly against You, and have not kept the commandments, the statutes, nor the ordinances which You commanded Your servant

Moses. Remember, I pray, the word that You commanded Your servant Moses, saying, "If you are unfaithful, I will scatter you among the nations; but if you return to Me, and keep My commandments and do them, though some of you were cast out to the farthest part of the heavens, yet I will gather them from there, and bring them to the place which I have chosen as a dwelling for My name." Now these are Your servants and Your people, whom You have redeemed by Your great power, and by Your strong hand. O Lord, I pray, please let Your ear be attentive to the prayer of Your servant, and to the prayer of Your servants who desire to fear Your name; and let Your servant prosper this day, I pray, and grant him mercy in the sight of this man.' For I was the king's cupbearer."

Assured of sins forgiven

PSALM 32:5—"I acknowledged my sin to You, and my iniquity I have not hidden. I said, 'I will confess my transgressions to the LORD,' and You forgave the iniquity of my sin."

God knows about foolishness

PSALM 69:5—"O God, You know my foolishness; and my sins are not hidden from You."

Meditation: **Out of the depths,** Psalm 130:1–6: "Out of the depths I have cried to You, O LORD; Lord, hear my voice! Let Your ears be attentive to the voice of my supplications. If You, LORD, should mark iniquities, O Lord, who could stand? But there is forgiveness with You, that You may be feared. I wait for the LORD, my soul waits, and in His word I do hope. My soul waits for the Lord more than those who watch for the morning—yes, more than those who watch for the morning."

Recognize and confess besetting sin

HEBREWS 12:1–2—"We also, since we are surrounded by so great a cloud of witnesses, let us lay aside every weight, and the sin which so easily ensnares us, and let us run with endurance the race that is set before us, looking unto Jesus, the author and finisher of our faith, who for the joy that was set before Him endured the cross, despising the shame, and has sat down at the right hand of the throne of God."

Shared confession

JAMES 5:16—"Confess your trespasses to one another, and pray for one another, that you may be healed. The effective, fervent prayer of a righteous man avails much."

CONFIDENCE

Your Bible exudes confidence. Inherent in your position as God's child is the positive impetus that is yours for the asking.

God is always with you

JOSHUA 1:9—"Have I not commanded you? Be strong and of good courage; do not be afraid, nor be dismayed, for the LORD your God is with you wherever you go."

Consistent confidence

PSALM 16:8—"I have set the LORD always before me; because He is at my right hand I shall not be moved."

Let yourself in on God's secret

PSALM 25:14—"The secret of the LORD is with those who fear Him, and He will show them His covenant."

Be patient; God's will is worth waiting for

PSALM 27:14—"Wait on the LORD; be of good courage, and He shall strengthen your heart; wait, I say, on the LORD!"

Fear of man, trust in the Lord

PROVERBS 29:25—"The fear of man brings a snare, but whoever trusts in the LORD shall be safe."

God knows those who trust Him

NAHUM 1:7—"The LORD is good, a stronghold in the day of trouble; and He knows those who trust in Him."

Ability at your disposal

PHILIPPIANS 4:13—"I can do all things through Christ who strengthens me."

Lifelong confidence

2 TIMOTHY 1:12—"For this reason I also suffer these things; nevertheless I am not ashamed, for I know whom I have believed and am persuaded that He is able to keep what I have committed to Him until that Day."

Meditation: **Pray boldly,** Hebrews 4:13–16: "There is no creature hidden from His sight, but all things are naked and open to the eyes of Him to whom we must give account. Seeing then that we have a great High Priest who has passed through the heavens, Jesus the Son of God, let us hold fast our confession. For we do not have a High Priest who cannot sympathize with our weaknesses, but was in all points tempted as we are, yet without sin. Let us therefore come boldly to the throne of grace, that we may obtain mercy and find grace to help in time of need."

CONFLICT

Overcome your conflicts by applying biblical principles. Also see Opposition.

The Lord fights your battles

DEUTERONOMY 3:22—"You must not fear them, for the LORD your God Himself fights for you."

Confronting an enemy

PSALM 27:1–3—"The LORD is my light and my salvation; whom shall I fear? The LORD is the strength of my life; of whom shall I be afraid?

When the wicked came against me to eat up my flesh, my enemies and foes, they stumbled and fell. Though an army may encamp against me, my heart shall not fear; though war may rise against me, in this I will be confident."

At peace with God and people

PROVERBS 16:7—"When a man's ways please the LORD, He makes even his enemies to be at peace with him."

Avoid conflict with your Lord

ISAIAH 45:9—"Woe to him who strives with his Maker! Let the potsherd strive with the potsherds of the earth! Shall the clay say to him who forms it, 'What are you making?' Or shall your handiwork say, 'He has no hands'?"

Meditation: **Inner spiritual conflict,** Romans 7:22–25: "I delight in the law of God according to the inward man. But I see another law in my members, warring against the law of my mind, and bringing me into captivity to the law of sin which is in my members. O wretched man that I am! Who will deliver me from this body of death? I thank God—through Jesus Christ our Lord! So then, with the mind I myself serve the law of God, but with the flesh the law of sin."

CONFUSION

Rise above confusion with a calm attitude and a clear mind.

Your resource to endure confusion

2 SAMUEL 22:29—"You are my lamp, O LORD; the LORD shall enlighten my darkness."

Darkness into light

PSALM 18:28—"You will light my lamp; the LORD my God will enlighten my darkness."

Confusion depicted

PSALM 82:5—"They do not know, nor do they understand; they walk about in darkness; all the foundations of the earth are unstable."

Guided steps

PROVERBS 20:24—"A man's steps are of the LORD; how then can a man understand his own way?"

Don't strive against God

ISAIAH 45:9—"Woe to him who strives with his Maker! Let the potsherd strive with the potsherds of the earth! Shall the clay say to him who forms it, 'What are you making?' Or shall your handiwork say, 'He has no hands'?"

Follow the Light

JOHN 8:12—"Jesus spoke to them again, saying, 'I am the light of the world. He who follows Me shall not walk in darkness, but have the light of life.'"

You can be steadfast and abounding

1 CORINTHIANS 15:58—"Be steadfast, immovable, always abounding in the work of the Lord, knowing that your labor is not in vain in the Lord."

The gift of clear thinking

2 TIMOTHY 1:7—"God has not given us a spirit of fear, but of power and of love and of a sound mind."

CONSOLATION

When the going is rough, let the Bible console you.

Meditation: **Learn a new song,** Psalm 40:1–3: "I waited patiently for the LORD; and He inclined to me, and heard my cry. He also brought me up out of a horrible pit, out of the miry clay, and set my feet upon a rock, and established my steps. He has put a new song in my mouth—praise to our God; many will see it and fear, and will trust in the LORD."

Refuge and strength

PSALM 46:1—"God is our refuge and strength, a very present help in trouble."

Turn to the Good Shepherd

PSALM 100:1–3—"Make a joyful shout to the LORD, all you lands! Serve the LORD with gladness; come before His presence with singing. Know that the LORD, He is God; it is He who has made us, and not we ourselves; we are His people and the sheep of His pasture."

Death of a Christian

PSALM 116:15—"Precious in the sight of the LORD is the death of His saints."

A place of rest

MATTHEW 11:28—"Come to Me, all you who labor and are heavy laden, and I will give you rest."

CONTENTMENT

Being content with what you have far exceeds the ability to obtain more and more without satisfaction.

Be thankful for the Lord's goodness

PSALM 107:8–9—"Oh, that men would give thanks to the LORD for His goodness, and for His wonderful works to the children of men! For He satisfies the longing soul, and fills the hungry soul with goodness."

Rejoice in the day God has made

PSALM 118:24—"This is the day the LORD has made; we will rejoice and be glad in it."

Family contentment

PSALM 128:3–4—"Your wife shall be like a fruitful vine in the very heart of your house, your children like olive plants all around your table. Behold, thus shall the man be blessed who fears the LORD."

Content with little

PROVERBS 15:16—"Better is a little with the fear of the LORD, than great treasure with trouble."

Let not your heart be troubled

JOHN 14:1–3—"Let not your heart be troubled; you believe in God, believe also in Me. In My Father's house are many mansions; if it were not so, I would have told you. I go to prepare a place for you. And if I go and prepare a place for you, I will come again and receive you to Myself; that where I am, there you may be also."

Meditation: **Long-lasting contentment,** Philippians 4:7–14: "The peace of God, which surpasses all understanding, will guard your hearts and minds through Christ Jesus. Finally, brethren, whatever things are true, whatever things are noble, whatever things are just, whatever things are pure, whatever things are lovely, whatever things are of good report, if there is any virtue and if there is anything praiseworthy—meditate on these things. The things which you learned and received and heard and saw in me, these do, and the God of peace will be with you. But I rejoiced in the Lord greatly that now at last your care for me has flourished again; though you surely did care, but you lacked opportunity. Not that I speak in regard to need, for I have learned in whatever state I am, to be content: I know how to be abased, and I know how to abound. Everywhere and in all things I have learned both to be full and to be hungry, both to abound and to suffer need. I can do all things through Christ who strengthens me. Nevertheless you have done well that you shared in my distress."

Godliness with contentment

1 TIMOTHY 6:6—"Godliness with contentment is great gain."

Be content, not covetous

HEBREWS 13:5—"Let your conduct be without covetousness; be

content with such things as you have. For He Himself has said, 'I will never leave you nor forsake you.'"

CONVERSION

The Bible helps you better understand what is involved when you become a factor in someone's conversion.

A child's need for conversion

1 SAMUEL 3:7—"Samuel did not yet know the LORD, nor was the word of the LORD yet revealed to him."

The Lord's abundant love and mercy

PSALM 51:1–2—"Have mercy upon me, O God, according to Your lovingkindness; according to the multitude of Your tender mercies, blot out my transgressions. Wash me thoroughly from my iniquity, and cleanse me from my sin."

Family division resulting from conversion

LUKE 12:52–53—"From now on five in one house will be divided: three against two, and two against three. Father will be divided against son and son against father, mother against daughter and daughter against mother, mother-in-law against her daughter-in-law and daughter-in-law against her mother-in-law."

Candidates for conversion

JOHN 1:11–12—"He came to His own, and His own did not receive Him. But as many as received Him, to them He gave the right to become children of God, to those who believe in His name."

The need to be born again

JOHN 3:1–7—"There was a man of the Pharisees named Nicodemus, a ruler of the Jews. This man came to Jesus by night and said to Him, 'Rabbi, we know that You are a teacher come from God; for no one can do these signs that You do unless God is with him.' Jesus answered and said to him, 'Most assuredly, I say to you, unless one is born again, he cannot see the kingdom of God.' Nicodemus said to Him, 'How can a man be born when he is old? Can he enter a second time into his mother's womb and be born?' Jesus answered, 'Most assuredly, I say to you, unless one is born of water and the Spirit, he cannot enter the kingdom of God. That which is born of the flesh is flesh, and that which is born of the Spirit is spirit. Do not marvel that I said to you, "You must be born again."'"

Facing the facts

JOHN 20:30–31—"Jesus did many other signs in the presence of His disciples, which are not written in this book; but these are written that you may believe that Jesus is the Christ, the Son of God, and that believing you may have life in His name."

Conversion provides changed life

2 CORINTHIANS 5:17—"If anyone is in Christ, he is a new creation; old things have passed away; behold, all things have become new."

COOPERATION
The Bible speaks helpfully on this subject.

Building together

NEHEMIAH 4:6—"We built the wall, and the entire wall was joined together up to half its height, for the people had a mind to work."

Agreement makes people agreeable

AMOS 3:3—"Can two walk together, unless they are agreed?"

Think cooperatively

1 CORINTHIANS 1:10—"I plead with you, brethren, by the name of our Lord Jesus Christ, that you all speak the same thing, and that there be no divisions among you, but that you be perfectly joined together in the same mind and in the same judgment."

Cooperating in humility

2 CORINTHIANS 4:5—"We do not preach ourselves, but Christ Jesus the Lord, and ourselves your bondservants for Jesus' sake."

Ready to work with gentle spirit

TITUS 3:1–2—"Remind them to be subject to rulers and authorities, to obey, to be ready for every good work, to speak evil of no one, to be peaceable, gentle, showing all humility to all men."

CORRECTION

Giving and receiving correction invite the fine touch the Bible gives. Also see Criticism.

Have a teachable attitude

JOB 6:24—"Teach me, and I will hold my tongue; cause me to understand wherein I have erred."

Some wise, others stupid

PROVERBS 12:1—"Whoever loves instruction loves knowledge, but he who hates correction is stupid."

Danger of refusing correction

PROVERBS 29:1—"He who is often rebuked, and hardens his neck, will suddenly be destroyed, and that without remedy."

Inviting the Lord's correction

JEREMIAH 10:24—"O LORD, correct me, but with justice; not in Your anger, lest You bring me to nothing."

Strong brother, weak brother

GALATIANS 6:1—"If a man is overtaken in any trespass, you who are spiritual restore such a one in a spirit of gentleness, considering yourself lest you also be tempted."

Gentle, patient teaching

2 TIMOTHY 2:24–26—"A servant of the Lord must not quarrel but be

gentle to all, able to teach, patient, in humility correcting those who are in opposition, if God perhaps will grant them repentance, so that they may know the truth, and that they may come to their senses and escape the snare of the devil, having been taken captive by him to do his will."

Parental correction

HEBREWS 12:7—"If you endure chastening, God deals with you as with sons; for what son is there whom a father does not chasten?"

COUNSEL

Needing counsel or giving it, you can find viable guidance in the Bible.

Seek God's counsel daily

1 KINGS 22:5—"Jehoshaphat said to the king of Israel, 'Please inquire for the word of the LORD today.'"

Counselor needing counsel

JOB 4:3–5—"Surely you have instructed many, and you have strengthened weak hands. Your words have upheld him who was stumbling, and you have strengthened the feeble knees; but now it comes upon you, and you are weary; it touches you, and you are troubled."

Let God's light become your light

PSALM 36:9—"With You is the fountain of life; in Your light we see light."

Daily Guidebook

PSALM 119:133—"Direct my steps by Your word."

Counsel put to good use

PROVERBS 9:9—"Give instruction to a wise man, and he will be still wiser; teach a just man, and he will increase in learning."

Listening to many counselors

PROVERBS 15:22—"Without counsel, plans go awry, but in the multitude of counselors they are established."

Meditation: **Counseled by the Holy Spirit,** John 14:15–17: "If you love Me, keep My commandments. And I will pray the Father, and He will give you another Helper, that He may abide with you forever—the Spirit of truth, whom the world cannot receive, because it neither sees Him nor knows Him; but you know Him, for He dwells with you and will be in you."

Sharing from experience

2 CORINTHIANS 1:3–4—"Blessed be the God and Father of our Lord Jesus Christ, the Father of mercies and God of all comfort, who comforts us in all our tribulation, that we may be able to comfort those who are in any trouble, with the comfort with which we ourselves are comforted by God."

Counseling others

GALATIANS 6:1–2—"If a man is overtaken in any trespass, you who are spiritual restore such a one in a spirit of gentleness, considering yourself lest you also be tempted. Bear one another's burdens, and so fulfill the law of Christ."

COURAGE

A Bible specialty, courage involves reinforcement beyond yourself. Also see Boldness.

The battle is the Lord's

EXODUS 14:14—"The LORD will fight for you, and you shall hold your peace."

All the courage you need

JOSHUA 1:9—"Have I not commanded you? Be strong and of good courage; do not be afraid, nor be dismayed, for the LORD your God is with you wherever you go."

Rewarded courage

2 CHRONICLES 15:7—"Be strong and do not let your hands be weak, for your work shall be rewarded!"

Ask the Lord for courage

PSALM 138:3—"In the day when I cried out, You answered me, and made me bold with strength in my soul."

Facing death courageously

ACTS 21:13—"Paul answered, 'What do you mean by weeping and breaking my heart? For I am ready not only to be bound, but also to die at Jerusalem for the name of the Lord Jesus.'"

Don't budge an inch

1 CORINTHIANS 15:58—"Be steadfast, immovable, always abounding in the work of the Lord, knowing that your labor is not in vain in the Lord."

Do not lose heart

2 CORINTHIANS 4:1—"Since we have this ministry, as we have received mercy, we do not lose heart."

No place for fear

2 TIMOTHY 1:7—"God has not given us a spirit of fear, but of power and of love and of a sound mind."

COVET

The Bible censures coveting and provides deliverance. Also see Envy, Jealousy.

Tenth commandment

EXODUS 20:17—"You shall not covet your neighbor's house; you shall not covet your neighbor's wife, nor his male servant, nor his female servant, nor his ox, nor his donkey, nor anything that is your neighbor's."

Antidote to covetousness

PSALM 119:36—"Incline my heart to Your testimonies, and not to covetousness."

Avoid envy

PROVERBS 23:17—"Do not let your heart envy sinners, but be zealous for the fear of the LORD all the day."

Unsatisfied greed

LUKE 12:15—"He said to them, 'Take heed and beware of covetousness, for one's life does not consist in the abundance of the things he possesses.'"

Love negates coveting

ROMANS 13:9—"The commandments, 'You shall not commit adultery,' 'You shall not murder,' 'You shall not steal,' 'You shall not bear false witness,' 'You shall not covet,' and if there is any other commandment, are all summed up in this saying, namely, 'You shall love your neighbor as yourself.'"

> Know the difference between praying and begging. Waiting for the answer to a prayer is also part of the answer.
>
> —OLIVER BARCLAY

CREATION

The universe around us is always cause for praise.

Praise the Creator for His creation

NEHEMIAH 9:6—"You alone are the LORD; You have made heaven, the heaven of heavens, with all their host, the earth and everything on it, the seas and all that is in them, and You preserve them all. The host of heaven worships You."

Humbled by creation

PSALM 8:3–4—"When I consider Your heavens, the work of Your fingers, the moon and the stars, which You have ordained, what is man that You are mindful of him, and the son of man that You visit him?"

STEPS Nugget

INSIDE LOOK AT COVETING

In jest I sometimes say, "I don't covet what you have. I just would like an exact duplicate."

My premise, of course, is wrong. The sin of covetousness is internal. Desire is the wrong, not the object desired. Looking deeper, one also detects a greater wrong, namely, competition in that another person upstages me by possessing something I do not have for myself.

The key is found in Hebrews 13:5: "Let your conduct be without covetousness; be content with such things as you have."

Be in awe of your Creator

PSALM 33:8–9—"Let all the earth fear the LORD; let all the inhabitants of the world stand in awe of Him. For He spoke, and it was done; He commanded, and it stood fast."

Creation illustrates God's mercy, faithfulness, and righteousness

PSALM 36:5–6—"Your mercy, O LORD, is in the heavens; Your faithfulness reaches to the clouds. Your righteousness is like the great mountains; Your judgments are a great deep; O LORD, You preserve man and beast."

Majestic mountains

PSALM 90:2—"Before the mountains were brought forth, or ever You had formed the earth and the world, even from everlasting to everlasting, You are God."

Mighty Creator

JEREMIAH 10:12—"He has made the earth by His power, He has established the world by His wisdom, and has stretched out the heavens at His discretion."

Creation challenges faith

HEBREWS 11:3—"By faith we understand that the worlds were framed by the word of God, so that the things which are seen were not made of things which are visible."

CRISIS

At the point of any crisis, your Bible becomes more resourceful.

Your Refuge and Strength

PSALM 46:1—"God is our refuge and strength, a very present help in trouble."

In the center of the storm

PSALM 138:7—"Though I walk in the midst of trouble, You will revive me; You will stretch out Your hand against the wrath of my enemies, and Your right hand will save me."

The positive side of hurting

PROVERBS 20:30—"Blows that hurt cleanse away evil, as do stripes the inner depths of the heart."

Crisis as a barometer of your need

PROVERBS 24:10—"If you faint in the day of adversity, your strength is small."

Crooked places made straight

ISAIAH 45:2—"I will go before you and make the crooked places straight; I will break in pieces the gates of bronze and cut the bars of iron."

The value of crises

JAMES 1:2–4—"Count it all joy when you fall into various trials, knowing that the testing of your faith produces patience. But let patience have its perfect work, that you may be perfect and complete, lacking nothing."

CRITICISM

Your Bible can teach you how to face and accept criticism. Also see Correction.

A good rule to follow

NUMBERS 23:8—"How shall I curse whom God has not cursed? And how shall I denounce whom the LORD has not denounced?"

Hold your tongue

JOB 6:24–25—"Teach me, and I will hold my tongue; cause me to understand wherein I have erred. How forceful are right words! But what does your arguing prove?"

Criticizing church leaders

PSALM 105:15—"Do not touch My anointed ones, and do My prophets no harm."

Some can't take criticism, but others can

PROVERBS 9:8—"Do not correct a scoffer, lest he hate you; rebuke a wise man, and he will love you."

A friend's criticism

PROVERBS 27:6, 9—"Faithful are the wounds of a friend, but the kisses of an enemy are deceitful . . . Ointment and perfume delight the heart, and the sweetness of a man's friend gives delight by hearty counsel."

Rebuke better than flattery

PROVERBS 28:23—"He who rebukes a man will find more favor afterward than he who flatters with the tongue."

Let the Lord be the judge

1 CORINTHIANS 4:3–4—"With me it is a very small thing that I should

be judged by you or by a human court. In fact, I do not even judge myself. For I know of nothing against myself, yet I am not justified by this; but He who judges me is the Lord."

How to live above criticism

TITUS 2:7–8—"In all things showing yourself to be a pattern of good works; in doctrine showing integrity, reverence, incorruptibility, sound speech that cannot be condemned, that one who is an opponent may be ashamed, having nothing evil to say of you."

Easy does it responding to criticism

JAMES 1:19—"Let every man be swift to hear, slow to speak, slow to wrath."

CULTS

Depend on the Bible for your attitude and action regarding cults. Also see Heresy.

Deceitful publications

JEREMIAH 8:8—"How can you say, 'We are wise, and the law of the LORD is with us'? Look, the false pen of the scribe certainly works falsehood."

Bad dreams

JEREMIAH 23:25–26—"I have heard what the prophets have said who prophesy lies in My name, saying, 'I have dreamed, I have dreamed!' How long will this be in the heart of the prophets who prophesy lies? Indeed they are prophets of the deceit of their own heart."

A son of hell

MATTHEW 23:15—"Woe to you, scribes and Pharisees, hypocrites! For you travel land and sea to win one proselyte, and when he is won, you make him twice as much a son of hell as yourselves."

Stern warning

GALATIANS 1:9—"If anyone preaches any other gospel to you than what you have received, let him be accursed."

Beware of deceitful teaching

COLOSSIANS 2:8—"Beware lest anyone cheat you through philosophy and empty deceit, according to the tradition of men, according to the basic principles of the world, and not according to Christ."

Taught by demons

1 TIMOTHY 4:1—"The Spirit expressly says that in latter times some will depart from the faith, giving heed to deceiving spirits and doctrines of demons."

Gently correcting those in error

2 TIMOTHY 2:24–26—"A servant of the Lord must not quarrel but be gentle to all, able to teach, patient, in humility correcting those who are in opposition, if God perhaps will grant them repentance, so that they may know the truth, and that they may come to their senses and escape the snare of the devil, having been taken captive by him to do his will."

Deceived persons deceive others

2 TIMOTHY 3:13—"Evil men and impostors will grow worse and worse, deceiving and being deceived."

Denying and defying truth

2 PETER 2:1–2—"There were also false prophets among the people, even as there will be false teachers among you, who will secretly bring in destructive heresies, even denying the Lord who bought them, and bring on themselves swift destruction. And many will follow their destructive ways, because of whom the way of truth will be blasphemed."

Led astray by error

2 PETER 3:17—"You therefore, beloved, since you know this beforehand, beware lest you also fall from your own steadfastness, being led away with the error of the wicked."

DANGER

Let danger open the doorway to courage and confidence. Also see Protection.

Secret hiding place

PSALM 27:5—"In the time of trouble He shall hide me in His pavilion; in the secret place of His tabernacle He shall hide me; He shall set me high upon a rock."

Guarded by angels

PSALM 91:11—"He shall give His angels charge over you, to keep you in all your ways."

Work through the fire

ISAIAH 43:2—"When you pass through the waters, I will be with you; and through the rivers, they shall not overflow you. When you walk through the fire, you shall not be burned, nor shall the flame scorch you."

How Jesus faced danger

JOHN 7:1—"After these things Jesus walked in Galilee; for He did not want to walk in Judea, because the Jews sought to kill Him."

DEATH

Exit from life or entrance to eternity? Your view makes all the difference.

Put things in order

2 KINGS 20:1—"In those days Hezekiah was sick and near death. And Isaiah the prophet, the son of Amoz, went to him and said to him, 'Thus says the LORD: "Set your house in order, for you shall die, and not live."'"

Blessed with full life

JOB 5:26—"You shall come to the grave at a full age, as a sheaf of grain ripens in its season."

Shadow of death

PSALM 23:4—"Yea, though I walk through the valley of the shadow of death, I will fear no evil; for You are with me; Your rod and Your staff, they comfort me."

Guidance through life unto death

PSALM 48:14—"This is God, our God forever and ever; He will be our guide even to death."

Nearing and fearing death

PSALM 88:1–5—"O LORD, God of my salvation, I have cried out day and night before You. Let my prayer come before You; incline Your ear to my cry. For my soul is full of troubles, and my life draws near to the grave. I am counted with those who go down to the pit; I am like a man who has no strength, adrift among the dead, like the slain who lie in the grave, whom You remember no more, and who are cut off from Your hand."

Death of a Christian

PSALM 116:15—"Precious in the sight of the LORD is the death of His saints."

Life is like a passing shadow

PSALM 144:3–4—"LORD, what is man, that You take knowledge of him? Or the son of man, that You are mindful of him? Man is like a breath; his days are like a passing shadow."

A time to die

ECCLESIASTES 3:1–2—"To everything there is a season, a time for every purpose under heaven: a time to be born, and a time to die; a time to plant, and a time to pluck what is planted."

Old age sustained

ISAIAH 46:4—"Even to your old age, I am He, and even to gray hairs I will carry you! I have made, and I will bear; even I will carry, and will deliver you."

Resurrection and life

JOHN 11:25–26—"Jesus said to her, 'I am the resurrection and the life. He who believes in Me, though he may die, he shall live. And whoever lives and believes in Me shall never die. Do you believe this?'"

Meditation: **Old body, new body,** 2 Corinthians 5:1–4: "We know that if our earthly house, this tent, is destroyed, we have a building from God, a house not made with hands, eternal in the heavens. For in this we groan, earnestly desiring to be clothed with our habitation which is from heaven, if indeed, having been clothed, we shall not be found naked. For we who are in this tent groan, being burdened, not because we want to be unclothed, but further clothed, that mortality may be swallowed up by life."

DEBT

Faced with insurmountable obligations? Your Lord promises to help you. Also see Bankruptcy, Provision.

Avoid going into debt

ROMANS 13:7–8—"Render therefore to all their due: taxes to whom taxes are due, customs to whom customs, fear to whom fear, honor to whom honor. Owe no one anything except to love one another, for he who loves another has fulfilled the law."

Rule of procedure

1 CORINTHIANS 10:31—"Whether you eat or drink, or whatever you do, do all to the glory of God."

Your status in the bank of heaven

PHILIPPIANS 4:19—"My God shall supply all your need according to His riches in glory by Christ Jesus."

DECEIT

How do you face deception? It can provide opportunity to honor your Lord.

Kiss of death

2 SAMUEL 20:9–10—"Joab said to Amasa, 'Are you in health, my brother?' And Joab took Amasa by the beard with his right hand to kiss him. But Amasa did not notice the sword that was in Joab's hand. And he struck him with it in the stomach, and his entrails poured out on the ground; and he did not strike him again. Thus he died. Then Joab and Abishai his brother pursued Sheba the son of Bichri."

Blessing of no deceit

PSALM 32:2—"Blessed is the man to whom the LORD does not impute iniquity, and in whose spirit there is no deceit."

Deceitful speech

PSALM 55:21—"The words of his mouth were smoother than butter, but war was in his heart; his words were softer than oil, yet they were drawn swords."

Confusing semantics

ISAIAH 5:20—"Woe to those who call evil good, and good evil; who put darkness for light, and light for darkness; who put bitter for sweet, and sweet for bitter!"

Camouflaged deceit

JEREMIAH 12:6—"Even your brothers, the house of your father, even they have dealt treacherously with you; yes, they have called a multitude after you. Do not believe them, even though they speak smooth words to you."

Pious pretense

LUKE 20:20—"They watched Him, and sent spies who pretended to be righteous, that they might seize on His words, in order to deliver Him to the power and the authority of the governor."

Satanic wiles

EPHESIANS 6:11—"Put on the whole armor of God, that you may be able to stand against the wiles of the devil."

Deceitful teaching

2 PETER 2:1–2—"There were also false prophets among the people, even as there will be false teachers among you, who will secretly bring in destructive heresies, even denying the Lord who bought them, and bring on themselves swift destruction. And many will follow their destructive ways, because of whom the way of truth will be blasphemed."

DECISION

When you need to make a decision, you need the insights of the Bible. Also see Choice.

Many plans, God's will

PROVERBS 19:21—"There are many plans in a man's heart, nevertheless the LORD's counsel—that will stand."

God's way and yours

PROVERBS 20:24— "A man's steps are of the LORD; how then can a man understand his own way?"

Ask the Lord to verify a decision

PROVERBS 21:2—"Every way of a man is right in his own eyes, but the LORD weighs the hearts."

Source for making best decisions

ISAIAH 55:8–9—"'My thoughts are not your thoughts, nor are your ways My ways,' says the LORD. 'For as the heavens are higher than the earth, so are My ways higher than your ways, and My thoughts than your thoughts.'"

Jesus prayed before choosing apostles

LUKE 6:12–13—"It came to pass in those days that He went out to the mountain to pray, and continued all night in prayer to God. And when it was day, He called His disciples to Himself; and from them He chose twelve whom He also named apostles."

Meditation: **Expertise in making a decision,** Philippians 1:9–10: "This I pray, that your love may abound still more and more in knowledge and all discernment, that you may approve the things that are excellent, that you may be sincere and without offense till the day of Christ."

Levelheaded decision making
2 TIMOTHY 1:7—"God has not given us a spirit of fear, but of power and of love and of a sound mind."

DEFEAT
Is there such a thing as defeat for the committed Christian? Also see Failure.

Example of being defeated by sin, forgiven by God
1 KINGS 8:33–34—"When Your people Israel are defeated before an enemy because they have sinned against You, and when they turn back to You and confess Your name, and pray and make supplication to You in this temple, then hear in heaven, and forgive the sin of Your people Israel, and bring them back to the land which You gave to their fathers."

> Prayer should be the key of the day and the lock of the night.
>
> —THOMAS FULLER

Lowest ebb of defeat
JOB 17:11—"My days are past, my purposes are broken off, even the thoughts of my heart."

Shame of defeat
PSALM 25:2—"O my God, I trust in You; let me not be ashamed; let not my enemies triumph over me."

Broken and contrite heart

PSALM 34:18—"The LORD is near to those who have a broken heart, and saves such as have a contrite spirit."

Keep your spirits high

2 CORINTHIANS 4:16—"We do not lose heart. Even though our outward man is perishing, yet the inward man is being renewed day by day."

DELAY

Slow progress and hindered plans may sometimes occur in the center of God's will for your life.

Patiently waiting in time of delay

PSALM 130:5–6—"I wait for the LORD, my soul waits, and in His word I do hope. My soul waits for the Lord more than those who watch for the morning—yes, more than those who watch for the morning."

On time in God's plan

HABAKKUK 2:3—"The vision is yet for an appointed time; but at the end it will speak, and it will not lie. Though it tarries, wait for it; because it will surely come, it will not tarry."

No permission for delay

MATTHEW 8:21–22—"Another of His disciples said to Him, 'Lord, let me first go and bury my father.' But Jesus said to him, 'Follow Me, and let the dead bury their own.'"

Given patience

2 THESSALONIANS 3:5—"Now may the Lord direct your hearts into the love of God and into the patience of Christ."

Reason for delayed answer to prayer

JAMES 4:3—"You ask and do not receive, because you ask amiss, that you may spend it on your pleasures."

DELIVERANCE

When you need deliverance, trust God. When you experience deliverance, praise Him.

Rock, Refuge, Deliverer

2 SAMUEL 22:2–3—"The LORD is my rock and my fortress and my deliverer; the God of my strength, in whom I will trust; my shield and the horn of my salvation, my stronghold and my refuge; my Savior, You save me from violence."

Meditation: **Nothing to fear,** Psalm 27:1–5: "The LORD is my light and my salvation; whom shall I fear? The LORD is the strength of my life; of whom shall I be afraid? When the wicked came against me to eat up my flesh, my enemies and foes, they stumbled and fell. Though an army may encamp against me, my heart shall not fear; though war may rise against me, in this I will be confident. One thing I have desired of the LORD, that will I seek: That I may dwell in the house of the LORD all the days of my life, to behold the beauty of the LORD, and to inquire in His temple. For in the time of trouble He shall hide me in His pavilion; in the secret place of His tabernacle He shall hide me; He shall set me high upon a rock."

Delivered from troublemakers

PSALM 35:1—"Plead my cause, O LORD, with those who strive with me; fight against those who fight against me."

God, our Refuge and Strength

PSALM 46:1–2—"God is our refuge and strength, a very present help in trouble. Therefore we will not fear, even though the earth be removed, and though the mountains be carried into the midst of the sea."

When you need protection

PSALM 57:1–2—"Be merciful to me, O God, be merciful to me! For

STEPS Nugget

WHO BELIEVES IN DEMONS?

When I'm asked to address a church-related group on the subject of demons, I begin with the statement: "If you don't believe in the existence of demons, open your Bible to the sixth chapter of Ephesians and tear it out." Then I proceed with a presentation on verses 10 through 16 of that chapter.

Have a look for yourself.

Also browse the Gospels, noting the numerous times Jesus faced the devil and his demons.

In the opinion of many people, demons are more active against Christians than against non-Christians. And they also assert that as children of God, we have the authority to rebuke demons.

I have never seen a Christian, indwelt by the Holy Spirit, who was demon possessed. I have observed many believers who were demon obsessed by the lust of the flesh, the lust of the eyes, and the pride of life, which we are warned against in 1 John 2:16.

my soul trusts in You; and in the shadow of Your wings I will make my refuge, until these calamities have passed by. I will cry out to God Most High, to God who performs all things for me."

Seek help only from God

PSALM 60:11—"Give us help from trouble, for the help of man is useless."

Total trust in God

PSALM 118:8–9—"It is better to trust in the LORD than to put confidence in man. It is better to trust in the LORD than to put confidence in princes."

> When it is hardest to pray, pray harder.
>
> —MARTIN LUTHER

Deliverance from sin

ROMANS 7:24–25—"O wretched man that I am! Who will deliver me from this body of death? I thank God—through Jesus Christ our Lord! So then, with the mind I myself serve the law of God, but with the flesh the law of sin."

Glory to God for deliverance

2 TIMOTHY 4:18—"The Lord will deliver me from every evil work and preserve me for His heavenly kingdom. To Him be glory forever and ever. Amen!"

DEMONS

Satan surely gloats over the nonchalance of many Christians toward demons, who are as active as angels in your life.

Rebuking a demon

MARK 9:25—"When Jesus saw that the people came running together, He rebuked the unclean spirit, saying to it: 'Deaf and dumb spirit, I command you, come out of him and enter him no more!'"

False angel of light

2 CORINTHIANS 11:14—"Satan himself transforms himself into an angel of light."

Your encounter with demons

EPHESIANS 6:12—"We do not wrestle against flesh and blood, but against principalities, against powers, against the rulers of the darkness of this age, against spiritual hosts of wickedness in the heavenly places."

Delivered from darkness

COLOSSIANS 1:13–14—"He has delivered us from the power of darkness and conveyed us into the kingdom of the Son of His love, in whom we have redemption through His blood, the forgiveness of sins."

Caught in Satan's trap

2 TIMOTHY 2:25–26—"In humility correcting those who are in opposition, if God perhaps will grant them repentance, so that they may know the truth, and that they may come to their senses and escape the snare of the devil, having been taken captive by him to do his will."

Demons believe

JAMES 2:19—"You believe that there is one God. You do well. Even the demons believe—and tremble!"

Submit to God; resist the devil

JAMES 4:7—"Submit to God. Resist the devil and he will flee from you."

DEPRAVITY

Never give up praying for those who are lost, however deep their lostness.

Born a sinner

PSALM 51:5—"I was brought forth in iniquity, and in sin my mother conceived me."

All are lost

PROVERBS 20:9—"Who can say, 'I have made my heart clean, I am pure from my sin'?"

Confused definitions

ISAIAH 5:20—"Woe to those who call evil good, and good evil; who put darkness for light, and light for darkness; who put bitter for sweet, and sweet for bitter!"

Who can be called good?

ISAIAH 64:6—"We are all like an unclean thing, and all our righteousnesses are like filthy rags."

Deceitful heart

JEREMIAH 17:9—"The heart is deceitful above all things, and desperately wicked; who can know it?"

Those who love darkness

JOHN 3:19—"This is the condemnation, that the light has come into the world, and men loved darkness rather than light, because their deeds were evil."

All have sinned

ROMANS 3:23—"All have sinned and fall short of the glory of God."

Understanding the natural man

1 CORINTHIANS 2:14—"The natural man does not receive the things of the Spirit of God, for they are foolishness to him; nor can he know them, because they are spiritually discerned."

One sin or all

JAMES 2:10—"Whoever shall keep the whole law, and yet stumble in one point, he is guilty of all."

DEPRESSION

In the depths of despair, you can have hope. Also see Anxiety, Stress.

Rescued from deep waters

2 SAMUEL 22:17—"He sent from above, He took me, He drew me out of many waters."

Gloom today, golden tomorrow

JOB 23:10—"He knows the way that I take; when He has tested me, I shall come forth as gold."

Your Lord cares about depression

PSALM 34:18—"The LORD is near to those who have a broken heart, and saves such as have a contrite spirit."

Broken spirit and happy heart

PROVERBS 17:22—"A merry heart does good, like medicine, but a broken spirit dries the bones."

Walking in darkness, seeing a light

ISAIAH 9:2—"The people who walked in darkness have seen a great light; those who dwelt in the land of the shadow of death, upon them a light has shined."

Solid anchor in stormy times

HEBREWS 6:19—"This hope we have as an anchor of the soul, both sure and steadfast, and which enters the Presence behind the veil."

Meditation: **Tough times have a purpose,** James 1:2–4: "Count it all joy when you fall into various trials, knowing that the testing of your faith produces patience. But let patience have its perfect work, that you may be perfect and complete, lacking nothing."

DESIRE

What do you choose—godly desires or worldly desires?

When God grants your desires

PSALM 37:4—"Delight yourself also in the LORD, and He shall give you the desires of your heart."

Greatest desire of all

PSALM 73:25—"Whom have I in heaven but You? And there is none upon earth that I desire besides You."

Desire delayed, then fulfilled

PROVERBS 13:12—"Hope deferred makes the heart sick, but when the desire comes, it is a tree of life."

In the night hours

ISAIAH 26:9—"With my soul I have desired You in the night, yes, by my spirit within me I will seek You early; for when Your judgments are in the earth, the inhabitants of the world will learn righteousness."

Meditation: **A purifying desire,** Philippians 3:7–8: "What things were gain to me, these I have counted loss for Christ. Yet indeed I also count all things loss for the excellence of the knowledge of Christ Jesus my Lord, for whom I have suffered the loss of all things, and count them as rubbish, that I may gain Christ."

Desire for money a potential evil

1 TIMOTHY 6:9–10—"Those who desire to be rich fall into temptation and a snare, and into many foolish and harmful lusts which drown men in destruction and perdition. For the love of money is a root of all kinds of evil, for which some have strayed from the faith in their greediness, and pierced themselves through with many sorrows."

Worldly desire versus doing God's will

1 JOHN 2:15–17—"Do not love the world or the things in the world. If anyone loves the world, the love of the Father is not in him. For all that is in the world—the lust of the flesh, the lust of the eyes, and the pride of life—is not of the Father but is of the world. And the world is passing away, and the lust of it; but he who does the will of God abides forever."

DESPAIR

Circumstances can bring the strongest Christians to the brink of despair. Also see Confusion, Crisis, Deliverance, Depression.

Trust in the Lord

PSALM 34:8—"Oh, taste and see that the LORD is good; blessed is the man who trusts in Him!"

Turn from despair to hope

PSALM 42:5—"Why are you cast down, O my soul? And why are you disquieted within me? Hope in God, for I shall yet praise Him for the help of His countenance."

Desperation prayer

PSALM 88:1–2—"O LORD, God of my salvation, I have cried out day and night before You. Let my prayer come before You; incline Your ear to my cry."

Daring to have hope

PROVERBS 13:12—"Hope deferred makes the heart sick, but when the desire comes, it is a tree of life."

Finding peace and rest

MATTHEW 11:28—"Come to Me, all you who labor and are heavy laden, and I will give you rest."

DETERMINATION

Determination involves your effort to do God's will in God's way for God's glory. Also see Courage.

Determination rewarded

2 CHRONICLES 15:7—"Be strong and do not let your hands be weak, for your work shall be rewarded!"

Ever onward in God's will

PSALM 44:18—"Our heart has not turned back, nor have our steps departed from Your way."

Priority determination

PSALM 119:10—"With my whole heart I have sought You; oh, let me not wander from Your commandments!"

Forward with God's help

ISAIAH 50:7—"The Lord GOD will help Me; therefore I will not be disgraced; therefore I have set My face like a flint, and I know that I will not be ashamed."

DISAGREEMENT

When you disagree with someone, you have an excellent opportunity to utilize Christian grace.

Hold your tongue and keep your cool

PROVERBS 17:27—"He who has knowledge spares his words, and a man of understanding is of a calm spirit."

Potential value of disagreement

PROVERBS 27:17—"As iron sharpens iron, so a man sharpens the countenance of his friend."

When it's wrong to go to court

1 CORINTHIANS 6:1–2—"Dare any of you, having a matter against another, go to law before the unrighteous, and not before the saints? Do you not know that the saints will judge the world? And if the world will be judged by you, are you unworthy to judge the smallest matters?"

Apply gentleness

2 TIMOTHY 2:24—"A servant of the Lord must not quarrel but be gentle to all, able to teach, patient."

DISAPPOINTMENT

Remember the saying, "Disappointment can be His appointment."

Mature attitude toward disappointment

JOB 1:21—"Naked I came from my mother's womb, and naked shall I return there. The LORD gave, and the LORD has taken away; blessed be the name of the LORD."

No fear of disappointment

PSALM 112:7—"He will not be afraid of evil tidings; his heart is steadfast, trusting in the LORD."

Disappointment and fulfillment

PROVERBS 13:12—"Hope deferred makes the heart sick, but when the desire comes, it is a tree of life."

Blessing from disappointment

ROMANS 5:3—"We also glory in tribulations, knowing that tribulation produces perseverance."

Sufficient grace for any disappointment

2 CORINTHIANS 12:9—"He said to me, 'My grace is sufficient for you, for My strength is made perfect in weakness.' Therefore most gladly I will rather boast in my infirmities, that the power of Christ may rest upon me."

Given patience

2 THESSALONIANS 3:5—"May the Lord direct your hearts into the love of God and into the patience of Christ."

Meditation: **Positive attitude facing disappointment,** James 1:2–6: "Count it all joy when you fall into various trials, knowing that the testing of your faith produces patience. But let patience have its perfect work, that you may be perfect and complete, lacking nothing. If any of you lacks wisdom, let him ask of God, who gives to all liberally and without reproach, and it will be given to him. But let him ask in faith, with no doubting, for he who doubts is like a wave of the sea driven and tossed by the wind."

DISCERNMENT
Ask God for discernment undergirded by integrity.

Prayer for discernment

PSALM 119:125—"I am Your servant; give me understanding, that I may know Your testimonies."

The Lord's ways are the right ways

HOSEA 14:9—"Who is wise? Let him understand these things. Who is prudent? Let him know them. For the ways of the LORD are right; the righteous walk in them, but transgressors stumble in them."

Shrewd discernment

MATTHEW 10:16—"I send you out as sheep in the midst of wolves. Therefore be wise as serpents and harmless as doves."

Human wisdom versus divine wisdom

COLOSSIANS 2:8—"Beware lest anyone cheat you through philosophy and empty deceit, according to the tradition of men, according to the basic principles of the world, and not according to Christ."

Gift of understanding

2 TIMOTHY 2:7—"May the Lord give you understanding in all things."

Correctly discerning Bible teaching

2 TIMOTHY 2:15—"Be diligent to present yourself approved to God, a worker who does not need to be ashamed, rightly dividing the word of truth."

Meditation: **Milk and meat,** Hebrews 5:12–14: "For though by this time you ought to be teachers, you need someone to teach you again the first principles of the oracles of God; and you have come to need milk and not solid food. For everyone who partakes only of milk is unskilled in the word of righteousness, for he is a babe. But solid food belongs to those who are of full age, that is, those who by reason of use have their senses exercised to discern both good and evil."

Ask God for discernment

JAMES 1:5—"If any of you lacks wisdom, let him ask of God, who gives to all liberally and without reproach, and it will be given to him."

DISCIPLESHIP

The ultimate status in life is to become a true disciple of Jesus Christ. Also see Commitment, Discipline, Obedience.

Full to the brim with righteousness

MATTHEW 5:6—"Blessed are those who hunger and thirst for righteousness, for they shall be filled."

Salt and light

MATTHEW 5:13–14—"You are the salt of the earth; but if the salt loses its flavor, how shall it be seasoned? It is then good for nothing but to be thrown out and trampled underfoot by men. You are the light of the world. A city that is set on a hill cannot be hidden."

Cost of discipleship

MATTHEW 16:24–25—"Jesus said to His disciples, 'If anyone desires to come after Me, let him deny himself, and take up his cross, and follow Me. For whoever desires to save his life will lose it, but whoever loses his life for My sake will find it.'"

Genuine trademark

JOHN 8:31—"Jesus said to those Jews who believed Him, 'If you abide in My word, you are My disciples indeed.'"

Becoming a servant

1 CORINTHIANS 9:19—"For though I am free from all men, I have made myself a servant to all, that I might win the more."

Crucified with Christ

GALATIANS 2:20—"I have been crucified with Christ; it is no longer I who live, but Christ lives in me; and the life which I now live in the flesh I live by faith in the Son of God, who loved me and gave Himself for me."

Serving one another

GALATIANS 5:13—"For you, brethren, have been called to liberty; only do not use liberty as an opportunity for the flesh, but through love serve one another."

Unselfishness

PHILIPPIANS 2:3—"Let nothing be done through selfish ambition or conceit, but in lowliness of mind let each esteem others better than himself."

DISCIPLINE

The edifying mental and physical calisthenics of discipline foster spiritual growth.

Bit and bridle

PSALM 32:8–9—"I will instruct you and teach you in the way you should go; I will guide you with My eye. Do not be like the horse or like the mule, which have no understanding, which must be harnessed with bit and bridle, else they will not come near you."

Disciplined speech

PSALM 141:3—"Set a guard, O LORD, over my mouth; keep watch over the door of my lips."

Meditation: **Accept the Lord's loving discipline,** Proverbs 3:11–12: "My son, do not despise the chastening of the LORD, nor detest His correction; for whom the LORD loves He corrects, just as a father the son in whom he delights."

Value of disciplining children

PROVERBS 22:15—"Foolishness is bound up in the heart of a child; the rod of correction will drive it far from him."

Neglected child

PROVERBS 29:15—"The rod and rebuke give wisdom, but a child left to himself brings shame to his mother."

Fathers discipline children

EPHESIANS 6:4—"Fathers, do not provoke your children to wrath, but bring them up in the training and admonition of the Lord."

Disciplined lifestyle

COLOSSIANS 2:6–7—"As you therefore have received Christ Jesus the Lord, so walk in Him, rooted and built up in Him and established in the faith, as you have been taught, abounding in it with thanksgiving."

Be serious about prayer

1 PETER 4:7—"The end of all things is at hand; therefore be serious and watchful in your prayers."

DISCOURAGEMENT

Faith offers you sure release from discouragement. Also see Encouragement.

Down in the dumps? Look up

PSALM 42:11—"Why are you cast down, O my soul? And why are you disquieted within me? Hope in God; for I shall yet praise Him, the help of my countenance and my God."

Your Lord knows; trust Him

PSALM 142:3—"When my spirit was overwhelmed within me, then You knew my path."

Meditation: **Utterly discouraged,** Psalm 143:4–8: "My spirit is overwhelmed within me; my heart within me is distressed. I remember the days of old; I meditate on all Your works; I muse on the work of Your hands. I spread out my hands to You; my soul longs for You like a thirsty land. Answer me speedily, O LORD; my spirit fails! Do not hide Your face from me, lest I be like those who go down into the pit. Cause me to hear Your lovingkindness in the morning, for in You do I trust; cause me to know the way in which I should walk, for I lift up my soul to You."

Heavy laden find rest

MATTHEW 11:28—"Come to Me, all you who labor and are heavy laden, and I will give you rest."

Your Lord makes no mistakes

ROMANS 8:28—"We know that all things work together for good to those who love God, to those who are the called according to His purpose."

On the winning team

1 CORINTHIANS 15:57–58—"Thanks be to God, who gives us the victory through our Lord Jesus Christ. Therefore, my beloved brethren, be steadfast, immovable, always abounding in the work of the Lord, knowing that your labor is not in vain in the Lord."

DISCRETION

The distinct mark of maturity in a Christian is discretion.

Learning discretion

PROVERBS 2:3–6—"Yes, if you cry out for discernment, and lift up your voice for understanding, if you seek her as silver, and search for her as for hidden treasures; then you will understand the fear of the LORD, and find the knowledge of God. For the LORD gives wisdom; from His mouth come knowledge and understanding."

Discreet speech

PROVERBS 10:32—"The lips of the righteous know what is acceptable, but the mouth of the wicked what is perverse."

Moral discretion

PROVERBS 11:6—"The righteousness of the upright will deliver them, but the unfaithful will be caught by their lust."

Divine guidelines

ISAIAH 28:26—"He instructs him in right judgment, his God teaches him."

Best source for discretion

1 JOHN 5:20—"We know that the Son of God has come and has given us an understanding, that we may know Him who is true; and we are in Him who is true, in His Son Jesus Christ. This is the true God and eternal life."

DISCRIMINATION

All are equal in God's sight.

Generic name for both sexes

GENESIS 5:2—"He created them male and female, and blessed them and called them Mankind in the day they were created."

Racial discrimination in Egypt

GENESIS 43:32—"They set him a place by himself, and them by themselves, and the Egyptians who ate with him by themselves; because the Egyptians could not eat food with the Hebrews, for that is an abomination to the Egyptians."

Jewish Christian view

ACTS 10:28—"He said to them, 'You know how unlawful it is for a Jewish man to keep company with or go to one of another nation. But God has shown me that I should not call any man common or unclean.'"

All share the same blood

ACTS 17:26—"He has made from one blood every nation of men to dwell on all the face of the earth, and has determined their preappointed times and the boundaries of their dwellings."

We are all one in Christ

GALATIANS 3:28—"There is neither Jew nor Greek, there is neither slave nor free, there is neither male nor female; for you are all one in Christ Jesus."

No partiality in Christ

EPHESIANS 6:9—"Masters, do the same things to them, giving up threatening, knowing that your own Master also is in heaven, and there is no partiality with Him."

DISOBEDIENCE

Whether by omission or commission, disobedience mars and scars.

Causing weariness to God

ISAIAH 7:13—"Is it a small thing for you to weary men, but will you weary my God also?"

Stale salt

MATTHEW 5:13—"You are the salt of the earth; but if the salt loses its flavor, how shall it be seasoned? It is then good for nothing but to be thrown out and trampled underfoot by men."

God's anger against disobedience

EPHESIANS 5:6—"Let no one deceive you with empty words, for because of these things the wrath of God comes upon the sons of disobedience."

Disobeying the gospel

2 THESSALONIANS 1:8—"In flaming fire taking vengeance on those who do not know God, and on those who do not obey the gospel of our Lord Jesus Christ."

Neglecting great salvation

HEBREWS 2:2–3—"For if the word spoken through angels proved

steadfast, and every transgression and disobedience received a just reward, how shall we escape if we neglect so great a salvation, which at the first began to be spoken by the Lord, and was confirmed to us by those who heard Him?"

Disobedient teaching

2 PETER 2:1—"There were also false prophets among the people, even as there will be false teachers among you, who will secretly bring in destructive heresies, even denying the Lord who bought them, and bring on themselves swift destruction."

DISSENSION

Dissension is all too common among Christians and equally unnecessary.

Dissension defined by Jesus

LUKE 11:23—"He who is not with Me is against Me, and he who does not gather with Me scatters."

Jesus accused of dissension

JOHN 7:12—"There was much complaining among the people concerning Him. Some said, 'He is good'; others said, 'No, on the contrary, He deceives the people.'"

Avoid doctrinal confrontation

ROMANS 16:17—"I urge you, brethren, note those who cause divisions and offenses, contrary to the doctrine which you learned, and avoid them."

Distorted teaching

1 TIMOTHY 1:3–4—"As I urged you when I went into Macedonia— remain in Ephesus that you may charge some that they teach no other doctrine, nor give heed to fables and endless genealogies, which cause disputes rather than godly edification which is in faith."

DIVORCE

Now at plague proportions, divorce is a specific Bible concern. Also see Marriage.

View of Jesus

MATTHEW 19:7–9—"They said to Him, 'Why then did Moses command to give a certificate of divorce, and to put her away?' He said to them, 'Moses, because of the hardness of your hearts, permitted you to divorce your wives, but from the beginning it was not so. And I say to you, whoever divorces his wife, except for sexual immorality, and marries another, commits adultery; and whoever marries her who is divorced commits adultery.'"

> Praying in the will of God is to want what He wants.
>
> —A. W. TOZER

Adultery and divorce

MARK 10:11–12—"Whoever divorces his wife and marries another commits adultery against her. And if a woman divorces her husband and marries another, she commits adultery."

Marital rapport

COLOSSIANS 3:18–19—"Wives, submit to your own husbands, as is fitting in the Lord. Husbands, love your wives and do not be bitter toward them."

Avoiding divorce

1 PETER 3:1—"Wives, likewise, be submissive to your own husbands, that even if some do not obey the word, they, without a word, may be won by the conduct of their wives."

STEPS Nugget

LAYOLOGY

I consider myself a student of layology rather than theology. Thus, I am classified as a layologian instead of a theologian. I have read several books on theology and see much importance in the study of doctrines and dispensations. I have close friends who are astute theologians, and I treasure their fellowship. Some assisted me as I was writing this book.

However, when I read my Bible, my foremost objective is not to affirm some doctrinal bias—whether I am pretrib or posttrib, Calvinist or Arminian—but to determine how Ken Anderson can be a better person today than he was yesterday, with actions and reactions that are genuinely Christian. Consequently I sometimes make practical applications of the Bible that are different from the majority opinion.

For example, in 1 Corinthians 3:2, Paul cajoled his followers, saying, "I fed you with milk and not with solid food." In the view of most Bible teachers—and correctly so—"milk" speaks of the simple truths, whereas "solid food" pertains to in-depth teachings, perhaps such as doctrines and dispensations.

Layology suggests another possible approach, however, in which "milk" involves significant truths categorized as doctrinal, dispensational, and the like, including opinions that may sometimes hinder fellowship between Christians.

On the other hand, my layology depicts *"solid food"* as Bible teachings that unite Christians, such as loving those with whom you disagree, learning patience, demonstrating compassion, reaching out to others, and consistently endeavoring to become a better person.

Healing power of love

1 PETER 4:8—"Above all things have fervent love for one another, for 'love will cover a multitude of sins.'"

DOCTRINE

Agree to disagree, yet be united by faith, hope, and love.

> ### How to Turn Doubting into Believing
>
> ---
>
> If you have many doubts but desire faith, read Appendix A: Proof Positive.

Differences of opinion

ROMANS 14:15—"If your brother is grieved because of your food, you are no longer walking in love. Do not destroy with your food the one for whom Christ died."

Meditation: **Spiritual babes in Pew Land,** 1 Corinthians 3:1–3: "I, brethren, could not speak to you as to spiritual people but as to carnal, as to babes in Christ. I fed you with milk and not with solid food; for until now you were not able to receive it, and even now you are still not able; for you are still carnal. For where there are envy, strife, and divisions among you, are you not carnal and behaving like mere men?"

Bedrock doctrine

1 CORINTHIANS 13:12–13—"Now we see in a mirror, dimly, but then face to face. Now I know in part, but then I shall know just as I also am known. And now abide faith, hope, love, these three; but the greatest of these is love."

Wavering faith

EPHESIANS 4:14—"That we should no longer be children, tossed to and fro and carried about with every wind of doctrine, by the trickery of men, in the cunning craftiness of deceitful plotting."

Disruptive preaching

PHILIPPIANS 1:15—"Some indeed preach Christ even from envy and strife, and some also from goodwill."

Demonic doctrine

1 TIMOTHY 4:1—"The Spirit expressly says that in latter times some will depart from the faith, giving heed to deceiving spirits and doctrines of demons."

Good doctrine

1 TIMOTHY 4:6—"If you instruct the brethren in these things, you will be a good minister of Jesus Christ, nourished in the words of faith and of the good doctrine which you have carefully followed."

Avoid foolish argument

2 TIMOTHY 2:23—"Avoid foolish and ignorant disputes, knowing that they generate strife."

DOUBT

Nothing dispels doubt like sincere searching for truth.

Be still and be sure

PSALM 46:10—"Be still, and know that I am God; I will be exalted among the nations, I will be exalted in the earth!"

Weakness of unbelief

ROMANS 3:3–4—"What if some did not believe? Will their unbelief make the faithfulness of God without effect? Certainly not! Indeed, let God be true but every man a liar."

Source of faith

ROMANS 10:17—"Faith comes by hearing, and hearing by the word of God."

Human wisdom tested

COLOSSIANS 2:8—"Beware lest anyone cheat you through philosophy and empty deceit, according to the tradition of men, according to the basic principles of the world, and not according to Christ."

Meditation: **Dynamic faith,** Hebrews 11:1–3, 6: "Faith is the substance of things hoped for, the evidence of things not seen. For by it the elders obtained a good testimony. By faith we understand that the worlds were framed by the word of God, so that the things which are seen were not made of things which are visible . . . But without faith it is impossible to please Him, for he who comes to God must believe that He is, and that He is a rewarder of those who diligently seek Him."

Sure of eternal life

1 JOHN 5:11–13—"This is the testimony: that God has given us eternal life, and this life is in His Son. He who has the Son has life; he who does not have the Son of God does not have life. These things I have written to you who believe in the name of the Son of God, that you may know that you have eternal life, and that you may continue to believe in the name of the Son of God."

EASTER

Discover your legacy in resurrection power.

Live the Easter lifestyle

ROMANS 6:4—"Just as Christ was raised from the dead by the glory of the Father, even so we also should walk in newness of life."

What if there were no Easter?

1 CORINTHIANS 15:13–14—"If there is no resurrection of the dead, then Christ is not risen. And if Christ is not risen, then our preaching is empty and your faith is also empty."

Meditation: **Charge your batteries with resurrection power,** Ephesians 1:15–21: "I also, after I heard of your faith in the Lord Jesus and your love for all the saints, do not cease to give thanks for you, making mention of you in my prayers: that the God of our Lord Jesus Christ, the Father of glory, may give to you the spirit of wisdom and revelation in the knowledge of Him, the eyes of your understanding being enlightened; that you may know what is the hope of His calling, what are the riches of the glory of His inheritance in the saints, and what is the exceeding greatness of His power toward us who believe, according to the working of His mighty power which He worked in Christ when He raised Him from the dead and seated Him at His right hand in the heavenly places, far above all principality and power and might and dominion, and every name that is named, not only in this age but also in that which is to come."

Easter prayer

PHILIPPIANS 3:7–11—"What things were gain to me, these I have counted loss for Christ. Yet indeed I also count all things loss for the excellence of the knowledge of Christ Jesus my Lord, for whom I have suffered the loss of all things, and count them as rubbish, that I may gain Christ and be found in Him, not having my own righteousness, which is from the law, but that which is through faith in Christ, the righteousness which is from God by faith; that I may know Him and the power of His resurrection, and the fellowship of His sufferings, being conformed to His death, if, by any means, I may attain to the resurrection from the dead."

Your own personal Easter

COLOSSIANS 3:1–3—"If then you were raised with Christ, seek those things which are above, where Christ is, sitting at the right hand of God. Set your mind on things above, not on things on the earth. For you died, and your life is hidden with Christ in God."

A living hope

1 PETER 1:3—"Blessed be the God and Father of our Lord Jesus

Christ, who according to His abundant mercy has begotten us again to a living hope through the resurrection of Jesus Christ from the dead."

EGO

As treacherous as cancer, ego can debilitate your soul. Also see Humility, Pride.

To God be the glory

PSALM 115:1—"Not unto us, O LORD, not unto us, but to Your name give glory, because of Your mercy, because of Your truth."

God is pure ego

ISAIAH 42:8—"I am the LORD, that is My name; and My glory I will not give to another, nor My praise to carved images."

Foolish ego game

2 CORINTHIANS 10:12—"We dare not class ourselves or compare ourselves with those who commend themselves. But they, measuring themselves by themselves, and comparing themselves among themselves, are not wise."

Meditation: **Christ's purifying example,** Philippians 2:3-11: "Let nothing be done through selfish ambition or conceit, but in lowliness of mind let each esteem others better than himself. Let each of you look out not only for his own interests, but also for the interests of others. Let this mind be in you which was also in Christ Jesus, who, being in the form of God, did not consider it robbery to be equal with God, but made Himself of no reputation, taking the form of a bondservant, and coming in the likeness of men. And being found in appearance as a man, He humbled Himself and became obedient to the point of death, even the death of the cross. Therefore God also has highly exalted Him and given Him the name which is above every name, that at the name of Jesus every knee should bow, of those in heaven, and of those on earth, and of those under the earth, and that every tongue should confess that Jesus Christ is Lord, to the glory of God the Father."

EMOTIONS

Emotions are the avenue and venue of spiritual intimacy.

Lamented disobedience

JOSHUA 7:6—"Joshua tore his clothes, and fell to the earth on his face before the ark of the LORD until evening, he and the elders of Israel; and they put dust on their heads."

Mind and heart

JOB 38:36—"Who has put wisdom in the mind? Or who has given understanding to the heart?"

Controlled emotions

PROVERBS 4:23—"Keep your heart with all diligence, for out of it spring the issues of life."

Sorrow and joy

ECCLESIASTES 3:4—"A time to weep, and a time to laugh; a time to mourn, and a time to dance."

Tears and supplication

JEREMIAH 31:9—"They shall come with weeping, and with supplications I will lead them. I will cause them to walk by the rivers of waters, in a straight way in which they shall not stumble."

Emotions of Jesus

JOHN 11:35—"Jesus wept."

Caring tears

ACTS 20:31—"Watch, and remember that for three years I did not cease to warn everyone night and day with tears."

Fervent spirit

ROMANS 12:11—"Not lagging in diligence, fervent in spirit, serving the Lord."

Joyful in troubled times

2 CORINTHIANS 7:4—"Great is my boldness of speech toward you, great is my boasting on your behalf. I am filled with comfort. I am exceedingly joyful in all our tribulation."

ENCOURAGEMENT

People prone to discouragement often respond most quickly to encouragement. Also see Commendation, Discouragement.

Be alert to encourage others

PROVERBS 3:27—"Do not withhold good from those to whom it is due, when it is in the power of your hand to do so."

The Lord encourages

ISAIAH 41:13—"I, the LORD your God, will hold your right hand, saying to you, 'Fear not, I will help you.'"

Sure therapy for anxious hearts

JOHN 16:33—"These things I have spoken to you, that in Me you may have peace. In the world you will have tribulation; but be of good cheer, I have overcome the world."

Mutual encouragement

PHILIPPIANS 2:1–2—"If there is any consolation in Christ, if any comfort of love, if any fellowship of the Spirit, if any affection and mercy, fulfill my joy by being like-minded, having the same love, being of one accord, of one mind."

Outreach to others benefits yourself

HEBREWS 10:24—"Let us consider one another in order to stir up love and good works."

ENEMY

Face your enemies with the Peacemaker by your side. Also see Opposition, Persecution.

Meditation: **Assurance when facing enemies,** Psalm 3:1–6: "LORD, how they have increased who trouble me! Many are they who rise up against me. Many are they who say of me, 'There is no help for him in God.' But You, O LORD, are a shield for me, my glory and the One who lifts up my head. I cried to the LORD with my voice, and He heard me from His holy hill. I lay down and slept; I awoke, for the LORD sustained me. I will not be afraid of ten thousands of people who have set themselves against me all around."

Peaceful sleep

PSALM 4:8—"I will both lie down in peace, and sleep; for You alone, O LORD, make me dwell in safety."

Pathway to peace with enemy

PROVERBS 16:7—"When a man's ways please the LORD, he makes even his enemies to be at peace with him."

Attitude toward enemy's failure

PROVERBS 24:17—"Do not rejoice when your enemy falls, and do not let your heart be glad when he stumbles."

Try the love attack

MATTHEW 5:43–44—"You have heard that it was said, 'You shall love your neighbor and hate your enemy.' But I say to you, love your enemies, bless those who curse you, do good to those who hate you, and pray for those who spitefully use you and persecute you."

Turn the other cheek

LUKE 6:29—"To him who strikes you on the one cheek, offer the other also. And from him who takes away your cloak, do not withhold your tunic either."

When God is on your side

ROMANS 8:31—"What then shall we say to these things? If God is for us, who can be against us?"

ENVY

The Bible can help you avoid the eye of envy. Also see Covet, Jealousy.

Never envy sinners

PROVERBS 23:17—"Do not let your heart envy sinners, but be zealous for the fear of the LORD all the day."

Envious neighbors

ECCLESIASTES 4:4—"I saw that for all toil and every skillful work a man is envied by his neighbor. This also is vanity and grasping for the wind."

Love cures envy

1 CORINTHIANS 13:4—"Love suffers long and is kind; love does not envy; love does not parade itself, is not puffed up."

Avoid the envy syndrome

GALATIANS 5:26—"Let us not become conceited, provoking one another, envying one another."

EVALUATION

Accurate evaluation is one of the first strides toward truth.

Judgment Day evaluation

ECCLESIASTES 12:13–14—"Let us hear the conclusion of the whole matter: Fear God and keep His commandments, for this is man's all. For God will bring every work into judgment, including every secret thing, whether good or evil."

Danger of judging others

ROMANS 2:1—"You are inexcusable, O man, whoever you are who

judge, for in whatever you judge another you condemn yourself; for you who judge practice the same things."

Self-evaluation

ROMANS 12:3—"I say, through the grace given to me, to everyone who is among you, not to think of himself more highly than he ought to think, but to think soberly, as God has dealt to each one a measure of faith."

Self-evaluation before taking Communion

1 CORINTHIANS 11:28—"Let a man examine himself, and so let him eat of the bread and drink of the cup."

Work for the Lord has value

1 CORINTHIANS 15:58—"Be steadfast, immovable, always abounding in the work of the Lord, knowing that your labor is not in vain in the Lord."

EVANGELISM

Life's greatest endeavor is proclaiming our Lord's message to others. Also see Outreach.

Many proclaimers

PSALM 68:11—"The Lord gave the word; great was the company of those who proclaimed it."

Awake or sleeping

PROVERBS 10:5—"He who gathers in summer is a wise son; he who sleeps in harvest is a son who causes shame."

Wise evangelists

PROVERBS 11:30—"The fruit of the righteous is a tree of life, and he who wins souls is wise."

Effectiveness guaranteed

ISAIAH 55:10–11—"For as the rain comes down, and the snow from heaven, and do not return there, but water the earth, and make it bring forth and bud, that it may give seed to the sower and bread to the eater, so shall My word be that goes forth from My mouth; it shall not return to Me void, but it shall accomplish what I please, and it shall prosper in the thing for which I sent it."

Orders from your CEO

MARK 16:15—"He said to them, 'Go into all the world and preach the gospel to every creature.'"

Meditation: **The evangelism procedure,** 1 Corinthians 3:6–9: "I planted, Apollos watered, but God gave the increase. So then neither he who plants is anything, nor he who waters, but God who gives the increase. Now he who plants and he who waters are one, and each one will receive his own reward according to his own labor. For we are God's fellow workers; you are God's field, you are God's building."

EVIL

We must face the debilitating, destructive reality of evil. Also see Demons.

Inherited evil nature

PSALM 51:5—"I was brought forth in iniquity, and in sin my mother conceived me."

Decisively avoiding evil

PROVERBS 4:14–15—"Do not enter the path of the wicked, and do not walk in the way of evil. Avoid it, do not travel on it; turn away from it and pass on."

Confident in evil

ISAIAH 47:10–11—"You have trusted in your wickedness; you have said, 'No one sees me'; your wisdom and your knowledge have warped you; and you have said in your heart, 'I am, and there is no one else besides me.' Therefore evil shall come upon you; you shall not know from where it arises. And trouble shall fall upon you; you will not be able to put it off. And desolation shall come upon you suddenly, which you shall not know."

Deliverance from evil

MATTHEW 6:13—"Do not lead us into temptation, but deliver us from the evil one. For Yours is the kingdom and the power and the glory forever. Amen."

Evil categorized

GALATIANS 5:19–21—"The works of the flesh are evident, which are: adultery, fornication, uncleanness, lewdness, idolatry, sorcery, hatred, contentions, jealousies, outbursts of wrath, selfish ambitions, dissensions, heresies, envy, murders, drunkenness, revelries, and the like; of which I tell you beforehand, just as I also told you in time past, that those who practice such things will not inherit the kingdom of God."

Protected from evil

2 THESSALONIANS 3:3—"The Lord is faithful, who will establish you and guard you from the evil one."

EXAMPLE

Becoming a model of right and righteousness is a high function of witness.

Father's example

PROVERBS 20:7—"The righteous man walks in his integrity; his children are blessed after him."

Mother's example

PROVERBS 31:26–28—"She opens her mouth with wisdom, and on her tongue is the law of kindness. She watches over the ways of her household, and does not eat the bread of idleness. Her children rise up and call her blessed; her husband also, and he praises her."

Meditation: **Salt and light,** Matthew 5:15–16: "Nor do they light a lamp and put it under a basket, but on a lampstand, and it gives light to all who are in the house. Let your light so shine before men, that they may see your good works and glorify your Father in heaven."

The Holy Spirit in you

GALATIANS 5:22–23—"The fruit of the Spirit is love, joy, peace, long-suffering, kindness, goodness, faithfulness, gentleness, self-control. Against such there is no law."

The mind of Christ

PHILIPPIANS 2:5–7—"Let this mind be in you which was also in Christ Jesus, who, being in the form of God, did not consider it robbery to be equal with God, but made Himself of no reputation, taking the form of a bondservant, and coming in the likeness of men."

Exemplary lifestyle

1 THESSALONIANS 4:11—"You also aspire to lead a quiet life, to mind your own business, and to work with your own hands, as we commanded you."

Meditation: **WWJD—what would Jesus do?** 1 Peter 2:21–24: "To this you were called, because Christ also suffered for us, leaving us an example, that you should follow His steps: 'Who committed no sin, nor was deceit found in His mouth'; who, when He was reviled, did not revile in return; when He suffered, He did not threaten, but committed Himself to Him who judges righteously; who Himself bore our sins in His own body on the tree, that we, having died to sins, might live for righteousness—by whose stripes you were healed."

FAILURE

Your sustaining Lord has never failed! Also see Disappointment, Discouragement.

Key to success

JOSHUA 1:8—"This Book of the Law shall not depart from your mouth, but you shall meditate in it day and night, that you may observe to do according to all that is written in it. For then you will make your way prosperous, and then you will have good success."

Friendship in times of failure

PROVERBS 17:17—"A friend loves at all times, and a brother is born for adversity."

Do not enjoy an enemy's failure

PROVERBS 24:17—"Do not rejoice when your enemy falls, and do not let your heart be glad when he stumbles."

Benefits from testing

JAMES 1:2–4—"Count it all joy when you fall into various trials, knowing that the testing of your faith produces patience.

Words That Rhyme with Faith

As I was flying to Los Angeles for my sister's funeral, a poem formed in my thoughts. It was subsequently published in the *Evangelical Beacon,* appeared on the cover of *Christian Reader,* then was reprinted in numerous periodicals.

Mirth
rhymes with
birth.
Strife
rhymes with
life,
and breath
with death.
I have not heard
or seen a word
to rhyme with faith.
And yet
my sorrow sees
that all of these—
mirth, birth,
strife, life,
breath, death—
all rhyme with faith
in words beyond our ears,
our tears,
our years.

But let patience have its perfect work, that you may be perfect and complete, lacking nothing."

Kept from falling

JUDE 24–25—"To Him who is able to keep you from stumbling, and to present you faultless before the presence of His glory with exceeding joy, to God our Savior, who alone is wise, be glory and majesty, dominion and power, both now and forever. Amen."

FAITH

Through the application of Bible precepts, faith can become sight.

Family faith in continuity

DEUTERONOMY 4:9—"Only take heed to yourself, and diligently keep yourself, lest you forget the things your eyes have seen, and lest they depart from your heart all the days of your life. And teach them to your children and your grandchildren."

Faith refined to gold

JOB 23:10—"He knows the way that I take; when He has tested me, I shall come forth as gold."

Facing problems with faith

PSALM 27:1—"The LORD is my light and my salvation; whom shall I fear? The LORD is the strength of my life; of whom shall I be afraid?"

Justified, peace with God

ROMANS 5:1—"Having been justified by faith, we have peace with God through our Lord Jesus Christ."

Source of faith

ROMANS 10:17—"Faith comes by hearing, and hearing by the word of God."

Meditation: **Assured faith, substance, and evidence,** Hebrews 11:1–6:

"Faith is the substance of things hoped for, the evidence of things not seen. For by it the elders obtained a good testimony. By faith we understand that the worlds were framed by the word of God, so that the things which are seen were not made of things which are visible. By faith Abel offered to God a more excellent sacrifice than Cain, through which he obtained witness that he was righteous, God testifying of his gifts; and through it he being dead still speaks. By faith Enoch was taken away so that he did not see death, 'and was not found, because God had taken him'; for before he was taken he had this testimony, that he pleased God. But without faith it is impossible to please Him, for he who comes to God must believe that He is, and that He is a rewarder of those who diligently seek Him."

Meditation: **Additives to faith,** 2 Peter 1:5–8: "For this very reason, giving all diligence, add to your faith virtue, to virtue knowledge, to knowledge self-control, to self-control perseverance, to perseverance godliness, to godliness brotherly kindness, and to brotherly kindness love. For if these things are yours and abound, you will be neither barren nor unfruitful in the knowledge of our Lord Jesus Christ."

FAITHFULNESS
Our Lord's faithfulness engenders our own.

Meditation: **Pledge of faithfulness,** Deuteronomy 26:16–19: "This day the LORD your God commands you to observe these statutes and judgments; therefore you shall be careful to observe them with all your heart and with all your soul. Today you have proclaimed the LORD to be your God, and that you will walk in His ways and keep His statutes, His commandments, and His judgments, and that you will obey His voice. Also today the LORD has proclaimed you to be His special people, just as He promised you, that you should keep all His commandments, and that He will set you high above all nations which He has made, in praise, in name, and in honor, and that you may be a holy people to the LORD your God, just as He has spoken."

Your Lord's great faithfulness

LAMENTATIONS 3:22–23—"Through the LORD's mercies we are not consumed, because His compassions fail not. They are new every morning; great is Your faithfulness."

> God is still on the throne, we're still on his footstool, and there is only knees distance between.
>
> —JIM ELLIOT

Meditation: **Deny yourself and follow,** Mark 8:34–36: "When He had called the people to Himself, with His disciples also, He said to them, 'Whoever desires to come after Me, let him deny himself, and take up his cross, and follow Me. For whoever desires to save his life will lose it, but whoever loses his life for My sake and the gospel's will save it. For what will it profit a man if he gains the whole world, and loses his own soul?'"

Fellowship of faithfulness

1 CORINTHIANS 1:9—"God is faithful, by whom you were called into the fellowship of His Son, Jesus Christ our Lord."

Standard for your faithfulness

1 CORINTHIANS 4:1–2—"Let a man so consider us, as servants of Christ and stewards of the mysteries of God. Moreover it is required in stewards that one be found faithful."

FAME
Celebrity status is a gift from God.

STEPS Nugget

PRAYING CONTINUALLY

In 1 Thessalonians 5:17, the Bible urges you to "pray without ceasing." How do you do that? It's simple and vastly enriching.

For example, you can pick up the telephone on the second ring instead of the first. This gives you four seconds to ask your Lord for His guidance. Or, when you meet someone, you can outwardly be warm and casual while inwardly you pray, "Can I help this person?"

Throughout the day, stay on PA—"prayer alert." Take deep breaths and express gratitude that your body is functioning normally. Whisper, "Thanks, Lord." As thoughts come to your mind, give them a brief, PA touch. Concerns. Needs. Challenges. Do your regular work and routines, but stay on PA.

Sense God's presence, thank Him, enjoy Him—for an entire day.

Wealth and honor come from God

1 CHRONICLES 29:12—"Both riches and honor come from You, and You reign over all. In Your hand is power and might; in Your hand it is to make great and to give strength to all."

God puts down, lifts up

PSALM 75:7—"God is the Judge: He puts down one, and exalts another."

First and last

MARK 10:31—"Many who are first will be last, and the last first."

Meditation: **Famous in ministry,** 1 Corinthians 3:4–15: "For when one says, 'I am of Paul,' and another, 'I am of Apollos,' are you not carnal? Who then is Paul, and who is Apollos, but ministers through whom you believed, as the Lord gave to each one? I planted, Apollos watered, but God gave the increase. So then neither he who plants is anything, nor he who waters, but God who gives the increase. Now he who plants and he who waters are one, and each one will receive his own reward according to his own labor. For we are God's fellow workers; you are God's field, you are God's building. According to the grace of God which was given to me, as a wise master builder I have laid the foundation, and another builds on it. But let each one take heed how he builds on it. For no other foundation can anyone lay than that which is laid, which is Jesus Christ. Now if anyone builds on this foundation with gold, silver, precious stones, wood, hay, straw, each one's work will become clear; for the Day will declare it, because it will be revealed by fire; and the fire will test each one's work, of what sort it is. If anyone's work which he has built on it endures, he will receive a reward. If anyone's work is burned, he will suffer loss; but he himself will be saved, yet so as through fire."

> Prayer lies at the root of all personal godliness.
>
> —WILLIAM CAREY

FAMILY

God created, loves, blesses, and depends on families. Also see Children, Father, Mother.

Family unity

GENESIS 13:8—"Abram said to Lot, 'Please let there be no strife between you and me, and between my herdsmen and your herdsmen; for we are brethren.'"

STEPS Nugget

FASTING

Many find fasting an edifying and invigorating experience. One day, such as Sunday, increases in significance if you donate the food money to a hunger program. All three meals should be denied with only water to drink.

Weekend fasts could allow a light Saturday morning breakfast and a Sunday evening snack. Drinking fruit juice is advisable during the two days.

Fasting for one week or more provides a discipleship experience. Prayer has special value; so does the Bible. Drink juice and water. End the fast with very light, digestible food for at least two days.

A period of fasting should be kept personal and private as much as possible. It is not a performance but an observance between you and your Lord.

In 2 Corinthians 11:27, the apostle Paul said that he was "in fastings often," but in 1 Corinthians 8:8, he cautioned, "Food does not commend us to God; for neither if we eat are we the better, nor if we do not eat are we the worse."

God's mercy to all generations

PSALM 100:5—"The LORD is good; His mercy is everlasting, and His truth endures to all generations."

To children's children

PSALM 103:17—"The mercy of the LORD is from everlasting to everlasting on those who fear Him, and His righteousness to children's children."

Blessed family

PSALM 128:3—"Your wife shall be like a fruitful vine in the very heart of your house, your children like olive plants all around your table."

Agreeable brothers

PSALM 133:1—"How good and how pleasant it is for brethren to dwell together in unity!"

Development of children

PSALM 144:12—"That our sons may be as plants grown up in their youth; that our daughters may be as pillars, sculptured in palace style."

Like father, like family

PROVERBS 20:7—"The righteous man walks in his integrity; his children are blessed after him."

Good training, good results

PROVERBS 22:6—"Train up a child in the way he should go, and when he is old he will not depart from it."

Continuity of family faith

JOEL 1:3—"Tell your children about it, let your children tell their children, and their children another generation."

Meditation: **Counsel to families,** Ephesians 6:1–4: "Children, obey your parents in the Lord, for this is right. 'Honor your father and mother,' which is the first commandment with promise: 'that it may be well with you and you may live long on the earth.' And you, fathers, do not provoke your children to wrath, but bring them up in the training and admonition of the Lord."

Childhood teaching

2 TIMOTHY 3:14–15—"You must continue in the things which you have learned and been assured of, knowing from whom you have learned them, and that from childhood you have known the Holy Scriptures, which are able to make you wise for salvation through faith which is in Christ Jesus."

FASTING
Many believe prayers become more effective when they are combined with fasting.

Joyful fasting

ZECHARIAH 8:19—"Thus says the LORD of hosts: 'The fast of the fourth month, the fast of the fifth, the fast of the seventh, and the fast of the tenth, shall be joy and gladness and cheerful feasts for the house of Judah. Therefore love truth and peace.'"

Meditation: **Example of Jesus,** Matthew 4:1–11: "Then Jesus was led up by the Spirit into the wilderness to be tempted by the devil. And when He had fasted forty days and forty nights, afterward He was hungry. Now when the tempter came to Him, he said, 'If You are the Son of God, command that these stones become bread.' But He answered and said, 'It is written, "Man shall not live by bread alone, but by every word that proceeds from the mouth of God."'" Then the devil took Him up into the holy city, set Him on the pinnacle of the temple, and said to Him, 'If You are the Son of God, throw Yourself down. For it is written—"He shall give His angels charge over you," and, "In their hands they shall bear you up, lest you dash your foot against a stone."' Jesus said to him, 'It is written again, "You shall not tempt the LORD your God."' Again, the devil took Him up on an exceedingly high mountain, and showed Him all the kingdoms of the world and their glory. And he said to Him, 'All these things I will give You if You will fall down and worship me.' Then Jesus said to him, 'Away with you, Satan! For it is written, "You shall worship the LORD your God, and Him only you shall serve."' Then the devil left Him, and behold, angels came and ministered to Him."

Feasting and fasting

LUKE 5:33–35—"Then they said to Him, 'Why do the disciples of

John fast often and make prayers, and likewise those of the Pharisees, but Yours eat and drink?' And He said to them, 'Can you make the friends of the bridegroom fast while the bridegroom is with them? But the days will come when the bridegroom will be taken away from them; then they will fast in those days.'"

Fasting evaluated

1 CORINTHIANS 8:8—"Food does not commend us to God; for neither if we eat are we the better, nor if we do not eat are we the worse."

FATHER

The Father is God's intended link between Him and the family. Also see Mother, Parents.

Father's prayer for the unborn

JUDGES 13:8—"Manoah prayed to the LORD, and said, 'O my Lord, please let the Man of God whom You sent come to us again and teach us what we shall do for the child who will be born.'"

Earthly father, heavenly Father

PSALM 103:13–14—"As a father pities his children, so the LORD pities those who fear Him. For He knows our frame; He remembers that we are dust."

Discipline models

PROVERBS 3:11–12—"My son, do not despise the chastening of the LORD, nor detest His correction; for whom the LORD loves He corrects, just as a father the son in whom he delights."

Meditation: **Father's teaching,** Proverbs 4:1–5: "Hear, my children, the instruction of a father, and give attention to know understanding; for I give you good doctrine: Do not forsake my law. When I was my father's son, tender and the only one in the sight of my mother, he also taught me, and said to me: 'Let your heart retain my words;

keep my commands, and live. Get wisdom! Get understanding! Do not forget, nor turn away from the words of my mouth.'"

> Nothing lies outside the reach of prayer except that which lies outside the will of God.
>
> —ANDREW MURRAY

Good father's influence

PROVERBS 20:7—"The righteous man walks in his integrity; his children are blessed after him."

Meditation: **Rapport between father and family,** Ephesians 6:1–4: "Children, obey your parents in the Lord, for this is right. 'Honor your father and mother,' which is the first commandment with promise: 'that it may be well with you and you may live long on the earth.' And you, fathers, do not provoke your children to wrath, but bring them up in the training and admonition of the Lord."

FEAR
Let your fear become the target of faith and confidence.

Contagious fear

DEUTERONOMY 20:8—"The officers shall speak further to the people, and say, 'What man is there who is fearful and fainthearted? Let him go and return to his house, lest the heart of his brethren faint like his heart.'"

Delivered from all fear

PSALM 34:4—"I sought the LORD, and He heard me, and delivered me from all my fears."

Be still and know God

PSALM 46:10—"Be still, and know that I am God; I will be exalted among the nations, I will be exalted in the earth!"

Give your fear to the Lord

PSALM 55:22—"Cast your burden on the LORD, and He shall sustain you; He shall never permit the righteous to be moved."

Safety in God's hand

ISAIAH 41:10—"Fear not, for I am with you; be not dismayed, for I am your God. I will strengthen you, yes, I will help you, I will uphold you with My righteous right hand."

Meditation: **Assuring words of Jesus,** Matthew 6:25–34: "I say to you, do not worry about your life, what you will eat or what you will drink; nor about your body, what you will put on. Is not life more than food and the body more than clothing? Look at the birds of the air, for they neither sow nor reap nor gather into barns; yet your heavenly Father feeds them. Are you not of more value than they? Which of you by worrying can add one cubit to his stature? So why do you worry about clothing? Consider the lilies of the field, how they grow: they neither toil nor spin; and yet I say to you that even Solomon in all his glory was not arrayed like one of these. Now if God so clothes the grass of the field, which today is, and tomorrow is thrown into the oven, will He not much more clothe you, O you of little faith? Therefore do not worry, saying, 'What shall we eat?' or 'What shall we drink?' or 'What shall we wear?' For after all these things the Gentiles seek. For your heavenly Father knows that you need all these things. But seek first the kingdom of God and His righteousness, and all these things shall be added to you. Therefore do not worry about tomorrow, for tomorrow will worry about its own things. Sufficient for the day is its own trouble."

FELLOWSHIP

No association on earth equals that of Christian fellowship.

Glorifying God together

PSALM 34:3—"Oh, magnify the LORD with me, and let us exalt His name together."

Meditation: **Brotherhood,** Psalm 133:1–3: "How good and how pleasant it is for brethren to dwell together in unity! It is like the precious oil upon the head, running down on the beard, the beard of Aaron, running down on the edge of his garments. It is like the dew of Hermon, descending upon the mountains of Zion; for there the LORD commanded the blessing—life forevermore."

Quorum for prayer

MATTHEW 18:20—"Where two or three are gathered together in My name, I am there in the midst of them."

Meditation: **Fellowship of forgiven sin,** 1 John 1:5–10: "This is the message which we have heard from Him and declare to you, that God is light and in Him is no darkness at all. If we say that we have fellowship with Him, and walk in darkness, we lie and do not practice the truth. But if we walk in the light as He is in the light, we have fellowship with one another, and the blood of Jesus Christ His Son cleanses us from all sin. If we say that we have no sin, we deceive ourselves, and the truth is not in us. If we confess our sins, He is faithful and just to forgive us our sins and to cleanse us from all unrighteousness. If we say that we have not sinned, we make Him a liar, and His word is not in us."

FINANCIAL

Know the difference between needs and wants. God does! Also see Provision.

Wealth of others evaluated

PSALM 49:16–17—"Do not be afraid when one becomes rich, when the glory of his house is increased; for when he dies he shall carry nothing away; his glory shall not descend after him."

Prayer for urgent financial need

PSALM 70:5—"I am poor and needy; make haste to me, O God! You are my help and my deliverer; O LORD, do not delay."

STEPS Nugget

UNDERSTANDING THE TRINITY

Matthew 28:19 documents the fact of the Trinity. The function of the Trinity appears to be as follows:

1. God the Father is the Source of all things (Job 11:7–9).

2. God the Son is the Creator of all things (Col. 1:15–16).

The Creator of the universe became the Carpenter of Nazareth to save us from our sins. We read in 2 Corinthians 8:9: "You know the grace of our Lord Jesus Christ, that though He was rich, yet for your sakes He became poor, that you through His poverty might become rich."

3. God the Holy Spirit is the power through whom all things are accomplished (Gen. 1:2; Eph. 1:19–20).

Content with little

PROVERBS 15:16—"Better is a little with the fear of the LORD, than great treasure with trouble."

Meditation: **Treasures in heaven,** Matthew 6:19–21: "Do not lay up for yourselves treasures on earth, where moth and rust destroy and where thieves break in and steal; but lay up for yourselves treasures in heaven, where neither moth nor rust destroys and where thieves do not break in and steal. For where your treasure is, there your heart will be also."

Avoid debt

ROMANS 13:8—"Owe no one anything except to love one another, for he who loves another has fulfilled the law."

Like money in the bank

PHILIPPIANS 4:19—"My God shall supply all your need according to His riches in glory by Christ Jesus."

FORGIVENESS

Consider the joy of being forgiven and forgiving others. Also see Repentance.

Plea for forgiveness

PSALM 6:2—"Have mercy on me, O LORD, for I am weak."

Meditation: **Out of the depths,** Psalm 130:1–6: "Out of the depths I have cried to You, O LORD; Lord, hear my voice! Let Your ears be attentive to the voice of my supplications. If You, LORD, should mark iniquities, O Lord, who could stand? But there is forgiveness with You, that You may be feared. I wait for the LORD, my soul waits, and in His word I do hope. My soul waits for the Lord more than those who watch for the morning—yes, more than those who watch for the morning."

God's willingness to forgive

PSALM 145:8—"The LORD is gracious and full of compassion, slow to anger and great in mercy."

Sins forgiven

ISAIAH 1:18—"'Come now, and let us reason together,' says the LORD, 'though your sins are like scarlet, they shall be as white as snow; though they are red like crimson, they shall be as wool.'"

Your willingness to forgive

MATTHEW 18:21–22—"Peter came to Him and said, 'Lord, how often shall my brother sin against me, and I forgive him? Up to seven times?' Jesus said to him, 'I do not say to you, up to seven times, but up to seventy times seven.'"

Forgive and be forgiven

MARK 11:25–26—"Whenever you stand praying, if you have anything against anyone, forgive him, that your Father in heaven may also forgive you your trespasses. But if you do not forgive, neither will your Father in heaven forgive your trespasses."

Darkness and light

1 JOHN 2:9–10—"He who says he is in the light, and hates his brother, is in darkness until now. He who loves his brother abides in the light, and there is no cause for stumbling in him."

FRIENDSHIP

Friends provide building blocks for character, personality, and effort.

Deep and enduring friendship

1 SAMUEL 20:42—"Jonathan said to David, 'Go in peace, since we have both sworn in the name of the LORD, saying, "May the LORD be between you and me, and between your descendants and my descendants, forever."' So he arose and departed, and Jonathan went into the city."

An all-weather friend

PROVERBS 17:17—"A friend loves at all times, and a brother is born for adversity."

Wounded by a friend

PROVERBS 27:6—"Faithful are the wounds of a friend, but the kisses of an enemy are deceitful."

Meditation: **The view of Jesus,** John 15:12–17: "This is My commandment, that you love one another as I have loved you. Greater love has no one than this, than to lay down one's life for his friends. You are My friends if you do whatever I command you. No longer do I call you servants, for a servant does not know what his master is doing; but I have called you friends, for all things that I heard from

My Father I have made known to you. You did not choose Me, but I chose you and appointed you that you should go and bear fruit, and that your fruit should remain, that whatever you ask the Father in My name He may give you. These things I command you, that you love one another."

Concerned prayer for friends

2 THESSALONIANS 1:11–12—"We also pray always for you that our God would count you worthy of this calling, and fulfill all the good pleasure of His goodness and the work of faith with power, that the name of our Lord Jesus Christ may be glorified in you, and you in Him, according to the grace of our God and the Lord Jesus Christ."

Dangerous friendships

JAMES 4:4—"Do you not know that friendship with the world is enmity with God? Whoever therefore wants to be a friend of the world makes himself an enemy of God."

FULFILLMENT

Fulfillment becomes possible only within the parameters of faith.

Assured fulfillment

PSALM 84:11—"The LORD God is a sun and shield; the LORD will give grace and glory; no good thing will He withhold from those who walk uprightly."

Meditation: **Strong as an eagle,** Psalm 103:1–5: "Bless the LORD, O my soul; and all that is within me, bless His holy name! Bless the LORD, O my soul, and forget not all His benefits: who forgives all your iniquities, who heals all your diseases, who redeems your life from destruction, who crowns you with lovingkindness and tender mercies, who satisfies your mouth with good things, so that your youth is renewed like the eagle's."

Gratitude enriches fulfillment

PSALM 107:8–9—"Oh, that men would give thanks to the LORD for His goodness, and for His wonderful works to the children of men! For He satisfies the longing soul, and fills the hungry soul with goodness."

Thirst satisfied

JOHN 4:13–14—"Jesus answered and said to her, 'Whoever drinks of this water will thirst again, but whoever drinks of the water that I shall give him will never thirst. But the water that I shall give him will become in him a fountain of water springing up into everlasting life.'"

Joy and peace in believing

ROMANS 15:13—"May the God of hope fill you with all joy and peace in believing, that you may abound in hope by the power of the Holy Spirit."

Meditation: **Find fulfillment in doing God's will,** Hebrews 13:20–21: "May the God of peace who brought up our Lord Jesus from the dead, that great Shepherd of the sheep, through the blood of the everlasting covenant, make you complete in every good work to do His will, working in you what is well pleasing in His sight, through Jesus Christ, to whom be glory forever and ever. Amen."

FUTURE

Trust the One who knows the future.

Present and future in your Lord's hands

PSALM 31:15—"My times are in Your hand."

Children not yet born

PSALM 102:18—"This will be written for the generation to come, that a people yet to be created may praise the LORD."

Bright future

PROVERBS 4:18—"The path of the just is like the shining sun, that shines ever brighter unto the perfect day."

No need to fear

ISAIAH 41:10—"Fear not, for I am with you; be not dismayed, for I am your God. I will strengthen you, yes, I will help you, I will uphold you with My righteous right hand."

End known from beginning

ISAIAH 46:9–10—"I am God, and there is none like Me, declaring the end from the beginning, and from ancient times things that are not yet done, saying, 'My counsel shall stand, and I will do all My pleasure.'"

God has plans for you

JEREMIAH 29:11—"I know the thoughts that I think toward you, says the LORD, thoughts of peace and not of evil, to give you a future and a hope."

What God has prepared

1 CORINTHIANS 2:9—"Eye has not seen, nor ear heard, nor have entered into the heart of man the things which God has prepared for those who love Him."

GENEROSITY

Giving, caring, and sharing validate the golden rule. Also see Golden Rule.

Willing generosity

PROVERBS 3:27–28—"Do not withhold good from those to whom it is due, when it is in the power of your hand to do so. Do not say to your neighbor, 'Go, and come back, and tomorrow I will give it,' when you have it with you."

Generosity brings blessing

PROVERBS 22:9—"He who has a generous eye will be blessed, for he gives of his bread to the poor."

Consistently generous

MATTHEW 5:42—"Give to him who asks you, and from him who wants to borrow from you do not turn away."

Meditation: **Keep it a secret,** Matthew 6:1–4: "Take heed that you do not do your charitable deeds before men, to be seen by them. Otherwise you have no reward from your Father in heaven. Therefore, when you do a charitable deed, do not sound a trumpet before you as the hypocrites do in the synagogues and in the streets, that they may have glory from men. Assuredly, I say to you, they have their reward. But when you do a charitable deed, do not let your left hand know what your right hand is doing, that your charitable deed may be in secret; and your Father who sees in secret will Himself reward you openly."

Giving and receiving

LUKE 6:38—"Give, and it will be given to you: good measure, pressed down, shaken together, and running over will be put into your bosom. For with the same measure that you use, it will be measured back to you."

Generosity with a smile

2 CORINTHIANS 9:6–7—"He who sows sparingly will also reap sparingly, and he who sows bountifully will also reap bountifully. So let each one give as he purposes in his heart, not grudgingly or of necessity; for God loves a cheerful giver."

GOALS

Life at its best involves setting goals in the will of God.

Whatever it takes

JOB 23:10—"He knows the way that I take; when He has tested me, I shall come forth as gold."

Meditation: **Living the life,** Psalm 119:1–6: "Blessed are the undefiled in the way, who walk in the law of the LORD! Blessed are those who keep His testimonies, who seek Him with the whole heart! They also do no iniquity; they walk in His ways. You have commanded us to keep Your precepts diligently. Oh, that my ways were directed to keep Your statutes! Then I would not be ashamed, when I look into all Your commandments."

Keeping on course

PROVERBS 4:25–26—"Let your eyes look straight ahead, and your eyelids look right before you. Ponder the path of your feet, and let all your ways be established."

Divinely guided goal setting

PROVERBS 19:21—"There are many plans in a man's heart, nevertheless the LORD's counsel—that will stand."

> If you love God, you cannot be at a loss for something to say to Him.
>
> —MATTHEW HENRY

Think big

ISAIAH 54:2–3—"Enlarge the place of your tent, and let them stretch out the curtains of your dwellings; do not spare; lengthen your cords, and strengthen your stakes. For you shall expand to the right and to the left, and your descendants will inherit the nations, and make the desolate cities inhabited."

Dangerous self-centered goals

JEREMIAH 45:4–5—"Thus says the LORD: 'Behold, what I have built I will break down, and what I have planted I will pluck up, that is, this whole land. And do you seek great things for yourself? Do not seek them; for behold, I will bring adversity on all flesh,' says the LORD. 'But I will give your life to you as a prize in all places, wherever you go.'"

Concentrate on your goal

PHILIPPIANS 3:13–14—"I do not count myself to have apprehended;

but one thing I do, forgetting those things which are behind and reaching forward to those things which are ahead, I press toward the goal for the prize of the upward call of God in Christ Jesus."

Doing God's will

HEBREWS 13:20–21—"May the God of peace who brought up our Lord Jesus from the dead, that great Shepherd of the sheep, through the blood of the everlasting covenant, make you complete in every good work to do His will, working in you what is well pleasing in His sight, through Jesus Christ, to whom be glory forever and ever. Amen."

GOD

Let your heavenly Father be strategic to your prayers. He knows your need.

The great Promise Keeper

1 CHRONICLES 17:23—"And now, O LORD, the word which You have spoken concerning Your servant and concerning his house, let it be established forever, and do as You have said."

In God's hand

PSALM 31:15—"My times are in Your hand."

Let God be exalted

PSALM 57:5—"Be exalted, O God, above the heavens; let Your glory be above all the earth."

God's abundant goodness

PSALM 86:15—"You, O Lord, are a God full of compassion, and gracious, longsuffering and abundant in mercy and truth."

Daily Guidebook

PSALM 119:133—"Direct my steps by Your word."

Meditation: **Unmeasured greatness,** Psalm 145:1–3: "I will extol You, my God, O King; and I will bless Your name forever and ever. Every day I will bless You, and I will praise Your name forever and ever. Great is the LORD, and greatly to be praised; and His greatness is unsearchable."

Exclusive glory

ISAIAH 42:8—"I am the LORD, that is My name; and My glory I will not give to another, nor My praise to carved images."

God knows those who trust Him

NAHUM 1:7—"The LORD is good, a stronghold in the day of trouble; and He knows those who trust in Him."

Good things from God

JAMES 1:17—"Every good gift and every perfect gift is from above, and comes down from the Father of lights, with whom there is no variation or shadow of turning."

Meditation: **God's love and ours,** 1 John 4:7–11: "Let us love one another, for love is of God; and everyone who loves is born of God and knows God. He who does not love does not know God, for God is love. In this the love of God was manifested toward us, that God has sent His only begotten Son into the world, that we might live through Him. In this is love, not that we loved God, but that He loved us and sent His Son to be the propitiation for our sins. Beloved, if God so loved us, we also ought to love one another."

GOD'S WILL

God wants you to know His will more than you desire to find it.

Finding God's will

PSALM 25:14—"The secret of the LORD is with those who fear Him, and He will show them His covenant."

Your responsibility and God's

PROVERBS 3:5–6—"Trust in the LORD with all your heart, and lean not on your own understanding; in all your ways acknowledge Him, and He shall direct your paths."

Qualifying for God's will

ROMANS 12:1—"Present your bodies a living sacrifice."

Sustaining God's will

1 CORINTHIANS 10:31—"Whether you eat or drink, or whatever you do, do all to the glory of God."

GOLDEN RULE

This universal rule of conduct is unique to the Christian lifestyle.

Love your neighbor

LEVITICUS 19:18—"You shall love your neighbor as yourself."

Inverse golden rule

PROVERBS 21:13—"Whoever shuts his ears to the cry of the poor will also cry himself and not be heard."

Avoid revenge

PROVERBS 24:29—"Do not say, 'I will do to him just as he has done to me; I will render to the man according to his work.'"

The golden rule

LUKE 6:31—"Just as you want men to do to you, you also do to them likewise."

Doing good to the undeserving

LUKE 6:35—"Love your enemies, do good, and lend, hoping for nothing in return; and your reward will be great, and you will be sons of the Most High. For He is kind to the unthankful and evil."

Variation of the golden rule

1 CORINTHIANS 10:24—"Let no one seek his own, but each one the other's well-being."

GOSSIP

Don't let your tongue become like serpent's fangs! Also see Slander.

Despised victim of gossip

JOB 17:6—"He has made me a byword of the people, and I have become one in whose face men spit."

Meditation: **Hurt by gossip,** Psalm 35:26–27: "Let them be ashamed and brought to mutual confusion who rejoice at my hurt; let them be clothed with shame and dishonor who exalt themselves against me. Let them shout for joy and be glad, who favor my righteous cause; and let them say continually, 'Let the LORD be magnified, who has pleasure in the prosperity of His servant.'"

Crushed emotions

PSALM 69:20—"Reproach has broken my heart, and I am full of heaviness; I looked for someone to take pity, but there was none; and for comforters, but I found none."

Disciplined speech prevents gossip

PSALM 141:3—"Set a guard, O LORD, over my mouth; keep watch over the door of my lips."

Deceitful mouth

PROVERBS 4:24—"Put away from you a deceitful mouth, and put perverse lips far from you."

Neighborhood gossip

1 TIMOTHY 5:13—"They learn to be idle, wandering about from house

to house, and not only idle but also gossips and busybodies, saying things which they ought not."

Uncontrolled tongue

JAMES 1:26—"If anyone among you thinks he is religious, and does not bridle his tongue but deceives his own heart, this one's religion is useless."

Bridled tongue

JAMES 3:5—"The tongue is a little member and boasts great things. See how great a forest a little fire kindles!"

GRATITUDE

Gratitude is a mark of maturity, an emblem of graciousness.

Meditation: **David's prayer of thanks,** 1 Chronicles 16:8–10: "Oh, give thanks to the LORD! Call upon His name; make known His deeds among the peoples! Sing to Him, sing psalms to Him; talk of all His wondrous works! Glory in His holy name; let the hearts of those rejoice who seek the LORD!"

Grateful for prayer being heard

PSALM 28:6–7—"Blessed be the LORD, because He has heard the voice of my supplications! The LORD is my strength and my shield; my heart trusted in Him, and I am helped; therefore my heart greatly rejoices, and with my song I will praise Him."

Morning and evening gratefulness

PSALM 92:1–2—"It is good to give thanks to the LORD, and to sing praises to Your name, O Most High; to declare Your lovingkindness in the morning, and Your faithfulness every night."

Give thanks to God

PSALM 107:1—"Oh, give thanks to the LORD, for He is good! For His mercy endures forever."

Grateful for spiritual growth

2 THESSALONIANS 1:3—"We are bound to thank God always for you, brethren, as it is fitting, because your faith grows exceedingly, and the love of every one of you all abounds toward each other."

GREED

Greed is akin to lust and the opposite of love and generosity. Also see Covet.

Total materialist

PSALM 52:7—"Here is the man who did not make God his strength, but trusted in the abundance of his riches, and strengthened himself in his wickedness."

High price of greed

PSALM 106:15—"He gave them their request, but sent leanness into their soul."

Family harmed by greed

PROVERBS 15:27—"He who is greedy for gain troubles his own house, but he who hates bribes will live."

Unsatisfied greed for silver

ECCLESIASTES 5:10—"He who loves silver will not be satisfied with silver; nor he who loves abundance, with increase."

Love of money

1 TIMOTHY 6:9–10—"Those who desire to be rich fall into temptation and a snare, and into many foolish and harmful lusts which drown men in destruction and perdition. For the love of money is a root of all kinds of evil, for which some have strayed from the faith in their greediness, and pierced themselves through with many sorrows."

GROWTH

The roots of spiritual growth reach deeply into the soil of prayer.

A young prophet's growth

1 SAMUEL 2:26—"The child Samuel grew in stature, and in favor both with the LORD and men."

Well-watered tree

JEREMIAH 17:7–8—"Blessed is the man who trusts in the LORD, and whose hope is the LORD. For he shall be like a tree planted by the waters, which spreads out its roots by the river, and will not fear when heat comes."

Example of Jesus

LUKE 2:52—"Jesus increased in wisdom and stature, and in favor with God and men."

Spiritual growth

2 PETER 3:18—"Grow in the grace and knowledge of our Lord and Savior Jesus Christ. To Him be the glory both now and forever. Amen."

GUIDANCE

In a world of electronic guidance systems, your Bible offers infinitely more accurate spiritual resources.

Dependable guidance

JOSHUA 1:8—"This Book of the Law shall not depart from your mouth, but you shall meditate in it day and night, that you may observe to do according to all that is written in it. For then you will make your way prosperous, and then you will have good success."

Follow the Lord's perfect way

2 SAMUEL 22:31—"As for God, His way is perfect; the word of the LORD is proven; He is a shield to all who trust in Him."

Meditation: **New leader's prayer for guidance,** 1 Kings 3:7–9: "O LORD my God, You have made Your servant king instead of my father David, but I am a little child; I do not know how to go out or come in. And Your servant is in the midst of Your people whom You have chosen, a great people, too numerous to be numbered or counted. Therefore give to Your servant an understanding heart to judge Your people, that I may discern between good and evil. For who is able to judge this great people of Yours?"

Guidance through tough times

JOB 23:10—"He knows the way that I take; when He has tested me, I shall come forth as gold."

Prayer for guidance

PSALM 25:4–5—"Show me Your ways, O LORD; teach me Your paths. Lead me in Your truth and teach me, for You are the God of my salvation; on You I wait all the day."

Finding God's will

PSALM 25:14—"The secret of the LORD is with those who fear Him, and He will show them His covenant."

Divinely guided steps

PSALM 37:23—"The steps of a good man are ordered by the LORD, and He delights in his way."

Dependable Guidebook

PSALM 119:133—"Direct my steps by Your word."

Sure formula for guidance

PROVERBS 3:5–6—"Trust in the LORD with all your heart, and lean not on your own understanding; in all your ways acknowledge Him, and He shall direct your paths."

Look to your Counselor

JOHN 16:13—"When He, the Spirit of truth, has come, He will guide you into all truth; for He will not speak on His own authority, but whatever He hears He will speak; and He will tell you things to come."

Guidance in prayer

ROMANS 8:26–27—"The Spirit also helps in our weaknesses. For we do not know what we should pray for as we ought, but the Spirit Himself makes intercession for us with groanings which cannot be uttered. Now He who searches the hearts knows what the mind of the Spirit is, because He makes intercession for the saints according to the will of God."

GUILT

Dealing with guilt provides a gauge of progress in Christian maturity.

Plea for mercy

PSALM 6:1–2—"O LORD, do not rebuke me in Your anger, nor chasten me in Your hot displeasure. Have mercy on me, O LORD, for I am weak; O LORD, heal me, for my bones are troubled."

> Work as if you were to live one hundred years. Pray as if you were to die tomorrow.
>
> —BENJAMIN FRANKLIN

Sins confessed and forgiven

PSALM 32:5—"I acknowledged my sin to You, and my iniquity I have not hidden. I said, 'I will confess my transgressions to the LORD,' and You forgave the iniquity of my sin."

Total cleansing

ISAIAH 1:18—"'Come now, and let us reason together,' says the LORD, 'though your sins are like scarlet, they shall be as white as snow; though they are red like crimson, they shall be as wool.'"

Hidden guilt

JOHN 3:20—"Everyone practicing evil hates the light and does not come to the light, lest his deeds should be exposed."

STEPS Nugget

SPIRITUAL HEALTH

The Bible speaks about physical well-being. Particularly in the Old Testament—such as the fifth commandment—we learn that longevity results from righteousness. On the other hand, the New Testament emphasizes spiritual wellness. Note 1 Timothy 4:8—"Bodily exercise profits a little, but godliness is profitable for all things."

My wife and I stood in the Piazza della Signoria of Florence and gazed in silent awe at Michelangelo's *David*. Across our minds went the psalmist's words—"I am fearfully and wonderfully made" (Ps. 139:14).

I have become increasingly convinced, however, that you and I are far more richly endowed for spiritual achievement than we are for mortal attainment.

Give thought to Romans 12:1–21; Ephesians 1:15–21; Colossians 1:9–14; and 2 Peter 3:18.

Realistic measure of guilt

JAMES 2:10—"Whoever shall keep the whole law, and yet stumble in one point, he is guilty of all."

HAPPINESS
Only the Bible points the way to genuine happiness. Also see Fulfillment, Joy.

Joy empowers

NEHEMIAH 8:10—"The joy of the LORD is your strength."

Assured happiness

PSALM 97:11—"Light is sown for the righteous, and gladness for the upright in heart."

Your Lord gives joy

JOHN 15:11—"These things I have spoken to you, that My joy may remain in you, and that your joy may be full."

Rejoice in the Lord

PHILIPPIANS 4:4—"Rejoice in the Lord always. Again I will say, rejoice!"

Spontaneous happiness

1 PETER 1:8—"Though now you do not see Him, yet believing, you rejoice with joy inexpressible and full of glory."

HATRED

Like poison, like a wildfire, hatred does its destructive work.

Sure cure for hatred

PROVERBS 10:12—"Hatred stirs up strife, but love covers all sins."

Resisting hatred

MATTHEW 5:38–39—"You have heard that it was said, 'An eye for an eye and a tooth for a tooth.' But I tell you not to resist an evil person. But whoever slaps you on your right cheek, turn the other to him also."

Darkness and blindness

1 JOHN 2:9–11—"He who says he is in the light, and hates his brother, is in darkness until now. He who loves his brother abides in the light, and there is no cause for stumbling in him. But he who hates his brother is in darkness and walks in darkness, and does not know where he is going, because the darkness has blinded his eyes."

You can't love God and hate your brother

1 JOHN 4:20—"If someone says, 'I love God,' and hates his brother, he

is a liar; for he who does not love his brother whom he has seen, how can he love God whom he has not seen?"

HEALING

Your Bible reveals your Lord's concern for people who need healing.

The great Healer

PSALM 103:1–3—"Bless the LORD, O my soul; and all that is within me, bless His holy name! Bless the LORD, O my soul, and forget not all His benefits: who forgives all your iniquities, who heals all your diseases."

Simple prayer

JEREMIAH 17:14—"Heal me, O LORD, and I shall be healed; save me, and I shall be saved, for You are my praise."

Seeking the Lord's will

MATTHEW 8:2–3—"A leper came and worshiped Him, saying, 'Lord, if You are willing, You can make me clean.' Then Jesus put out His hand and touched him, saying, 'I am willing; be cleansed.' Immediately his leprosy was cleansed."

Faith to be healed

MATTHEW 9:20–22—"Suddenly, a woman who had a flow of blood for twelve years came from behind and touched the hem of His garment. For she said to herself, 'If only I may touch His garment, I shall be made well.' But Jesus turned around, and when He saw her He said, 'Be of good cheer, daughter; your faith has made you well.' And the woman was made well from that hour."

Method of prayer for the sick

JAMES 5:14–15—"Is anyone among you sick? Let him call for the elders of the church, and let them pray over him, anointing him with oil in the name of the Lord. And the prayer of faith will save the sick, and the Lord will raise him up. And if he has committed sins, he will be forgiven."

HEALTH

Physical well-being is no prerequisite for spiritual well-being. Also see Sickness.

God made you

PSALM 139:14—"I will praise You, for I am fearfully and wonderfully made; marvelous are Your works, and that my soul knows very well."

Purpose of poor health

2 CORINTHIANS 4:17—"Our light affliction, which is but for a moment, is working for us a far more exceeding and eternal weight of glory."

Ill health promoted ministry

GALATIANS 4:13—"You know that because of physical infirmity I preached the gospel to you at the first."

Prosperity and good health

3 JOHN 2—"I pray that you may prosper in all things and be in health, just as your soul prospers."

HERESY

Truth and error are in deadly combat. Also see Cults.

Root cause for heresy

MATTHEW 22:29—"Jesus answered and said to them, 'You are mistaken, not knowing the Scriptures nor the power of God.'"

Heretical infiltration

GALATIANS 2:4–5—"This occurred because of false brethren secretly brought in (who came in by stealth to spy out our liberty which we have in Christ Jesus, that they might bring us into bondage), to whom we did not yield submission even for an hour, that the truth of the gospel might continue with you."

Be on guard

COLOSSIANS 2:8—"Beware lest anyone cheat you through philosophy and empty deceit, according to the tradition of men, according to the basic principles of the world, and not according to Christ."

> Our estimation of prayer is shown by how much time we give to it.
>
> —E. M. BOUNDS

Heresy resistant

HEBREWS 13:9—"Do not be carried about with various and strange doctrines. For it is good that the heart be established by grace, not with foods which have not profited those who have been occupied with them."

Meditation: **Beware! Danger ahead,** 2 Peter 2:1–3: "There were also false prophets among the people, even as there will be false teachers among you, who will secretly bring in destructive heresies, even denying the Lord who bought them, and bring on themselves swift destruction. And many will follow their destructive ways, because of whom the way of truth will be blasphemed. By covetousness they will exploit you with deceptive words; for a long time their judgment has not been idle, and their destruction does not slumber."

HOLINESS

By continual closeness to Christ, you can experience holiness.

Prepared for prayer

PSALM 24:3–5—"Who may ascend into the hill of the LORD? Or who may stand in His holy place? He who has clean hands and a pure heart, who has not lifted up his soul to an idol, nor sworn deceitfully. He shall receive blessing from the LORD, and righteousness from the God of his salvation."

Lust of the flesh subdued

GALATIANS 5:16—"Walk in the Spirit, and you shall not fulfill the lust of the flesh."

Fruit of the Spirit

GALATIANS 5:22–23—"The fruit of the Spirit is love, joy, peace, long-suffering, kindness, goodness, faithfulness, gentleness, self-control. Against such there is no law."

Living a life of holiness

COLOSSIANS 3:16–17—"Let the word of Christ dwell in you richly in all wisdom, teaching and admonishing one another in psalms and hymns and spiritual songs, singing with grace in your hearts to the Lord. And whatever you do in word or deed, do all in the name of the Lord Jesus, giving thanks to God the Father through Him."

Personal initiative toward holiness

1 PETER 2:1–2—"Laying aside all malice, all deceit, hypocrisy, envy, and all evil speaking, as newborn babes, desire the pure milk of the word, that you may grow thereby."

HOLY SPIRIT

The Holy Spirit is available at all times to make your prayers more effective.

Breath of God

JOB 32:8—"There is a spirit in man, and the breath of the Almighty gives him understanding."

Inner guidance

EZEKIEL 36:27—"I will put My Spirit within you and cause you to walk in My statutes, and you will keep My judgments and do them."

Dynamic resource

ZECHARIAH 4:6—"'Not by might nor by power, but by My Spirit,' says the LORD of hosts."

Assured salvation

ROMANS 8:16—"The Spirit Himself bears witness with our spirit that we are children of God."

Meditation: **The Holy Spirit in you,** 1 Corinthians 2:11–13: "For what man knows the things of a man except the spirit of the man which is in him? Even so no one knows the things of God except the Spirit of God. Now we have received, not the spirit of the world, but the Spirit who is from God, that we might know the things that have been freely given to us by God. These things we also speak, not in words which man's wisdom teaches but which the Holy Spirit teaches, comparing spiritual things with spiritual."

Your body, the Holy Spirit's temple

1 CORINTHIANS 6:19–20—"Do you not know that your body is the temple of the Holy Spirit who is in you, whom you have from God, and you are not your own? For you were bought at a price; therefore glorify God in your body and in your spirit, which are God's."

Fruit of the Spirit

GALATIANS 5:22–23—"The fruit of the Spirit is love, joy, peace, long-suffering, kindness, goodness, faithfulness, gentleness, self-control. Against such there is no law."

Do not grieve the Holy Spirit

EPHESIANS 4:30—"Do not grieve the Holy Spirit of God, by whom you were sealed for the day of redemption."

HOME

A Christ-centered home is a Bible-centered home. Also see Family.

Blessed house

1 CHRONICLES 17:27—"You have been pleased to bless the house of Your servant, that it may continue before You forever; for You have blessed it, O LORD, and it shall be blessed forever."

Elements of a good home

PROVERBS 24:3–4—"Through wisdom a house is built, and by understanding it is established; by knowledge the rooms are filled with all precious and pleasant riches."

Home schooling

EPHESIANS 6:4—"Fathers, do not provoke your children to wrath, but bring them up in the training and admonition of the Lord."

Guest room

PHILEMON 22—"Prepare a guest room for me, for I trust that through your prayers I shall be granted to you."

HONESTY

Honesty is the hallmark and heartbeat of a Bible-centered lifestyle.

Requirement for worship

PSALM 24:3–4—"Who may ascend into the hill of the LORD? Or who may stand in His holy place? He who has clean hands and a pure heart."

Penalty for dishonesty

PSALM 101:7—"He who works deceit shall not dwell within my house; he who tells lies shall not continue in my presence."

Guidance principle

PROVERBS 11:3—"The integrity of the upright will guide them, but the perversity of the unfaithful will destroy them."

Clean outside, dirty inside

LUKE 11:39—"The Lord said to him, 'Now you Pharisees make the outside of the cup and dish clean, but your inward part is full of greed and wickedness.'"

Set free by truth

JOHN 8:32—"You shall know the truth, and the truth shall make you free."

HOPE

Whatever the circumstances, you need never lose hope.

In the worst of circumstances

JOB 19:25–26—"I know that my Redeemer lives, and He shall stand at last on the earth; and after my skin is destroyed, this I know, that in my flesh I shall see God."

Courage, strength, and hope

PSALM 31:24—"Be of good courage, and He shall strengthen your heart, all you who hope in the LORD."

Hope strong since youth

PSALM 71:5—"You are my hope, O Lord GOD; You are my trust from my youth."

Nothing too hard for the Lord

JEREMIAH 32:17—"Ah, Lord GOD! Behold, You have made the heavens and the earth by Your great power and outstretched arm. There is nothing too hard for You."

Meditation: **The Blessed Hope,** Titus 2:11–13: "The grace of God that brings salvation has appeared to all men, teaching us that, denying ungodliness and worldly lusts, we should live soberly, righteously, and godly in the present age, looking for the blessed hope and glorious appearing of our great God and Savior Jesus Christ."

Your soul's anchor

HEBREWS 6:19—"This hope we have as an anchor of the soul, both sure and steadfast, and which enters the Presence behind the veil."

Living hope

1 PETER 1:3–4—"Blessed be the God and Father of our Lord Jesus Christ, who according to His abundant mercy has begotten us again to a living hope through the resurrection of Jesus Christ from the dead, to an inheritance incorruptible and undefiled and that does not fade away, reserved in heaven for you."

Purifying hope

1 JOHN 3:2–3—"Now we are children of God; and it has not yet been revealed what we shall be, but we know that when He is revealed, we shall be like Him, for we shall see Him as He is. And everyone who has this hope in Him purifies himself, just as He is pure."

HOSPITALITY

Open the door to your house and your heart.

Hospitality withheld

PSALM 101:7—"He who works deceit shall not dwell within my house; he who tells lies shall not continue in my presence."

Cup of cold water

MARK 9:41—"Whoever gives you a cup of water to drink in My name, because you belong to Christ, assuredly, I say to you, he will by no means lose his reward."

Hospitality that cannot be returned

LUKE 14:13–14—"When you give a feast, invite the poor, the maimed, the lame, the blind. And you will be blessed, because they cannot repay you; for you shall be repaid at the resurrection of the just."

Hospitable leader

TITUS 1:7–8—"A bishop must be blameless, as a steward of God, not self-willed, not quick-tempered, not given to wine, not violent, not greedy for money, but hospitable, a lover of what is good, sober-minded, just, holy, self-controlled."

Angels at your door

HEBREWS 13:2—"Do not forget to entertain strangers, for by so doing some have unwittingly entertained angels."

Cheerful hospitality

1 PETER 4:9—"Be hospitable to one another without grumbling."

HUMILITY

Humility thrives in the realization of God's greatness and your smallness.

Meditation: **Prayer of King David,** 2 Samuel 7:18–22: "King David went in and sat before the LORD; and he said: 'Who am I, O Lord GOD? And what is my house, that You have brought me this far? And yet this was a small thing in Your sight, O Lord GOD; and You have also spoken of Your servant's house for a great while to come. Is this the manner of man, O Lord GOD? Now what more can David say to You? For You, Lord GOD, know Your servant. For Your word's sake, and according to Your own heart, You have done all these great things, to make Your servant know them. Therefore You are great, O Lord GOD. For there is none like You, nor is there any God besides You, according to all that we have heard with our ears.'"

Broken before the Lord

PSALM 51:17—"The sacrifices of God are a broken spirit, a broken and a contrite heart—these, O God, You will not despise."

Glory only in the Lord

JEREMIAH 9:23–24—"Thus says the LORD: 'Let not the wise man glory in his wisdom, let not the mighty man glory in his might, nor let the rich man glory in his riches; but let him who glories glory in this, that he understands and knows Me, that I am the LORD, exercising lovingkindness, judgment, and righteousness in the earth. For in these I delight.'"

Disciple not above teacher

MATTHEW 10:24—"A disciple is not above his teacher, nor a servant above his master."

Become as little children

MATTHEW 18:4—"Whoever humbles himself as this little child is the greatest in the kingdom of heaven."

Servant leadership

MATTHEW 23:11–12—"He who is greatest among you shall be your servant. And whoever exalts himself will be humbled, and he who humbles himself will be exalted."

He increases, I decrease

JOHN 3:30—"He must increase, but I must decrease."

Avoid selfish ambition

PHILIPPIANS 2:3—"Let nothing be done through selfish ambition or conceit, but in lowliness of mind let each esteem others better than himself."

Meditation: **Example of Jesus,** Philippians 2:5–11: "Let this mind be in you which was also in Christ Jesus, who, being in the form of God, did not consider it robbery to be equal with God, but made Himself of no reputation, taking the form of a bondservant, and coming in the likeness of men. And being found in appearance as a man, He humbled Himself and became obedient to the point of death, even the death of the cross. Therefore God also has highly exalted Him and given Him the name which is above every name, that at the name of Jesus every knee should bow, of those in heaven, and of those on earth, and of those under the earth, and that every tongue should confess that Jesus Christ is Lord, to the glory of God the Father."

Humble yourself

JAMES 4:10—"Humble yourselves in the sight of the Lord, and He will lift you up."

HYPOCRISY
Anything so viable as faith is sure to have counterfeits.

Lips betray heart
PROVERBS 26:23—"Fervent lips with a wicked heart are like earthenware covered with silver dross."

Flagrant hypocrisy
JEREMIAH 7:9–10—"Will you steal, murder, commit adultery, swear falsely, burn incense to Baal, and walk after other gods whom you do not know, and then come and stand before Me in this house which is called by My name, and say, 'We are delivered to do all these abominations'?"

Hearers but not doers
EZEKIEL 33:31—"They come to you as people do, they sit before you as My people, and they hear your words, but they do not do them; for with their mouth they show much love, but their hearts pursue their own gain."

Putting on a show
MATTHEW 6:1—"Take heed that you do not do your charitable deeds before men, to be seen by them. Otherwise you have no reward from your Father in heaven."

Clean outside, dirty inside
LUKE 11:39—"The Lord said to him, 'Now you Pharisees make the outside of the cup and dish clean, but your inward part is full of greed and wickedness.'"

Empty profession
TITUS 1:16—"They profess to know God, but in works they deny Him, being abominable, disobedient, and disqualified for every good work."

Meditation: **Best seats in the house,** James 2:2–4: "If there should come into your assembly a man with gold rings, in fine apparel, and there should also come in a poor man in filthy clothes, and you pay attention to the one wearing the fine clothes and say to him, 'You sit here in a good place,' and say to the poor man, 'You stand there,' or, 'Sit here at my footstool,' have you not shown partiality among yourselves, and become judges with evil thoughts?"

IMMORALITY

Human conduct is subject to God's mercy. Also see Morality.

The Bible's mandate

EXODUS 20:17—"You shall not covet your neighbor's house; you shall not covet your neighbor's wife, nor his male servant, nor his female servant, nor his ox, nor his donkey, nor anything that is your neighbor's."

Reduced in value

PROVERBS 6:26—"By means of a harlot a man is reduced to a crust of bread; and an adulteress will prey upon his precious life."

Dangerous association

ECCLESIASTES 7:26—"I find more bitter than death the woman whose heart is snares and nets, whose hands are fetters. He who pleases God shall escape from her, but the sinner shall be trapped by her."

God sees in the dark

EZEKIEL 8:12—"He said to me, 'Son of man, have you seen what the elders of the house of Israel do in the dark, every man in the room of his idols? For they say, "The LORD does not see us, the LORD has forsaken the land."'"

Immoral thoughts and acts

MATTHEW 5:27–28—"You have heard that it was said to those of old, 'You shall not commit adultery.' But I say to you that whoever looks at a woman to lust for her has already committed adultery with her in his heart."

Bodily discipline

1 CORINTHIANS 9:27—"I discipline my body and bring it into subjection, lest, when I have preached to others, I myself should become disqualified."

Intro

You may want to spend a few moments preparing your mind and heart for prayer. The following selections offer options—either as the opening phrase of your communication or as a separate overture.

Requesting the Lord's attention, I Kings 8:28—"Yet regard the prayer of Your servant and his supplication, O LORD my God, and listen to the cry and the prayer which Your servant is praying before You today."

If you are a leader, muse Nehemiah's prologue, Nehemiah 1:4–11—"So it was, when I heard these words, that I sat down and wept, and mourned for many days; I was fasting and praying before the God of heaven. And I said: 'I pray, LORD God of heaven, O great and awesome God, You who keep Your covenant and mercy with those who love You and observe Your commandments, please let Your ear be attentive and Your eyes open, that You may hear the prayer of Your servant which I pray before You now, day and night, for the children of Israel Your servants, and confess the sins of the children of Israel which we have sinned against You. Both my father's house and I have sinned. We have acted very corruptly against You, and have not kept the commandments, the statutes, nor the ordinances which You commanded Your servant Moses. Remember, I pray, the word that You commanded Your servant Moses, saying, "If you are unfaithful, I will scatter you among the nations; but if you return to Me, and keep My commandments and do them, though some of you were cast out to the farthest part of the heavens, yet I will gather them from there, and bring them to the place which I have chosen as a dwelling for My name." Now these are Your servants and Your people, whom You have redeemed by Your great power, and by Your strong hand.

O Lord, I pray, please let Your ear be attentive to the prayer of Your servant, and to the prayer of Your servants who desire to fear Your name; and let Your servant prosper this day, I pray, and grant him mercy in the sight of this man.' For I was the king's cupbearer."

Good morning, Lord, Psalm 5:1–3—"Give ear to my words, O LORD, consider my meditation. Give heed to the voice of my cry, my King and my God, for to You I will pray. My voice You shall hear in the morning, O LORD; in the morning I will direct it to You, and I will look up."

Tell the Lord you love Him, Psalm 18:1–3—"I will love You, O LORD, my strength. The LORD is my rock and my fortress and my deliverer; my God, my strength, in whom I will trust; my shield and the horn of my salvation, my stronghold. I will call upon the LORD, who is worthy to be praised; so shall I be saved from my enemies."

Words and thoughts pleasing to the Lord, Psalm 19:14—"Let the words of my mouth and the meditation of my heart be acceptable in Your sight, O LORD, my strength and my Redeemer."

Humbly ask God for His attention, Psalm 27:7–8—"Hear, O LORD, when I cry with my voice! Have mercy also upon me, and answer me. When You said, 'Seek My face,' my heart said to You, 'Your face, LORD, I will seek.'"

Be still and know you are in God's presence, Psalm 46:10—"Be still, and know that I am God; I will be exalted among the nations, I will be exalted in the earth!"

Going through tough times? Here's help, Psalm 57:1–2—"Be merciful to me, O God, be merciful to me! For my soul trusts in You; and in the shadow of Your wings I will make my refuge, until these calamities have passed by. I will cry out to God Most High, to God who performs all things for me."

Exalt the Lord as you prepare to pray, Psalm 57:5—"Be exalted, O God, above the heavens; let Your glory be above all the earth."

Early morning prayer, Psalm 63:1—"O God, You are my God; early will I seek You; my soul thirsts for You; my flesh longs for You."

It is God's plan to bless you, Psalm 84:11—"The LORD God is a sun and shield; the LORD will give grace and glory; no good thing will He withhold from those who walk uprightly."

Desperation prayer, Psalm 88:1–2—"O LORD, God of my salvation, I have cried out day and night before You. Let my prayer come before You; incline Your ear to my cry."

Please, God, hear my prayer, Psalm 102:1–2—"Hear my prayer, O LORD, and let my cry come to You. Do not hide Your face from me in the day of my trouble; incline Your ear to me; in the day that I call, answer me speedily."

Praising the Lord, Psalm 103:1–2—"Bless the LORD, O my soul; and all that is within me, bless His holy name! Bless the LORD, O my soul, and forget not all His benefits."

You can be sure God listens, Psalm 116:1–2—"I love the LORD, because He has heard my voice and my supplications. Because He has inclined His ear to me, therefore I will call upon Him as long as I live."

Enduring mercy, Psalm 118:28—"You are my God, and I will praise You; You are my God, I will exalt You."

Heart-searching encounter, Psalm 139:23–24—"Search me, O God, and know my heart; try me, and know my anxieties; and see if there is any wicked way in me, and lead me in the way everlasting."

Praise God for His greatness, Psalm 145:3—"Great is the LORD, and greatly to be praised; and His greatness is unsearchable."

The Lord's glory, Isaiah 42:8—"I am the LORD, that is My name; and My glory I will not give to another."

God knows those who trust Him, Nahum 1:7—"The LORD is good, a stronghold in the day of trouble; and He knows those who trust in Him."

How to approach God, Hebrews 4:14–16—"Seeing then that we have a great High Priest who has passed through the heavens, Jesus the Son of God, let us hold fast our confession. For we do not have a High Priest who cannot sympathize with our weaknesses, but was in all points tempted as we are, yet without sin. Let us therefore come boldly to the throne of grace, that we may obtain mercy and find grace to help in time of need."

INVESTMENT

In this age of intense interest in stocks and bonds, investing becomes a prayer item.

Investment options

MATTHEW 6:19–20—"Do not lay up for yourselves treasures on earth, where moth and rust destroy and where thieves break in and steal; but lay up for yourselves treasures in heaven, where neither moth nor rust destroys and where thieves do not break in and steal."

Satan trembles when he sees the weakest saint upon his knees.

—WILLIAM COWPER

Wise use of wealth

1 TIMOTHY 6:17–18—"Command those who are rich in this present age not to be haughty, nor to trust in uncertain riches but in the living God, who gives us richly all things to enjoy. Let them do good, that they be rich in good works, ready to give, willing to share."

JEALOUSY

Like a poison, jealousy can decimate your spiritual well-being. Also see Covet, Envy.

Your jealous God

EXODUS 34:14—"You shall worship no other god, for the LORD, whose name is Jealous, is a jealous God."

STEPS Nugget

COMPUTERIZED PRAYER

The greatest computer ever built is the human brain. Only a fraction of its potential is ever put to use by the most intelligent people. I believe our brains were so designed to enhance our pursuit of the seventh sense. (See page 91.)

But I have discovered yet another use for this marvelous facility, which I call *computerized prayer*.

In the Lord's goodness to me, my ministry has taken me to more than one hundred countries, in scores of which I am enriched by friends among national Christians. I keep a large map of the world on the wall where I now sit. Half a moment ago I turned my attention from the computer screen to that map. For five minutes, I took a panoramic look at such points as Australia, Bolivia, China, Denmark, Egypt, Finland, Japan, Liberia, and Madagascar. In those few moments, as though by computer chip, I lift hundreds of friends to the throne.

Even now, moments later, my heart senses a lingering radiance.

Success of others

PSALM 37:7—"Rest in the LORD, and wait patiently for Him; do not fret because of him who prospers in his way, because of the man who brings wicked schemes to pass."

Little is much

PSALM 37:16—"A little that a righteous man has is better than the riches of many wicked."

God puts down, exalts

PSALM 75:7—"God is the Judge: He puts down one, and exalts another."

Correct attitude

GALATIANS 6:4—"Let each one examine his own work, and then he will have rejoicing in himself alone, and not in another."

> We cannot talk to God unless we walk with Him when we are not talking.
>
> —OSWALD CHAMBERS

JESUS

Remind yourself of the Good Shepherd's role in your prayers.

Gentle Shepherd

ISAIAH 40:11—"He will feed His flock like a shepherd; He will gather the lambs with His arm, and carry them in His bosom, and gently lead those who are with young."

The way, the truth, the life

JOHN 14:6—"Jesus said to him, 'I am the way, the truth, and the life. No one comes to the Father except through Me.'"

Last words of Jesus

ACTS 1:7–8—"He said to them, 'It is not for you to know times or seasons which the Father has put in His own authority. But you shall receive power when the Holy Spirit has come upon you; and you shall be witnesses to Me in Jerusalem, and in all Judea and Samaria, and to the end of the earth.'"

Meditation: **Christ as Creator,** Colossians 1:15–18: "He is the image of the invisible God, the firstborn over all creation. For by Him all things were created that are in heaven and that are on earth, visible and invisible, whether thrones or dominions or principalities or powers. All things were created through Him and for Him. And He is before all things, and in Him all things consist. And He is the head of the body, the church, who is the beginning, the firstborn from the dead, that in all things He may have the preeminence."

One Mediator between God and you

1 TIMOTHY 2:5—"There is one God and one Mediator between God and men, the Man Christ Jesus."

Praising Jesus, the Lamb

REVELATION 5:12—"Worthy is the Lamb who was slain to receive power and riches and wisdom, and strength and honor and glory and blessing!"

JOY

Whatever your circumstances, let the hymns of heaven fortify and fulfill.

Joy brings strength

NEHEMIAH 8:10—"The joy of the LORD is your strength."

Weeping turns to joy

PSALM 30:5—"Weeping may endure for a night, but joy comes in the morning."

No good thing withheld

PSALM 84:11—"The LORD God is a sun and shield; the LORD will give grace and glory; no good thing will He withhold from those who walk uprightly."

Joy in giving

2 CORINTHIANS 9:7—"Let each one give as he purposes in his heart, not grudgingly or of necessity; for God loves a cheerful giver."

Consistent joy

PHILIPPIANS 4:4—"Rejoice in the Lord always. Again I will say, rejoice!"

Meditation: **Benefits from tough times,** James 1:2–5: "Count it all joy when you fall into various trials, knowing that the testing of your faith produces patience. But let patience have its perfect work, that you may be perfect and complete, lacking nothing. If any of you lacks wisdom, let him ask of God, who gives to all liberally and without reproach, and it will be given to him."

KINDNESS
Bible-based compassion and caring enrich the human touch.

Kindness to strangers
LEVITICUS 19:34—"The stranger who dwells among you shall be to you as one born among you, and you shall love him as yourself; for you were strangers in the land of Egypt: I am the LORD your God."

Neighborhood attitude
PROVERBS 14:21—"He who despises his neighbor sins; but he who has mercy on the poor, happy is he."

Meditation: **Kindness in action,** Romans 12:19–21: "Beloved, do not avenge yourselves, but rather give place to wrath; for it is written, 'Vengeance is Mine, I will repay,' says the Lord. Therefore 'If your enemy is hungry, feed him; if he is thirsty, give him a drink; for in so doing you will heap coals of fire on his head.' Do not be overcome by evil, but overcome evil with good."

Love is kind
1 CORINTHIANS 13:4—"Love suffers long and is kind; love does not envy; love does not parade itself, is not puffed up."

Not weary doing good
GALATIANS 6:9–10—"Let us not grow weary while doing good, for in due season we shall reap if we do not lose heart. Therefore, as we have

opportunity, let us do good to all, especially to those who are of the household of faith."

KNOWLEDGE

Knowledge is the Holy Spirit's terrain for guidance and conduct.

Secret information

DEUTERONOMY 29:29—"The secret things belong to the LORD our God."

Sorrowful knowledge

ECCLESIASTES 1:18—"For in much wisdom is much grief, and he who increases knowledge increases sorrow."

Knowledge and obedience

JOHN 13:17—"If you know these things, blessed are you if you do them."

Greatest knowledge

PHILIPPIANS 3:8—"I also count all things loss for the excellence of the knowledge of Christ Jesus my Lord, for whom I have suffered the loss of all things, and count them as rubbish, that I may gain Christ."

LEADERSHIP

Responsibility, opportunity, and blessing—all are parts of leadership.

The Bible, the key to leadership

JOSHUA 1:8—"This Book of the Law shall not depart from your mouth, but you shall meditate in it day and night, that you may observe to do according to all that is written in it. For then you will make your way prosperous, and then you will have good success."

Special anointing

PSALM 45:7—"You love righteousness and hate wickedness; therefore God, Your God, has anointed You with the oil of gladness more than Your companions."

Servant leadership

MATTHEW 23:11–12—"He who is greatest among you shall be your servant. And whoever exalts himself will be humbled, and he who humbles himself will be exalted."

In-depth qualities

COLOSSIANS 1:9–10—"For this reason we also, since the day we heard it, do not cease to pray for you, and to ask that you may be filled with the knowledge of His will in all wisdom and spiritual understanding; that you may walk worthy of the Lord, fully pleasing Him, being fruitful in every good work and increasing in the knowledge of God."

Leadership qualifications

TITUS 1:7–9—"A bishop must be blameless, as a steward of God, not self-willed, not quick-tempered, not given to wine, not violent, not greedy for money, but hospitable, a lover of what is good, sober-minded, just, holy, self-controlled, holding fast the faithful word as he has been taught, that he may be able, by sound doctrine, both to exhort and convict those who contradict."

LONELINESS

What to do, where to turn, and how to escape feelings of loneliness.

Your Lord, always with you

DEUTERONOMY 31:8—"The LORD, He is the One who goes before you. He will be with you, He will not leave you nor forsake you; do not fear nor be dismayed."

Lonely sleeplessness

PSALM 102:7—"I lie awake, and am like a sparrow alone on the housetop."

Jesus alone on the cross

MARK 15:34—"At the ninth hour Jesus cried out with a loud voice, saying, 'Eloi, Eloi, lama sabachthani?' which is translated, 'My God, My God, why have You forsaken Me?'"

Tears of loneliness

2 TIMOTHY 1:3–4—"I thank God, whom I serve with a pure conscience, as my forefathers did, as without ceasing I remember you in my prayers night and day, greatly desiring to see you, being mindful of your tears, that I may be filled with joy."

A Friend at your heart's door

REVELATION 3:20—"I stand at the door and knock. If anyone hears My voice and opens the door, I will come in to him and dine with him, and he with Me."

LOVE

According to the Bible itself—1 Corinthians 13:13—love is the greatest force in human relationships.

Greater than life itself

PSALM 63:3—"Your lovingkindness is better than life, my lips shall praise You."

Unquenchable love

SONG OF SONGS 8:7—"Many waters cannot quench love, nor can the floods drown it."

Love God, neighbor

MATTHEW 22:36–39—"'Teacher, which is the great commandment in the law?' Jesus said to him, "'You shall love the LORD your God with all your heart, with all your soul, and with all your mind.'" This is the first and great commandment. And the second is like it: "'You shall love your neighbor as yourself.'""

Meditation: **Abiding love,** John 15:9–12: "As the Father loved Me, I also have loved you; abide in My love. If you keep My commandments, you will abide in My love, just as I have kept My Father's commandments and abide in His love. These things I have spoken to you, that My joy may remain in you, and that your joy may be full. This is My commandment, that you love one another as I have loved you."

Love is the greatest

1 CORINTHIANS 13:13—"Now abide faith, hope, love, these three; but the greatest of these is love."

Give love priority

COLOSSIANS 3:14—"Put on love, which is the bond of perfection."

Brotherly love

1 THESSALONIANS 4:9—"Concerning brotherly love you have no need that I should write to you, for you yourselves are taught by God to love one another."

Forgiving love

1 PETER 4:8—"Above all things have fervent love for one another, for 'love will cover a multitude of sins.'"

MARRIAGE

Base your marriage on the Bible and you undergird the relationship with harmony, purpose, and fulfillment.

Strategic premise for marriage

PSALM 34:3—"Oh, magnify the LORD with me, and let us exalt His name together."

Loving intimacy

PROVERBS 5:18—"Let your fountain be blessed, and rejoice with the wife of your youth."

It is good to find a wife

PROVERBS 18:22—"He who finds a wife finds a good thing, and obtains favor from the LORD."

Garden of love

SONG OF SONGS 4:16—"Awake, O north wind, and come, O south! Blow upon my garden, that its spices may flow out. Let my beloved come to his garden and eat its pleasant fruits."

Enduring marriage

MARK 10:7–9—"'For this reason a man shall leave his father and mother and be joined to his wife, and the two shall become one flesh'; so then they are no longer two, but one flesh. Therefore what God has joined together, let not man separate."

MATURITY

The Bible's foremost purpose is to help you experience spiritual growth.

Lose to gain

MATTHEW 16:24—"Jesus said to His disciples, 'If anyone desires to come after Me, let him deny himself, and take up his cross, and follow Me.'"

Steadfast, abounding

1 CORINTHIANS 15:58—"Be steadfast, immovable, always abounding in the work of the Lord, knowing that your labor is not in vain in the Lord."

Mature thinking

PHILIPPIANS 4:8—"Whatever things are true, whatever things are noble, whatever things are just, whatever things are pure, whatever things are lovely, whatever things are of good report, if there is any virtue and if there is anything praiseworthy—meditate on these things."

Meditation: **In-depth Christian growth,** Colossians 1:9–12: "For this reason we also, since the day we heard it, do not cease to pray for you, and to ask that you may be filled with the knowledge of His will in all wisdom and spiritual understanding; that you may walk worthy of the Lord, fully pleasing Him, being fruitful in every good work and increasing in the knowledge of God; strengthened with all might, according to His glorious power, for all patience and longsuffering with joy; giving thanks to the Father who has qualified us to be partakers of the inheritance of the saints in the light."

Walking in mature faith

COLOSSIANS 2:6–7—"As you therefore have received Christ Jesus the Lord, so walk in Him, rooted and built up in Him and established in the faith, as you have been taught, abounding in it with thanksgiving."

Meditation: **Subdue carnal nature,** Colossians 3:5–8: "Put to death your members which are on the earth: fornication, uncleanness, passion, evil desire, and covetousness, which is idolatry. Because of these things the wrath of God is coming upon the sons of disobedience, in which you yourselves once walked when you lived in them. But now you yourselves are to put off all these: anger, wrath, malice, blasphemy, filthy language out of your mouth."

Endure hardness

2 TIMOTHY 2:3–5—"You therefore must endure hardship as a good soldier of Jesus Christ. No one engaged in warfare entangles himself with the affairs of this life, that he may please him who enlisted him as a soldier. And also if anyone competes in athletics, he is not crowned unless he competes according to the rules."

Mature in God's will

HEBREWS 13:20–21—"May the God of peace who brought up our Lord Jesus from the dead, that great Shepherd of the sheep, through the blood of the everlasting covenant, make you complete in every good work to do His will, working in you what is well pleasing in His sight, through Jesus Christ, to whom be glory forever and ever. Amen."

Mature additives to faith

2 PETER 1:5–7—"For this very reason, giving all diligence, add to your faith virtue, to virtue knowledge, to knowledge self-control, to self-control perseverance, to perseverance godliness, to godliness brotherly kindness, and to brotherly kindness love."

MEDITATION

All major religions emphasize some kind of meditation. Only when you meditate on Scripture, however, do you tap into the forces of creation, the Holy Spirit's unction, and the mind of Christ. The procedure is simple but by no means elementary.

I have found Bible passages such as 1 Timothy 6:6–10 conducive to meditation:

> Godliness with contentment is great gain. For we brought nothing into this world, and it is certain we can carry nothing out. And having food and clothing, with these we shall be content. But those who desire to be rich fall into temptation and a snare, and into many foolish and harmful lusts which drown men in destruction and perdition. For the love of money is a root of all kinds of evil.

1. I pray, asking that my mind and heart be emptied of any distracting thoughts and cares. I also ask to be receptive to whatever the Holy Spirit wishes me to learn.

2. I read the text, often making that reading a continuing phrase of my prayer. I pay close attention to the learning points. I have discovered that since the Bible is a living Book (Heb. 4:12), I can expect its teachings to enrich and motivate me.

3. I pray my way through the learning points.

"Godliness with contentment is great gain." I mull over the statement for several moments, inviting the Holy Spirit to help me fully grasp the meaning. Such times can stir my emotions, but it is the kind of sentiment I cherish and find positive and productive.

"We brought nothing into this world, and it is certain we can carry nothing out." I take inventory of remembered friends and acquaintances and people in the world around me. I think of the newborn and the aged—the emptiness of hands at the moment of birth and at the hour of death. *Nothing*. I think a long time about that word.

"Having food and clothing, with these we shall be content." Content only with "food and clothing"? Hardly! God's children are not ascetics; we are people of abundance. "Godliness with contentment"—that is the key!

Again and again I read the text, pondering each word. Meditation is feasting or, if you prefer, a delightful way to charge one's batteries.

Silent approach to God

PSALM 62:5–7—"My soul, wait silently for God alone, for my expectation is from Him. He only is my rock and my salvation; He is my defense; I shall not be moved. In God is my salvation and my glory; the rock of my strength, and my refuge, is in God."

Preparation to consulting Scripture

PSALM 119:15–16—"I will meditate on Your precepts, and contemplate Your ways. I will delight myself in Your statutes; I will not forget Your word."

Laying it all on the line

PSALM 139:23–24—"Search me, O God, and know my heart; try me, and know my anxieties; and see if there is any wicked way in me, and lead me in the way everlasting."

What God expects of you

MICAH 6:8—"He has shown you, O man, what is good; and what does the LORD require of you but to do justly, to love mercy, and to walk humbly with your God?"

Ponder the Beatitudes

MATTHEW 5:3–10—"Blessed are the poor in spirit, for theirs is the kingdom of heaven. Blessed are those who mourn, for they shall be comforted. Blessed are the meek, for they shall inherit the earth. Blessed are those who hunger and thirst for righteousness, for they shall be filled. Blessed are the merciful, for they shall obtain mercy. Blessed are the pure in heart, for they shall see God. Blessed are the peacemakers, for they shall be called sons of God. Blessed are those who are persecuted for righteousness' sake, for theirs is the kingdom of heaven."

The cost of discipleship

MATTHEW 10:37–39—"He who loves father or mother more than Me is not worthy of Me. And he who loves son or daughter more than Me is not worthy of Me. And he who does not take his cross and follow after Me is not worthy of Me. He who finds his life will lose it, and he who loses his life for My sake will find it."

Tired? Discouraged? Find rest in the Lord

MATTHEW 11:28–30—"Come to Me, all you who labor and are heavy laden, and I will give you rest. Take My yoke upon you and learn from Me, for I am gentle and lowly in heart, and you will find rest for your souls. For My yoke is easy and My burden is light."

Abiding in Christ

JOHN 15:5–7—"I am the vine, you are the branches. He who abides in Me, and I in him, bears much fruit; for without Me you can do nothing. If anyone does not abide in Me, he is cast out as a branch and is withered; and they gather them and throw them into the fire, and they are burned. If you abide in Me, and My words abide in you, you will ask what you desire, and it shall be done for you."

Holy Spirit's role in prayer

ROMANS 8:26–28—"The Spirit also helps in our weaknesses. For we do not know what we should pray for as we ought, but the Spirit Himself makes intercession for us with groanings which cannot be uttered. Now

He who searches the hearts knows what the mind of the Spirit is, because He makes intercession for the saints according to the will of God. And we know that all things work together for good to those who love God, to those who are the called according to His purpose."

How to commit your life to Christ

ROMANS 12:1–2—"I beseech you therefore, brethren, by the mercies of God, that you present your bodies a living sacrifice, holy, acceptable to God, which is your reasonable service. And do not be conformed to this world, but be transformed by the renewing of your mind, that you may prove what is that good and acceptable and perfect will of God."

Love is the greatest

1 CORINTHIANS 13:11–13—"When I was a child, I spoke as a child, I understood as a child, I thought as a child; but when I became a man, I put away childish things. For now we see in a mirror, dimly, but then face to face. Now I know in part, but then I shall know just as I also am known. And now abide faith, hope, love, these three; but the greatest of these is love."

Crucified with Christ

GALATIANS 2:20—"I have been crucified with Christ; it is no longer I who live, but Christ lives in me; and the life which I now live in the flesh I live by faith in the Son of God, who loved me and gave Himself for me."

Fruit of the Spirit in your life

GALATIANS 5:22–23, 25—"The fruit of the Spirit is love, joy, peace, longsuffering, kindness, goodness, faithfulness, gentleness, self-control. Against such there is no law . . . If we live in the Spirit, let us also walk in the Spirit."

Faith in four dimensions!

EPHESIANS 3:17–19—"That Christ may dwell in your hearts through faith; that you, being rooted and grounded in love, may be able to comprehend with all the saints what is the width and length and depth and height—to know the love of Christ which passes knowledge; that you may be filled with all the fullness of God."

Thinking the way Jesus thought

PHILIPPIANS 2:5–8—"Let this mind be in you which was also in Christ Jesus, who, being in the form of God, did not consider it robbery to be equal with God, but made Himself of no reputation, taking the form of a bondservant, and coming in the likeness of men. And being found in appearance as a man, He humbled Himself and became obedient to the point of death, even the death of the cross."

Gain from loss

PHILIPPIANS 3:7–8—"What things were gain to me, these I have counted loss for Christ. Yet indeed I also count all things loss for the excellence of the knowledge of Christ Jesus my Lord, for whom I have suffered the loss of all things, and count them as rubbish, that I may gain Christ."

> The self-sufficient do not pray, the self-satisfied will not pray, the self-righteous cannot pray.
>
> —LEONARD RAVENHILL

Goal setting

PHILIPPIANS 3:13–14—"I do not count myself to have apprehended; but one thing I do, forgetting those things which are behind and reaching forward to those things which are ahead, I press toward the goal for the prize of the upward call of God in Christ Jesus."

Positive prayer

PHILIPPIANS 4:6–7—"Be anxious for nothing, but in everything by prayer and supplication, with thanksgiving, let your requests be made known to God; and the peace of God, which surpasses all understanding, will guard your hearts and minds through Christ Jesus."

Accentuate the positive

PHILIPPIANS 4:8—"Whatever things are true, whatever things are noble, whatever things are just, whatever things are pure, whatever things are lovely, whatever things are of good report, if there is any virtue and if there is anything praiseworthy—meditate on these things."

In-depth Christian growth

COLOSSIANS 1:9–12—"For this reason we also, since the day we heard it, do not cease to pray for you, and to ask that you may be filled with the knowledge of His will in all wisdom and spiritual understanding; that you may walk worthy of the Lord, fully pleasing Him, being fruitful in every good work and increasing in the knowledge of God; strengthened with all might, according to His glorious power, for all patience and longsuffering with joy; giving thanks to the Father who has qualified us to be partakers of the inheritance of the saints in the light."

Christ as Creator

COLOSSIANS 1:15–18—"He is the image of the invisible God, the first-born over all creation. For by Him all things were created that are in heaven and that are on earth, visible and invisible, whether thrones or dominions or principalities or powers. All things were created through Him and for Him. And He is before all things, and in Him all things consist. And He is the head of the body, the church, who is the beginning, the firstborn from the dead, that in all things He may have the preeminence."

Walking in mature faith

COLOSSIANS 2:6–7—"As you therefore have received Christ Jesus the Lord, so walk in Him, rooted and built up in Him and established in the faith, as you have been taught, abounding in it with thanksgiving."

Godliness with contentment

1 TIMOTHY 6:6–8—"Godliness with contentment is great gain. For we brought nothing into this world, and it is certain we can carry nothing out. And having food and clothing, with these we shall be content."

Tough commitment

2 TIMOTHY 2:3–7—"You therefore must endure hardship as a good soldier of Jesus Christ. No one engaged in warfare entangles himself with the affairs of this life, that he may please him who enlisted him as a soldier. And also if anyone competes in athletics, he is not crowned unless he competes according to the rules. The hardworking farmer must be first to partake of the crops. Consider what I say, and may the Lord give you understanding in all things."

Assured faith, substance, evidence

HEBREWS 11:1, 3, 6—"Faith is the substance of things hoped for, the evidence of things not seen . . . By faith we understand that the worlds were framed by the word of God, so that the things which are seen were not made of things which are visible . . . But without faith it is impossible to please Him, for he who comes to God must believe that He is, and that He is a rewarder of those who diligently seek Him."

Not only hearers, but doers

JAMES 1:22–25—"Be doers of the word, and not hearers only, deceiving yourselves. For if anyone is a hearer of the word and not a doer, he is like a man observing his natural face in a mirror; for he observes himself, goes away, and immediately forgets what kind of man he was. But he who looks into the perfect law of liberty and continues in it, and is not a forgetful hearer but a doer of the work, this one will be blessed in what he does."

Additives to faith

2 PETER 1:5–8—"Giving all diligence, add to your faith virtue, to virtue knowledge, to knowledge self-control, to self-control perseverance, to

perseverance godliness, to godliness brotherly kindness, and to brotherly kindness love. For if these things are yours and abound, you will be neither barren nor unfruitful in the knowledge of our Lord Jesus Christ."

Becoming like Christ

1 JOHN 3:2–3—"Now we are children of God; and it has not yet been revealed what we shall be, but we know that when He is revealed, we shall be like Him, for we shall see Him as He is. And everyone who has this hope in Him purifies himself, just as He is pure."

Considering God's love and ours

1 JOHN 4:7–11—"Beloved, let us love one another, for love is of God; and everyone who loves is born of God and knows God. He who does not love does not know God, for God is love. In this the love of God was manifested toward us, that God has sent His only begotten Son into the world, that we might live through Him. In this is love, not that we loved God, but that He loved us and sent His Son to be the propitiation for our sins. Beloved, if God so loved us, we also ought to love one another."

MERCY

God's mercy is yours for your time of need and is available upon request.

Plea for mercy

PSALM 6:1–2—"O LORD, do not rebuke me in Your anger, nor chasten me in Your hot displeasure. Have mercy on me, O LORD, for I am weak."

Mercy requested

PSALM 41:4—"LORD, be merciful to me; heal my soul, for I have sinned against You."

Dimensions of mercy

PSALM 57:1—"Be merciful to me, O God, be merciful to me! For my soul trusts in You; and in the shadow of Your wings I will make my refuge, until these calamities have passed by."

Delight in mercy

MICAH 7:18–19—"Who is a God like You, pardoning iniquity and passing over the transgression of the remnant of His heritage? He does not retain His anger forever, because He delights in mercy. He will again have compassion on us, and will subdue our iniquities. You will cast all our sins into the depths of the sea."

Mercy to sinners

2 PETER 3:9—"The Lord is not slack concerning His promise, as some count slackness, but is longsuffering toward us, not willing that any should perish but that all should come to repentance."

MORALITY

Morality is a requirement for channels open to blessing and guidance. Also see Immorality.

Making moral covenant

JOB 31:1—"I have made a covenant with my eyes; why then should I look upon a young woman?"

Total morality

ROMANS 13:14—"Put on the Lord Jesus Christ, and make no provision for the flesh, to fulfill its lusts."

Spiritual fruit

GALATIANS 5:22–23—"The fruit of the Spirit is love, joy, peace, longsuffering, kindness, goodness, faithfulness, gentleness, self-control. Against such there is no law."

Companion to faith

2 PETER 1:5–7—"Add to your faith virtue, to virtue knowledge, to knowledge self-control, to self-control perseverance, to perseverance godliness, to godliness brotherly kindness, and to brotherly kindness love."

MORNING

The new day often marks the continuity of yesterday's blessings.

Early morning prayer

PSALM 63:1–3—"O God, You are my God; early will I seek You; my soul thirsts for You; my flesh longs for You in a dry and thirsty land where there is no water. So I have looked for You in the sanctuary, to see Your power and Your glory. Because Your lovingkindness is better than life, my lips shall praise You."

Morning heart search

PSALM 139:23–24—"Search me, O God, and know my heart; try me, and know my anxieties; and see if there is any wicked way in me, and lead me in the way everlasting."

Morning assurance

PSALM 143:8—"Cause me to hear Your lovingkindness in the morning, for in You do I trust; cause me to know the way in which I should walk, for I lift up my soul to You."

New every morning

LAMENTATIONS 3:22–23—"Through the LORD's mercies we are not consumed, because His compassions fail not. They are new every morning; great is Your faithfulness."

MOTHER

A mother is God's designed light and warmth in the home. Also see Father, Parents.

Remember mother's teaching

PROVERBS 6:20—"My son, keep your father's command, and do not forsake the law of your mother."

Parental discipline

PROVERBS 29:15—"The rod and rebuke give wisdom, but a child left to himself brings shame to his mother."

Meditation: **Exemplary mother,** Proverbs 31:27–30: "She watches over the ways of her household, and does not eat the bread of idleness. Her children rise up and call her blessed; her husband also, and he praises her: 'Many daughters have done well, but you excel them all.' Charm is deceitful and beauty is passing, but a woman who fears the LORD, she shall be praised."

Childbirth

JOHN 16:21—"A woman, when she is in labor, has sorrow because her hour has come; but as soon as she has given birth to the child, she no longer remembers the anguish, for joy that a human being has been born into the world."

NATURE
God's creative skill and artistry are evident in nature.

Nature praises the Creator

PSALM 69:34—"Let heaven and earth praise Him, the seas and everything that moves in them."

Lord of nature

JEREMIAH 31:35—"Thus says the LORD, who gives the sun for a light by day, the ordinances of the moon and the stars for a light by night, who disturbs the sea, and its waves roar."

Visible wonders

AMOS 4:13—"Behold, He who forms mountains, and creates the wind, who declares to man what his thought is, and makes the morning darkness, who treads the high places of the earth—the LORD God of hosts is His name."

Nature's Creator

COLOSSIANS 1:16—"By Him all things were created that are in heaven and that are on earth, visible and invisible, whether thrones or dominions or principalities or powers. All things were created through Him and for Him."

NEIGHBORS

In a shrinking world, you have increasingly more neighbors.

Honesty concerning neighbor

EXODUS 20:16—"You shall not bear false witness against your neighbor."

Damaged property

EXODUS 22:5—"If a man causes a field or vineyard to be grazed, and lets loose his animal, and it feeds in another man's field, he shall make restitution from the best of his own field and the best of his own vineyard."

> Could you be content to meet a loved one only in public?
>
> —J. HUDSON TAYLOR

Keeping up with the Joneses

ECCLESIASTES 4:4—"I saw that for all toil and every skillful work a man is envied by his neighbor. This also is vanity and grasping for the wind."

Dishonest to neighbor

JEREMIAH 9:8—"One speaks peaceably to his neighbor with his mouth, but in his heart he lies in wait."

Love God, neighbor

MARK 12:30–31—"'You shall love the LORD your God with all your heart, with all your soul, with all your mind, and with all your strength.' This is the first commandment. And the second, like it, is this: 'You shall love your neighbor as yourself.' There is no other commandment greater than these."

STEPS Nugget

EXTRA BUT OFTEN ORDINARY

As long as they occupy space on Planet Earth, Christians experience tension and stress. They face times of disappointment and discouragement. They struggle with anger and resentment. They can become envious and jealous. They can have hurt feelings. Make mistakes. Often fail. Some more than others.

Don't expect to become some kind of pristine saint. Instead, see yourself as an ordinary human being who enjoys extra benefits by integrating the Bible into your life through prayer.

Prior to his death, the apostle Paul told his understudy, "I have fought the good fight" (2 Tim. 4:7). Earlier, in 1 Timothy 6:12, he challenged his young friend to "fight the good fight of faith."

What kind of fight was Paul talking about?

Doctrines?

Interpretations?

Policies?

No.

Paul was a normal human being determined to overcome his human weaknesses and become a committed Christian. His fight was against spiritual forces and his carnality.

So don't mind being an ordinary person who has the extraordinary joy of living out the Bible's precepts and promises through prayer—making yourself a better person than you could ever otherwise be.

NEW YEAR

The new year brings greetings, resolutions, and Day One for new spiritual ventures and adventures. Also see Future.

New song

PSALM 40:3—"He has put a new song in my mouth—praise to our God; many will see it and fear, and will trust in the LORD."

Bright path ahead

PROVERBS 4:18—"The path of the just is like the shining sun, that shines ever brighter unto the perfect day."

Meditation: **Uncertain future,** James 4:13–15: "Come now, you who say, 'Today or tomorrow we will go to such and such a city, spend a year there, buy and sell, and make a profit'; whereas you do not know what will happen tomorrow. For what is your life? It is even a vapor that appears for a little time and then vanishes away. Instead you ought to say, 'If the Lord wills, we shall live and do this or that.'"

OBEDIENCE

The line of command in your spiritual development assures you an enriching and maturing two-way relationship with your Lord. Think of it—rapport with the Creator of the universe!

Principles of obedience

DEUTERONOMY 10:12—"What does the LORD your God require of you, but to fear the LORD your God, to walk in all His ways and to love Him, to serve the LORD your God with all your heart and with all your soul?"

Intimate Scripture

DEUTERONOMY 30:14—"The word is very near you, in your mouth and in your heart, that you may do it."

Learning obedience

PSALM 119:34—"Give me understanding, and I shall keep Your law; indeed, I shall observe it with my whole heart."

Avoid trying to obey two masters

MATTHEW 6:24—"No one can serve two masters; for either he will hate the one and love the other, or else he will be loyal to the one and despise the other. You cannot serve God and mammon."

Faithful stewards

1 CORINTHIANS 4:2—"It is required in stewards that one be found faithful."

Don't just go to church; live the life

JAMES 1:22 "Be doers of the word, and not hearers only, deceiving yourselves."

OLD AGE

Those who live in the will of God become a day younger with each sunset. Also see Birthday.

Much work to be done

JOSHUA 13:1—"Joshua was old, advanced in years. And the LORD said to him: 'You are old, advanced in years, and there remains very much land yet to be possessed.'"

Plea for help

PSALM 71:9—"Do not cast me off in the time of old age; do not forsake me when my strength fails."

Meditation: **Facing old age,** 2 Corinthians 4:16–18: "We do not lose heart. Even though our outward man is perishing, yet the inward man is being renewed day by day. For our light affliction, which is but for a moment, is working for us a far more exceeding and eternal weight of glory, while we do not look at the things which are seen, but at the things which are not seen. For the things which are seen are temporary, but the things which are not seen are eternal."

Exemplary old age

TITUS 2:1–3—"Speak the things which are proper for sound doctrine: that the older men be sober, reverent, temperate, sound in faith, in love, in patience; the older women likewise, that they be reverent in behavior, not slanderers, not given to much wine, teachers of good things."

If you want God to hear you when you pray, you must hear Him when He speaks.

—THOMAS BROOKS

OPPOSITION

Sometimes those who oppose us become catalysts for good in our lives.

Confronting an enemy

PSALM 27:1—"The LORD is my light and my salvation; whom shall I fear? The LORD is the strength of my life; of whom shall I be afraid?"

Stronghold in trouble

PSALM 37:39—"The salvation of the righteous is from the LORD; He is their strength in the time of trouble."

Walking through opposition

PSALM 138:7—"Though I walk in the midst of trouble, You will revive me; You will stretch out Your hand against the wrath of my enemies, and Your right hand will save me."

At peace with an enemy

PROVERBS 16:7—"When a man's ways please the LORD, He makes even his enemies to be at peace with him."

Persecution, a source of blessing

MATTHEW 5:11–12—"Blessed are you when they revile and persecute you, and say all kinds of evil against you falsely for My sake. Rejoice and be exceedingly glad, for great is your reward in heaven, for so they persecuted the prophets who were before you."

Forgive before prayer

MARK 11:25—"Whenever you stand praying, if you have anything against anyone, forgive him, that your Father in heaven may also forgive you your trespasses."

OPPRESSION

Through the refining fire come otherwise unattainable blessings. Also see Testing.

Refuge for the oppressed

PSALM 9:9—"The LORD also will be a refuge for the oppressed, a refuge in times of trouble."

Oppressing the poor

PROVERBS 14:31—"He who oppresses the poor reproaches his Maker, but he who honors Him has mercy on the needy."

Enemies without cause

LAMENTATIONS 3:52—"My enemies without cause hunted me down like a bird."

Meditation: **Benefits from testing,** James 1:2–4: "Count it all joy when you fall into various trials, knowing that the testing of your faith produces patience. But let patience have its perfect work, that you may be perfect and complete, lacking nothing."

OUTREACH

A Christian's prime purpose for living is to touch others with sharing and blessing. Also see Evangelism.

Tell God's wonders

PSALM 9:1—"I will praise You, O LORD, with my whole heart; I will tell of all Your marvelous works."

Winning souls

PROVERBS 11:30—"The fruit of the righteous is a tree of life, and he who wins souls is wise."

Reaching many

DANIEL 12:3—"Those who are wise shall shine like the brightness of the firmament, and those who turn many to righteousness like the stars forever and ever."

Fishers of men

MARK 1:17—"Jesus said to them, 'Follow Me, and I will make you become fishers of men.'"

Pray for laborers

LUKE 10:2—"The harvest truly is great, but the laborers are few; therefore pray the Lord of the harvest to send out laborers into His harvest."

Meditation: **One lost sheep,** Luke 15:4–7: "What man of you, having a hundred sheep, if he loses one of them, does not leave the ninety-nine in the wilderness, and go after the one which is lost until he finds it? And when he has found it, he lays it on his shoulders, rejoicing. And when he comes home, he calls together his friends and neighbors, saying to them, 'Rejoice with me, for I have found my sheep which was lost!' I say to you that likewise there will be more joy in heaven over one sinner who repents than over ninety-nine just persons who need no repentance."

Last words of Jesus

ACTS 1:7–8—"He said to them, 'It is not for you to know times or seasons which the Father has put in His own authority. But you shall receive power when the Holy Spirit has come upon you; and you shall be witnesses to Me in Jerusalem, and in all Judea and Samaria, and to the end of the earth.'"

Not ashamed of the gospel

ROMANS 1:16—"I am not ashamed of the gospel of Christ, for it is the power of God to salvation for everyone who believes, for the Jew first and also for the Greek."

Not weary doing good

GALATIANS 6:9–10—"Let us not grow weary while doing good, for in due season we shall reap if we do not lose heart. Therefore, as we have opportunity, let us do good to all, especially to those who are of the household of faith."

PAIN

Pain is a potential means for blessing and understanding. Also see Comfort, Suffering.

Come forth as gold

JOB 23:10—"He knows the way that I take; when He has tested me, I shall come forth as gold."

Severe pain

JOB 30:17—"My bones are pierced in me at night, and my gnawing pains take no rest."

Given patience

2 THESSALONIANS 3:5—"May the Lord direct your hearts into the love of God and into the patience of Christ."

No more pain

REVELATION 21:4—"God will wipe away every tear from their eyes; there shall be no more death, nor sorrow, nor crying. There shall be no more pain, for the former things have passed away."

PARENTS

Parents are a bridge between past and future, a link between earth and heaven.

Influence of parents

PROVERBS 6:20–22—"My son, keep your father's command, and do not forsake the law of your mother. Bind them continually upon your heart; tie them around your neck. When you roam, they will lead you; when you sleep, they will keep you; and when you awake, they will speak with you."

Wise child

PROVERBS 23:24—"The father of the righteous will greatly rejoice, and he who begets a wise child will delight in him."

Parents teach children

JOEL 1:3—"Tell your children about it, let your children tell their children, and their children another generation."

Bad influence over children

MARK 9:42—"Whoever causes one of these little ones who believe in Me to stumble, it would be better for him if a millstone were hung around his neck, and he were thrown into the sea."

Parents transmit faith to child

2 TIMOTHY 3:14–15—"You must continue in the things which you have learned and been assured of, knowing from whom you have learned them, and that from childhood you have known the Holy Scriptures, which are able to make you wise for salvation through faith which is in Christ Jesus."

PATIENCE

In whatever circumstances, trust in your Lord.

Patience softens anger

PSALM 4:4—"Be angry, and do not sin. Meditate within your heart on your bed, and be still."

Hope delayed

PROVERBS 13:12—"Hope deferred makes the heart sick, but when the desire comes, it is a tree of life."

When God says to wait

ISAIAH 30:18—"The LORD will wait, that He may be gracious to you; and therefore He will be exalted, that He may have mercy on you. For the LORD is a God of justice; blessed are all those who wait for Him."

Steadfast, abounding

1 CORINTHIANS 15:58—"Be steadfast, immovable, always abounding in the work of the Lord, knowing that your labor is not in vain in the Lord."

Purpose of suffering

2 CORINTHIANS 4:17–18—"Our light affliction, which is but for a moment, is working for us a far more exceeding and eternal weight of glory, while we do not look at the things which are seen, but at the things which are not seen. For the things which are seen are temporary, but the things which are not seen are eternal."

Patience rewarded

JAMES 5:11—"We count them blessed who endure. You have heard of the perseverance of Job and seen the end intended by the Lord—that the Lord is very compassionate and merciful."

PERSECUTION

Persecution is always a learning site, often a source of blessing.

Stronghold during persecution

PSALM 37:39—"The salvation of the righteous is from the LORD; He is their strength in the time of trouble."

Persecution rewarded

LUKE 6:22–23—"Blessed are you when men hate you, and when they exclude you, and revile you, and cast out your name as evil, for the Son of Man's sake. Rejoice in that day and leap for joy! For indeed your reward is great in heaven, for in like manner their fathers did to the prophets."

Meditation: **Persecution to be expected,** John 15:18–20: "If the world hates you, you know that it hated Me before it hated you. If you were of the world, the world would love its own. Yet because you are not of the world, but I chose you out of the world, therefore the world hates you. Remember the word that I said to you, 'A servant is not greater than his master.' If they persecuted Me, they will also persecute you. If they kept My word, they will keep yours also."

Endure hardness

2 TIMOTHY 2:3–5—"You therefore must endure hardship as a good soldier of Jesus Christ. No one engaged in warfare entangles himself with the affairs of this life, that he may please him who enlisted him as a soldier. And also if anyone competes in athletics, he is not crowned unless he competes according to the rules."

Part of the program

2 TIMOTHY 3:12—"All who desire to live godly in Christ Jesus will suffer persecution."

No fear of man

HEBREWS 13:6—"We may boldly say: 'The LORD is my helper; I will not fear. What can man do to me?'"

PRAISE

Praise opens the door to answered prayer. Also see Worship.

Worthy of praise

2 SAMUEL 22:4—"I will call upon the LORD, who is worthy to be praised."

Meditation: **David's prayer of praise,** 1 Chronicles 29:10–13: "Therefore David blessed the LORD before all the assembly; and

David said: 'Blessed are You, LORD God of Israel, our Father, forever and ever. Yours, O LORD, is the greatness, the power and the glory, the victory and the majesty; for all that is in heaven and in earth is Yours; Yours is the kingdom, O LORD, and You are exalted as head over all. Both riches and honor come from You, and You reign over all. In Your hand is power and might; in Your hand it is to make great and to give strength to all. Now therefore, our God, we thank You and praise Your glorious name.'"

Gratitude for an answer

PSALM 28:6–7—"Blessed be the LORD, because He has heard the voice of my supplications! The LORD is my strength and my shield; my heart trusted in Him, and I am helped; therefore my heart greatly rejoices, and with my song I will praise Him."

Thinking about God's greatness

PSALM 86:10–12—"You are great, and do wondrous things; You alone are God. Teach me Your way, O LORD; I will walk in Your truth; unite my heart to fear Your name. I will praise You, O Lord my God, with all my heart, and I will glorify Your name forevermore."

Greatness beyond measurement

PSALM 145:2–3—"Every day I will bless You, and I will praise Your name forever and ever. Great is the LORD, and greatly to be praised; and His greatness is unsearchable."

Exclusive glory and praise

ISAIAH 42:8—"I am the LORD, that is My name; and My glory I will not give to another."

Praising Jesus, the Lamb

REVELATION 5:12–13—"'Worthy is the Lamb who was slain to receive power and riches and wisdom, and strength and honor and glory and blessing!' And every creature which is in heaven and on the earth and under the earth and such as are in the sea, and all that are in them,

I heard saying: 'Blessing and honor and glory and power be to Him who sits on the throne, and to the Lamb, forever and ever!'"

PREGNANCY

A pregnancy is a participation in the wonders of Genesis.

Patiently awaiting conception

1 SAMUEL 1:20—"It came to pass in the process of time that Hannah conceived and bore a son, and called his name Samuel, saying, 'Because I have asked for him from the LORD.'"

Embryo development

PSALM 139:13–14—"You formed my inward parts; You covered me in my mother's womb. I will praise You, for I am fearfully and wonderfully made; marvelous are Your works, and that my soul knows very well."

Pregnancy's Gentle Shepherd

ISAIAH 40:11—"He will feed His flock like a shepherd; He will gather the lambs with His arm, and carry them in His bosom, and gently lead those who are with young."

Destiny of the fetus

JEREMIAH 1:5—"Before I formed you in the womb I knew you; before you were born I sanctified you."

Drama of birth

JOHN 16:21—"A woman, when she is in labor, has sorrow because her hour has come; but as soon as she has given birth to the child, she no longer remembers the anguish, for joy that a human being has been born into the world."

PRIDE

Exhibiting pride is flaunting the heavenly Father by taking to oneself glory that belongs only to Him. Also see Ego.

To God be the glory

PSALM 115:1—"Not unto us, O LORD, not unto us, but to Your name give glory, because of Your mercy, because of Your truth."

Holier than thou

ISAIAH 65:5—"Who say, 'Keep to yourself, do not come near me, for I am holier than you!' These are smoke in My nostrils, a fire that burns all the day."

God designed you

1 CORINTHIANS 4:7—"Who makes you differ from another? And what do you have that you did not receive? Now if you did indeed receive it, why do you boast as if you had not received it?"

Phony self-esteem

GALATIANS 6:3—"If anyone thinks himself to be something, when he is nothing, he deceives himself."

Avoid boasting

GALATIANS 6:14—"God forbid that I should boast except in the cross of our Lord Jesus Christ, by whom the world has been crucified to me, and I to the world."

Selfish ambition

PHILIPPIANS 2:3—"Let nothing be done through selfish ambition or conceit, but in lowliness of mind let each esteem others better than himself."

Meditation: **Example of Jesus,** Philippians 2:5–8: "Let this mind be in you which was also in Christ Jesus, who, being in the form of God, did not consider it robbery to be equal with God, but made Himself of no reputation, taking the form of a bondservant, and coming in the likeness of men. And being found in appearance as a man, He humbled Himself and became obedient to the point of death, even the death of the cross."

PRIORITY

Being able to set priorities is the guided skill of putting first things first.
Also see Choice.

Divine priority

MICAH 6:8—"He has shown you, O man, what is good; and what does the LORD require of you but to do justly, to love mercy, and to walk humbly with your God?"

Stewardship priority

MATTHEW 6:19–20—"Do not lay up for yourselves treasures on earth, where moth and rust destroy and where thieves break in and steal; but lay up for yourselves treasures in heaven, where neither moth nor rust destroys and where thieves do not break in and steal."

Meditation: **Last words of Jesus,** Acts 1:6–8: "When they had come together, they asked Him, saying, 'Lord, will You at this time restore the kingdom to Israel?' And He said to them, 'It is not for you to know times or seasons which the Father has put in His own authority. But you shall receive power when the Holy Spirit has come upon you; and you shall be witnesses to Me in Jerusalem, and in all Judea and Samaria, and to the end of the earth.'"

Dangerous priority

1 TIMOTHY 6:10—"The love of money is a root of all kinds of evil, for which some have strayed from the faith in their greediness, and pierced themselves through with many sorrows."

Doing God's will

HEBREWS 13:20–21—"May the God of peace who brought up our Lord Jesus from the dead, that great Shepherd of the sheep, through the blood of the everlasting covenant, make you complete in every good work to do His will, working in you what is well pleasing in His sight, through Jesus Christ, to whom be glory forever and ever. Amen."

STEPS Nugget

TO WHOM AM I SPEAKING?

"Lord."

"Heavenly Father."

"Dear Jesus."

"O God."

Perhaps you have heard prayers begun with each of these appellations.

A clergyman friend believes he has the right to address his prayers directly to the Holy Spirit. I believe so strongly in personal angels, I have given mine a name, yet I would not think of praying to him. I recall a Swedish immigrant to the rural community of my childhood who began each prayer, "Yah, Fadder." Indeed, in Romans 8:15, we are taught, "You received the Spirit of adoption by whom we cry out, 'Abba, Father,'" the word *abba* being an intimate word for "father." Tribesmen in Papua New Guinea begin their prayers with "Papa God." And note Jesus' words in Mark 14:36—"Abba, Father, all things are possible for You."

One radio preacher began his broadcast prayer, "O Thou Infinite Heart." Another, "Great Lover of my soul."

In my study of the Bible, I have found "Lord" used most frequently, especially in the Psalms. So I almost always introduce my prayers with that meaningful heading.

But I do not think of it as a rule or requirement.

Nor need you.

PRISON

These prayer guidelines are for those concerned about people in custody.

Showing compassion to captives

2 CHRONICLES 28:15—"The men who were designated by name rose up and took the captives, and from the spoil they clothed all who were naked among them, dressed them and gave them sandals, gave them food and drink, and anointed them; and they let all the feeble ones ride on donkeys. So they brought them to their brethren at Jericho, the city of palm trees. Then they returned to Samaria."

Meditation: **Prison evangelism,** Acts 16:25–31: "At midnight Paul and Silas were praying and singing hymns to God, and the prisoners were listening to them. Suddenly there was a great earthquake, so that the foundations of the prison were shaken; and immediately all the doors were opened and everyone's chains were loosed. And the keeper of the prison, awaking from sleep and seeing the prison doors open, supposing the prisoners had fled, drew his sword and was about to kill himself. But Paul called with a loud voice, saying, 'Do yourself no harm, for we are all here.' Then he called for a light, ran in, and fell down trembling before Paul and Silas. And he brought them out and said, 'Sirs, what must I do to be saved?' So they said, 'Believe on the Lord Jesus Christ, and you will be saved, you and your household.'"

Prison fellowship

COLOSSIANS 4:10—"Aristarchus my fellow prisoner greets you, with Mark the cousin of Barnabas (about whom you received instructions: if he comes to you, welcome him)."

Empathy for prisoners

HEBREWS 13:3—"Remember the prisoners as if chained with them—those who are mistreated—since you yourselves are in the body also."

Satan in chains

REVELATION 20:1–2—"Then I saw an angel coming down from

heaven, having the key to the bottomless pit and a great chain in his hand. He laid hold of the dragon, that serpent of old, who is the Devil and Satan, and bound him for a thousand years."

PROMISE

Only by faith can you sense the validity of God's promises. Also see Assurance.

Unfailing promises

1 KINGS 8:56—"Blessed be the LORD, who has given rest to His people Israel, according to all that He promised. There has not failed one word of all His good promise, which He promised through His servant Moses."

Rock-solid promise

PSALM 18:2—"The LORD is my rock and my fortress and my deliverer; my God, my strength, in whom I will trust; my shield and the horn of my salvation, my stronghold."

No good thing withheld

PSALM 84:11—"The LORD God is a sun and shield; the LORD will give grace and glory; no good thing will He withhold from those who walk uprightly."

Your response to God's promises

2 CORINTHIANS 7:1—"Having these promises, beloved, let us cleanse ourselves from all filthiness of the flesh and spirit, perfecting holiness in the fear of God."

PROTECTION

We are not so much hidden from danger as protected in and through it.

Rock, Refuge, Deliverer

2 SAMUEL 22:4—"I will call upon the LORD, who is worthy to be praised; so shall I be saved from my enemies."

Ask for protection

PSALM 16:1—"Preserve me, O God, for in You I put my trust."

Apple of God's eye

PSALM 17:6–8—"I have called upon You, for You will hear me, O God; incline Your ear to me, and hear my speech. Show Your marvelous lovingkindness by Your right hand, O You who save those who trust in You from those who rise up against them. Keep me as the apple of Your eye; hide me under the shadow of Your wings."

Protected reputation

PSALM 25:21—"Let integrity and uprightness preserve me, for I wait for You."

Songs of deliverance

PSALM 32:7—"You are my hiding place; You shall preserve me from trouble; You shall surround me with songs of deliverance."

Stronghold in trouble

PSALM 37:39—"The salvation of the righteous is from the LORD; He is their strength in the time of trouble."

Angelic protection

PSALM 91:11—"He shall give His angels charge over you, to keep you in all your ways."

Protected from all evil

PSALM 121:7–8—"The LORD shall preserve you from all evil; He shall preserve your soul. The LORD shall preserve your going out and your coming in from this time forth, and even forevermore."

Prayer of Jesus

JOHN 17:15—"I do not pray that You should take them out of the world, but that You should keep them from the evil one."

Supreme Guardian

2 THESSALONIANS 3:3—"The Lord is faithful, who will establish you and guard you from the evil one."

PROVISION

Prayer connects you to the ultimate Resource.

Jehovah-jireh—the Lord provides

GENESIS 22:14—"Abraham called the name of the place, The-LORD-Will-Provide; as it is said to this day, 'In the Mount of the LORD it shall be provided.'"

Ebenezer

1 SAMUEL 7:12—"Samuel took a stone and set it up between Mizpah and Shen, and called its name Ebenezer, saying, 'Thus far the LORD has helped us.'"

Lifetime provision

PSALM 37:25—"I have been young, and now am old; yet I have not seen the righteous forsaken, nor his descendants begging bread."

Free provision

ISAIAH 55:1–2—"Everyone who thirsts, come to the waters; and you who have no money, come, buy and eat. Yes, come, buy wine and milk without money and without price. Why do you spend money for what is not bread, and your wages for what does not satisfy? Listen carefully to Me, and eat what is good, and let your soul delight itself in abundance."

Daily mercies

LAMENTATIONS 3:22–23—"Through the LORD's mercies we are not consumed, because His compassions fail not. They are new every morning; great is Your faithfulness."

Meditation: **Nature's provision, Luke 12:22–28: "He said to His** disciples, 'Therefore I say to you, do not worry about your life, what you will eat; nor about the body, what you will put on. Life is more than food, and the body is more than clothing. Consider the ravens, for they neither sow nor reap, which have neither storehouse nor barn; and God feeds them. Of how much more value are you than the birds? And which of you by worrying can add one cubit to his stature? If you then are not able to do the least, why are you anxious for the rest? Consider the lilies, how they grow: they neither toil nor spin; and yet I say to you, even Solomon in all his glory was not arrayed like one of these. If then God so clothes the grass, which today is in the field and tomorrow is thrown into the oven, how much more will He clothe you, O you of little faith?'"

Sufficiency and abundance

2 CORINTHIANS 9:8—"God is able to make all grace abound toward you, that you, always having all sufficiency in all things, may have an abundance for every good work."

Needs supplied

PHILIPPIANS 4:19—"My God shall supply all your need according to His riches in glory by Christ Jesus."

PURITY

The Bible often admonishes us to walk in purity. Also see Cleansing.

Unclean cannot produce clean

JOB 14:4—"Who can bring a clean thing out of an unclean? No one!"

Walk in purity

GALATIANS 5:16—"Walk in the Spirit, and you shall not fulfill the lust of the flesh."

Get rid of impure speech

EPHESIANS 5:3–4—"Fornication and all uncleanness or covetousness, let it not even be named among you, as is fitting for saints; neither filthiness, nor foolish talking, nor coarse jesting, which are not fitting, but rather giving of thanks."

Motivated purity

TITUS 2:11–13—"The grace of God that brings salvation has appeared to all men, teaching us that, denying ungodliness and worldly lusts, we should live soberly, righteously, and godly in the present age, looking for the blessed hope and glorious appearing of our great God and Savior Jesus Christ."

Truth and love

1 PETER 1:22—"Since you have purified your souls in obeying the truth through the Spirit in sincere love of the brethren, love one another fervently with a pure heart."

QUESTIONS

Unanswered questions drive us to faith. Also see Secrets.

Difficult answers

DEUTERONOMY 29:29—"The secret things belong to the LORD our God, but those things which are revealed belong to us."

Patiently waiting

PSALM 27:14—"Wait on the LORD; be of good courage, and He shall strengthen your heart; wait, I say, on the LORD!"

Wise men stumped

JEREMIAH 8:9—"The wise men are ashamed, they are dismayed and taken. Behold, they have rejected the word of the LORD; so what wisdom do they have?"

Question answered in ten days

JEREMIAH 42:7—"It happened after ten days that the word of the LORD came to Jeremiah."

God has the answers

DANIEL 2:20—"Blessed be the name of God forever and ever, for wisdom and might are His."

Any more questions?

JAMES 1:5—"If any of you lacks wisdom, let him ask of God, who gives to all liberally and without reproach, and it will be given to him."

REJECTION

Your Lord, spurned by His own Father, offers you acceptance, grace, and mercy.

Parental rejection

PSALM 27:10—"When my father and my mother forsake me, then the LORD will take care of me."

Concern about one's older years

PSALM 71:17–18—"O God, You have taught me from my youth; and to this day I declare Your wondrous works. Now also when I am old and grayheaded, O God, do not forsake me, until I declare Your strength to this generation, Your power to everyone who is to come."

Citywide rejection

MATTHEW 23:37—"O Jerusalem, Jerusalem, the one who kills the prophets and stones those who are sent to her! How often I wanted to gather your children together, as a hen gathers her chicks under her wings, but you were not willing!"

RELATIONSHIP

As a Christian, you are entitled to full relationship, identification, and privileges in God's family.

Apple of God's eye

PSALM 17:8—"Keep me as the apple of Your eye; hide me under the shadow of Your wings."

Shepherd and sheep

JOHN 10:14—"I am the good shepherd; and I know My sheep, and am known by My own."

Relationship by choice

JOHN 15:16—"You did not choose Me, but I chose you and appointed you that you should go and bear fruit, and that your fruit should remain, that whatever you ask the Father in My name He may give you."

Fulfilled relationship

1 JOHN 3:2—"Beloved, now we are children of God; and it has not yet been revealed what we shall be, but we know that when He is revealed, we shall be like Him, for we shall see Him as He is."

RENEWAL

Feel as if you're in a rut, spinning your wheels, speaking the language but not living the life? Prayer can change that and renew your spirit.

Clay in the Potter's hand

ISAIAH 64:8—"O LORD, You are our Father; we are the clay, and You our potter; and all we are the work of Your hand."

Think it over

LAMENTATIONS 3:40—"Let us search out and examine our ways, and turn back to the LORD."

The Lord renews hard hearts

EZEKIEL 11:19—"I will give them one heart, and I will put a new spirit within them."

Meditation: **Life at its best,** abiding in Christ, John 15:1–5: "I am the true vine, and My Father is the vinedresser. Every branch in Me that does not bear fruit He takes away; and every branch that bears fruit He prunes, that it may bear more fruit. You are already clean because of the word which I have spoken to you. Abide in Me, and I in you. As the branch cannot bear fruit of itself, unless it abides in the vine, neither can you, unless you abide in Me. I am the vine, you are the branches. He who abides in Me, and I in him, bears much fruit; for without Me you can do nothing."

Renewal involves your living sacrifice

ROMANS 12:1–2—"I beseech you therefore, brethren, by the mercies of God, that you present your bodies a living sacrifice, holy, acceptable to God, which is your reasonable service. And do not be conformed to this world, but be transformed by the renewing of your mind, that you may prove what is that good and acceptable and perfect will of God."

> If you are a stranger to prayer, you are a stranger to the greatest power known to humanity.
>
> —BILLY SUNDAY

Ultimate renewal, crucified with Christ

GALATIANS 2:20—"I have been crucified with Christ; it is no longer I who live, but Christ lives in me; and the life which I now live in the flesh I live by faith in the Son of God, who loved me and gave Himself for me."

Renewal lifestyle, the fruit of the Spirit

GALATIANS 5:22–23—"The fruit of the Spirit is love, joy, peace, long-suffering, kindness, goodness, faithfulness, gentleness, self-control. Against such there is no law."

Get rid of your worst sin

HEBREWS 12:1–2—"We also, since we are surrounded by so great a cloud of witnesses, let us lay aside every weight, and the sin which so easily ensnares us, and let us run with endurance the race that is set before us, looking unto Jesus, the author and finisher of our faith, who for the joy that was set before Him endured the cross, despising the shame, and has sat down at the right hand of the throne of God."

REPENTANCE
Open the door to God's mercy; unleash the wonders of His grace.

Prayer of repentance
EZRA 9:5–8—"At the evening sacrifice I arose from my fasting; and having torn my garment and my robe, I fell on my knees and spread out my hands to the LORD my God. And I said: 'O my God, I am too ashamed and humiliated to lift up my face to You, my God; for our iniquities have risen higher than our heads, and our guilt has grown up to the heavens. Since the days of our fathers to this day we have been very guilty, and for our iniquities we, our kings, and our priests have been delivered into the hand of the kings of the lands, to the sword, to captivity, to plunder, and to humiliation, as it is this day. And now for a little while grace has been shown from the LORD our God, to leave us a remnant to escape, and to give us a peg in His holy place, that our God may enlighten our eyes and give us a measure of revival in our bondage.'"

Seeking revival
PSALM 85:6—"Will You not revive us again, that Your people may rejoice in You?"

Meditation: **Out of the depths,** Psalm 130:1–4: "Out of the depths I have cried to You, O LORD; Lord, hear my voice! Let Your ears be attentive to the voice of my supplications. If You, LORD, should mark iniquities, O Lord, who could stand? But there is forgiveness with You, that You may be feared."

Restored hearts
LAMENTATIONS 5:21—"Turn us back to You, O LORD, and we will be restored; renew our days as of old."

Resist evil

JAMES 4:7–8—"Submit to God. Resist the devil and he will flee from you. Draw near to God and He will draw near to you. Cleanse your hands, you sinners; and purify your hearts, you double-minded."

RIDICULE

Winds of ridicule deepen roots of faith. Also see Gossip, Persecution.

Ridiculed by friends

JOB 12:4—"I am one mocked by his friends, who called on God, and He answered him, the just and blameless who is ridiculed."

Youthful resilience

PSALM 129:2—"Many a time they have afflicted me from my youth; yet they have not prevailed against me."

No fear of men

ISAIAH 51:7—"Listen to Me, you who know righteousness, you people in whose heart is My law: Do not fear the reproach of men, nor be afraid of their insults."

Ridicule at the cross

LUKE 23:35—"The rulers with them sneered, saying, 'He saved others; let Him save Himself if He is the Christ, the chosen of God.'"

ROMANCE

Needed more than moonlight and roses are your Lord's guidance and blessing. Also see Marriage.

A woman says yes

GENESIS 24:57–58—"They said, 'We will call the young woman and ask her personally.' Then they called Rebekah and said to her, 'Will you go with this man?' And she said, 'I will go.'"

Finding a wife

PROVERBS 18:22—"He who finds a wife finds a good thing, and obtains favor from the LORD."

In awe of romance

PROVERBS 30:18–19—"There are three things which are too wonderful for me, yes, four which I do not understand: the way of an eagle in the air, the way of a serpent on a rock, the way of a ship in the midst of the sea, and the way of a man with a virgin."

Romantic anticipation

SONG OF SONGS 2:14—"O my dove, in the clefts of the rock, in the secret places of the cliff, let me see your face, let me hear your voice; for your voice is sweet, and your face is lovely."

How to overcome lust

ROMANS 13:14—"Put on the Lord Jesus Christ, and make no provision for the flesh, to fulfill its lusts."

SECOND COMING

The Second Coming is the great hope of the church. Also see Hope.

Secret Second Coming

MARK 13:32—"Of that day and hour no one knows, not even the angels in heaven, nor the Son, but only the Father."

A place prepared

JOHN 14:1–3—"Let not your heart be troubled; you believe in God, believe also in Me. In My Father's house are many mansions; if it were not so, I would have told you. I go to prepare a place for you. And if I go and prepare a place for you, I will come again and receive you to Myself; that where I am, there you may be also."

Loving preparation

1 THESSALONIANS 3:12–13—"May the Lord make you increase and abound in love to one another and to all, just as we do to you, so that He may establish your hearts blameless in holiness before our God and Father at the coming of our Lord Jesus Christ with all His saints."

Purifying hope

TITUS 2:11–13—"The grace of God that brings salvation has appeared to all men, teaching us that, denying ungodliness and worldly lusts, we should live soberly, righteously, and godly in the present age, looking for the blessed hope and glorious appearing of our great God and Savior Jesus Christ."

SECRETS

Imagine, things known only to you and your heavenly Father.

Sacred secrets

DEUTERONOMY 29:29—"The secret things belong to the LORD our God, but those things which are revealed belong to us."

The secret place

PSALM 91:1—"He who dwells in the secret place of the Most High shall abide under the shadow of the Almighty."

Your mind-reading Lord

PSALM 94:11—"The LORD knows the thoughts of man, that they are futile."

Broken secrets

PROVERBS 11:13—"A talebearer reveals secrets, but he who is of a faithful spirit conceals a matter."

God knows all

HEBREWS 4:13—"There is no creature hidden from His sight, but all things are naked and open to the eyes of Him to whom we must give account."

SHAME

Shame is a positive emotion related to renewal and repentance. Also see
Humility.

Remorse for sin

EZRA 9:6–8—"O my God, I am too ashamed and humiliated to lift up
my face to You, my God; for our iniquities have risen higher than our
heads, and our guilt has grown up to the heavens. Since the days of our
fathers to this day we have been very guilty, and for our iniquities we,
our kings, and our priests have been delivered into the hand of the kings
of the lands, to the sword, to captivity, to plunder, and to humiliation, as
it is this day. And now for a little while grace has been shown from the
LORD our God, to leave us a remnant to escape, and to give us a peg in
His holy place, that our God may enlighten our eyes and give us a measure of revival in our bondage."

Release from shame

PSALM 34:5—"They looked to Him and were radiant, and their faces
were not ashamed."

Deep sense of shame

PSALM 44:15—"My dishonor is continually before me, and the shame
of my face has covered me."

Unable to blush

JEREMIAH 6:15—"'Were they ashamed when they had committed
abomination? No! They were not at all ashamed; nor did they know how
to blush. Therefore they shall fall among those who fall; at the time I
punish them, they shall be cast down,' says the LORD."

SICKNESS

A time to pause for reflection and renewal is a time of sickness. Also see
Health, Suffering.

Sustained in sickness

PSALM 41:3—"The LORD will strengthen him on his bed of illness."

Enduring sickness

ROMANS 5:3–4—"We also glory in tribulations, knowing that tribulation produces perseverance; and perseverance, character; and character, hope."

Sickness now, future glory

ROMANS 8:18—"I consider that the sufferings of this present time are not worthy to be compared with the glory which shall be revealed in us."

Meditation: **Purpose of suffering,** 2 Corinthians 4:17–18: "Our light affliction, which is but for a moment, is working for us a far more exceeding and eternal weight of glory, while we do not look at the things which are seen, but at the things which are not seen. For the things which are seen are temporary, but the things which are not seen are eternal."

SLANDER

Character assassination, ministry impairment, personal hurt—your Lord knows all about it. Also see Gossip.

Tongue-lashing

JOB 5:21—"You shall be hidden from the scourge of the tongue, and you shall not be afraid of destruction when it comes."

Many slanderers

PSALM 31:13—"I hear the slander of many; fear is on every side; while they take counsel together against me."

Insolent slander

PSALM 94:4—"They utter speech, and speak insolent things; all the workers of iniquity boast in themselves."

Dishonest attack

PSALM 109:1–2—"Do not keep silent, O God of my praise! For the mouth of the wicked and the mouth of the deceitful have opened against me; they have spoken against me with a lying tongue."

Do not slander others

JAMES 4:11—"Do not speak evil of one another, brethren. He who speaks evil of a brother and judges his brother, speaks evil of the law and judges the law. But if you judge the law, you are not a doer of the law but a judge."

SLEEP

No sleep is as peaceful as the sleep that follows prayer.

Have a sweet sleep

PROVERBS 3:24—"When you lie down, you will not be afraid; yes, you will lie down and your sleep will be sweet."

SORROW

Comfort and joy emerge from the same fountain. Also see Comfort, Death.

Sorrow prevents sleep

PSALM 6:6—"I am weary with my groaning; all night I make my bed swim; I drench my couch with my tears."

Broken heart healed

PSALM 34:17–18—"The righteous cry out, and the LORD hears, and delivers them out of all their troubles. The LORD is near to those who have a broken heart, and saves such as have a contrite spirit."

Be still and know God

PSALM 46:10—"Be still, and know that I am God; I will be exalted among the nations, I will be exalted in the earth!"

Give your burden to the Lord

PSALM 55:22—"Cast your burden on the LORD, and He shall sustain you; He shall never permit the righteous to be moved."

Heart stricken

PSALM 102:4—"My heart is stricken and withered like grass, so that I forget to eat my bread."

Jesus knows your sorrow

ISAIAH 53:3–4—"He is despised and rejected by men, a Man of sorrows and acquainted with grief . . . Surely He has borne our griefs and carried our sorrows; yet we esteemed Him stricken, smitten by God, and afflicted."

Comfort for those who mourn

MATTHEW 5:4—"Blessed are those who mourn, for they shall be comforted."

Meditation: **Your troubled heart,** John 14:1–3: "Let not your heart be troubled; you believe in God, believe also in Me. In My Father's house are many mansions; if it were not so, I would have told you. I go to prepare a place for you. And if I go and prepare a place for you, I will come again and receive you to Myself; that where I am, there you may be also."

Sorrow brings repentance

2 CORINTHIANS 7:9—"I rejoice, not that you were made sorry, but that your sorrow led to repentance. For you were made sorry in a godly manner, that you might suffer loss from us in nothing."

STEWARDSHIP

Stewardship is a privilege, a responsibility, and a source of earthly and eternal enrichment.

Praise and stewardship

PSALM 96:8—"Give to the LORD the glory due His name; bring an offering, and come into His courts."

Rewarded stewardship

PROVERBS 3:9—"Honor the LORD with your possessions, and with the firstfruits of all your increase."

Meditation: **Robbing and testing God,** Malachi 3:8, 10: "'Will a man rob God? Yet you have robbed Me! But you say, "In what way have we robbed You?" In tithes and offerings . . . Bring all the tithes into the storehouse, that there may be food in My house, and try Me now in this,' says the LORD of hosts, 'if I will not open for you the windows of heaven and pour out for you such blessing that there will not be room enough to receive it.'"

Giving and receiving

LUKE 6:38—"Give, and it will be given to you: good measure, pressed down, shaken together, and running over will be put into your bosom. For with the same measure that you use, it will be measured back to you."

Meditation: **Widow's mite,** Luke 21:1–4: "He looked up and saw the rich putting their gifts into the treasury, and He saw also a certain poor widow putting in two mites. So He said, 'Truly I say to you that this poor widow has put in more than all; for all these out of their abundance have put in offerings for God, but she out of her poverty put in all the livelihood that she had.'"

Cheerful giving

2 CORINTHIANS 9:7—"Let each one give as he purposes in his heart, not grudgingly or of necessity; for God loves a cheerful giver."

STRENGTH

Whatever the demand, however limiting your weakness, your Lord promises strength. Also see Ability, Asking, Confidence, Victory.

One strong, another weak

2 SAMUEL 3:1—"David grew stronger and stronger, and the house of Saul grew weaker and weaker."

God-given strength

PSALM 18:32—"It is God who arms me with strength, and makes my way perfect."

Strong as an ox

PSALM 92:10—"But my horn You have exalted like a wild ox; I have been anointed with fresh oil."

Renewed strength

ISAIAH 40:31—"Those who wait on the LORD shall renew their strength; they shall mount up with wings like eagles, they shall run and not be weary, they shall walk and not faint."

All-sufficient strength

JEREMIAH 32:27—"Behold, I am the LORD, the God of all flesh. Is there anything too hard for Me?"

Holy Spirit provides strength

ZECHARIAH 4:6—"'Not by might nor by power, but by My Spirit,' says the LORD of hosts."

Sufficient strength

PHILIPPIANS 4:13—"I can do all things through Christ who strengthens me."

STRESS

At the center of pressure or panic, find peace. Also see Anxiety.

Refinement through stress

JOB 23:10—"He knows the way that I take; when He has tested me, I shall come forth as gold."

Your Lord can handle your load

PSALM 55:22—"Cast your burden on the LORD, and He shall sustain you; He shall never permit the righteous to be moved."

Keep a stiff upper lip

PSALM 57:7—"My heart is steadfast, O God, my heart is steadfast; I will sing and give praise."

In up to your neck

PSALM 69:1—"Save me, O God! For the waters have come up to my neck."

Meditation: **Restored confidence,** Psalm 100:1–3: "Make a joyful shout to the LORD, all you lands! Serve the LORD with gladness; come before His presence with singing. Know that the LORD, He is God; it is He who has made us, and not we ourselves; we are His people and the sheep of His pasture."

Renewed strength

ISAIAH 40:31—"Those who wait on the LORD shall renew their strength; they shall mount up with wings like eagles, they shall run and not be weary, they shall walk and not faint."

Meditation: **Ultimate Resource,** Matthew 11:28–30: "Come to Me, all you who labor and are heavy laden, and I will give you rest. Take My yoke upon you and learn from Me, for I am gentle and lowly in heart, and you will find rest for your souls. For My yoke is easy and My burden is light."

Prayer in time of stress

PHILIPPIANS 4:6–7—"Be anxious for nothing, but in everything by prayer and supplication, with thanksgiving, let your requests be made known to God; and the peace of God, which surpasses all understanding, will guard your hearts and minds through Christ Jesus."

STRUGGLE

It's the wind that drives strong roots into the soil.

Flesh versus spirit

ROMANS 7:18–19—"I know that in me (that is, in my flesh) nothing good dwells; for to will is present with me, but how to perform what is good I do not find. For the good that I will to do, I do not do; but the evil I will not to do, that I practice."

Fight the good fight

1 TIMOTHY 6:12—"Fight the good fight of faith, lay hold on eternal life, to which you were also called and have confessed the good confession in the presence of many witnesses."

Meditation: **End-time struggles,** 2 Timothy 3:1–5: "Know this, that in the last days perilous times will come: For men will be lovers of themselves, lovers of money, boasters, proud, blasphemers, disobedient to parents, unthankful, unholy, unloving, unforgiving, slanderers, without self-control, brutal, despisers of good, traitors, headstrong, haughty, lovers of pleasure rather than lovers of God, having a form of godliness but denying its power. And from such people turn away!"

SUCCESS

The sweet taste of success needs the anointing touch of divine blessing. Also see Accomplishment.

Creator's success

GENESIS 1:25—"God made the beast of the earth according to its kind, cattle according to its kind, and everything that creeps on the earth according to its kind. And God saw that it was good."

Assured success

PSALM 1:3—"He shall be like a tree planted by the rivers of water, that brings forth its fruit in its season, whose leaf also shall not wither; and whatever he does shall prosper."

First things first

MATTHEW 6:33—"Seek first the kingdom of God and His righteousness, and all these things shall be added to you."

Success benediction

HEBREWS 13:20–21—"Now may the God of peace who brought up our Lord Jesus from the dead, that great Shepherd of the sheep, through the blood of the everlasting covenant, make you complete in every good work to do His will, working in you what is well pleasing in His sight, through Jesus Christ, to whom be glory forever and ever. Amen."

SUFFERING

Sometimes the best view of the mountaintop is from the deepest point in the valley. Also see Pain, Persecution, Sickness.

> The man who kneels to God can stand up to anything.
>
> —LEWIS H. EVANS

Severe testing

PROVERBS 17:3—"The refining pot is for silver and the furnace for gold, but the LORD tests the hearts."

Greater understanding

ISAIAH 55:8–9—"'My thoughts are not your thoughts, nor are your ways My ways,' says the LORD. 'For as the heavens are higher than the earth, so are My ways higher than your ways, and My thoughts than your thoughts.'"

Suffering precedes glory

ROMANS 8:18—"I consider that the sufferings of this present time are not worthy to be compared with the glory which shall be revealed in us."

Purpose of suffering

2 CORINTHIANS 4:17–18—"Our light affliction, which is but for a moment, is working for us a far more exceeding and eternal weight of glory, while we do not look at the things which are seen, but at the things which are not seen. For the things which are seen are temporary, but the things which are not seen are eternal."

> Prayer will make a man cease from sin, or sin will entice a man to cease from prayer.
>
> —JOHN BUNYAN

Meditation: **Benefits from suffering,** James 1:2–5: "Count it all joy when you fall into various trials, knowing that the testing of your faith produces patience. But let patience have its perfect work, that you may be perfect and complete, lacking nothing. If any of you lacks wisdom, let him ask of God, who gives to all liberally and without reproach, and it will be given to him."

TEMPTATION

Temptation is the battlefield where victories are won. Also see Carnality, Defeat, Deliverance.

Resistance resource

PROVERBS 2:10–12—"When wisdom enters your heart, and knowledge is pleasant to your soul, discretion will preserve you; understanding will keep you, to deliver you from the way of evil, from the man who speaks perverse things."

Do your part

ROMANS 6:12–13—"Do not let sin reign in your mortal body, that you should obey it in its lusts. And do not present your members as instruments of unrighteousness to sin, but present yourselves to God as being alive from the dead, and your members as instruments of righteousness to God."

STEPS Nugget

EFFECTIVE PRAYER REQUIRES HARD WORK

Luke 6:12 records how strenuously Jesus prayed. Luke 22:44 reports in the Garden of Gethsemane, He literally sweat drops of blood. The Lord Jesus, the one to whom we now address our intercession, experienced for Himself the rigorous effort required in effective prayer.

Sometime, during informal fellowship with other Christians, introduce the subject of prayer. Hear how many will speak—often with lament—of difficulty encountered in prayer. Inabaility to concentrate. Restlessness. Boredom.

My first prayer occurs early each morning. My mind fresh and focused, I have an uplifting time. However, at the beginning of intercession, my mind will sometimes begin to wander or go stark blank. In times past I would rebuke the evil one—addressing him as Herr Azazel or one of his lesser names—but now I allow him no place at all. Instead, from *Confession* in the topics section, I select James 5:16: "The effective, fervent prayer of a righteous man avails much."

My prayer goes like this: "I can't pray fervently with a confused head, Lord. Please liberate my mind. Set my thought in order. I want to come close, Lord."

Ususally, that does it. My rapport with heaven returns. My heart surges with adoration for my available Lord.

Or distraction may persist. I may continue struggling. This once disturbed me. No more. Instead, I force myself to concentrate, wrestle with each item. If the difficulty continues, I turn to Romans 8:26 (under *Guidance)*: "We do not know what we should pray . . . but the Spirit Himself makes intercession for us."

In any case, prayer is not an easy task. It is work—hard work—but very rewarding!

Handling temptation

1 CORINTHIANS 10:13—"No temptation has overtaken you except such as is common to man; but God is faithful, who will not allow you to be tempted beyond what you are able, but with the temptation will also make the way of escape, that you may be able to bear it."

Empathy and resource

HEBREWS 4:15–16—"We do not have a High Priest who cannot sympathize with our weaknesses, but was in all points tempted as we are, yet without sin. Let us therefore come boldly to the throne of grace, that we may obtain mercy and find grace to help in time of need."

TESTING

Times of adversity provide calisthenics for the soul.

Sure refuge

PSALM 46:1—"God is our refuge and strength, a very present help in trouble."

Rest in the Lord

PSALM 57:1–2—"Be merciful to me, O God, be merciful to me! For my soul trusts in You; and in the shadow of Your wings I will make my refuge, until these calamities have passed by. I will cry out to God Most High, to God who performs all things for me."

Refining meltdown

PROVERBS 17:3—"The refining pot is for silver and the furnace for gold, but the LORD tests the hearts."

Walk through the fire

ISAIAH 43:2—"When you pass through the waters, I will be with you; and through the rivers, they shall not overflow you. When you walk through the fire, you shall not be burned, nor shall the flame scorch you."

Potter and clay

ISAIAH 64:8—"O LORD, You are our Father; we are the clay, and You our potter; and all we are the work of Your hand."

God knows those who trust Him

NAHUM 1:7—"The LORD is good, a stronghold in the day of trouble; and He knows those who trust in Him."

Find rest

MATTHEW 11:28—"Come to Me, all you who labor and are heavy laden, and I will give you rest."

Sufficient grace for testing

2 CORINTHIANS 12:9—"'My grace is sufficient for you, for My strength is made perfect in weakness.' Therefore most gladly I will rather boast in my infirmities, that the power of Christ may rest upon me."

Meditation: **Face testing with peace,** Philippians 4:6–8: "Be anxious for nothing, but in everything by prayer and supplication, with thanksgiving, let your requests be made known to God; and the peace of God, which surpasses all understanding, will guard your hearts and minds through Christ Jesus. Finally, brethren, whatever things are true, whatever things are noble, whatever things are just, whatever things are pure, whatever things are lovely, whatever things are of good report, if there is any virtue and if there is anything praiseworthy—meditate on these things."

Accept testing

1 PETER 4:12–13—"Do not think it strange concerning the fiery trial which is to try you, as though some strange thing happened to you; but rejoice to the extent that you partake of Christ's sufferings, that when His glory is revealed, you may also be glad with exceeding joy."

TIMIDITY

Human shyness need not prevent spiritual boldness. Also see Boldness, Courage.

Speechless

JOB 29:10—"The voice of nobles was hushed, and their tongue stuck to the roof of their mouth."

Foolish timidity

JOHN 12:42–43—"Even among the rulers many believed in Him, but because of the Pharisees they did not confess Him, lest they should be put out of the synagogue; for they loved the praise of men more than the praise of God."

> Prayer is being on friendly terms with God.
>
> —MOTHER TERESA

Unashamed to witness

ROMANS 1:16—"I am not ashamed of the gospel of Christ, for it is the power of God to salvation for everyone who believes, for the Jew first and also for the Greek."

Knocking knees

1 CORINTHIANS 2:3—"I was with you in weakness, in fear, and in much trembling."

No need to be timid

2 TIMOTHY 1:7—"God has not given us a spirit of fear, but of power and of love and of a sound mind."

TRAUMA

Struggles may produce scars but also stars. Also see Testing.

Resource during trauma

PSALM 37:39—"The salvation of the righteous is from the LORD; He is their strength in the time of trouble."

Hope when all seems hopeless

PSALM 42:11—"Why are you cast down, O my soul? And why are you disquieted within me? Hope in God; for I shall yet praise Him."

Give your trauma to the Lord

PSALM 55:22—"Cast your burden on the LORD, and He shall sustain you; He shall never permit the righteous to be moved."

In up to your neck

PSALM 69:1—"Save me, O God! For the waters have come up to my neck."

Keep the faith

2 CORINTHIANS 4:8–10—"We are hard-pressed on every side, yet not crushed; we are perplexed, but not in despair; persecuted, but not forsaken; struck down, but not destroyed—always carrying about in the body the dying of the Lord Jesus, that the life of Jesus also may be manifested in our body."

TROUBLE

Whatever its magnitude, trouble is no match for the dynamics of your Bible. Also see Testing.

Delivered from multiple troubles

JOB 5:19—"He shall deliver you in six troubles, yes, in seven no evil shall touch you."

Golden finale to trouble

JOB 23:10—"He knows the way that I take; when He has tested me, I shall come forth as gold."

Day of trouble

PSALM 86:7—"In the day of my trouble I will call upon You, for You will answer me."

Meeting trouble head-on

PSALM 138:7—"Though I walk in the midst of trouble, You will revive me; You will stretch out Your hand against the wrath of my enemies, and Your right hand will save me."

Troubles teach you to help others

2 CORINTHIANS 1:3–4—"Blessed be the God and Father of our Lord Jesus Christ, the Father of mercies and God of all comfort, who comforts us in all our tribulation, that we may be able to comfort those who are in any trouble, with the comfort with which we ourselves are comforted by God."

TRUST

To trust is to have confidence; to have confidence is to be at peace.

Whatever it takes

JOB 13:15—"Though He slay me, yet will I trust Him."

Trust in the Lord

PSALM 28:7—"The LORD is my strength and my shield; my heart trusted in Him, and I am helped; therefore my heart greatly rejoices, and with my song I will praise Him."

Timely trust

PSALM 31:15—"My times are in Your hand."

Trust strong since youth

PSALM 71:5—"You are my hope, O Lord GOD; You are my trust from my youth."

Upheld by God's strength

ISAIAH 41:10—"Fear not, for I am with you; be not dismayed, for I am your God. I will strengthen you, yes, I will help you, I will uphold you with My righteous right hand."

Clay in the Potter's hands

ISAIAH 45:9—"Woe to him who strives with his Maker! Let the potsherd strive with the potsherds of the earth! Shall the clay say to him who forms it, 'What are you making?' Or shall your handiwork say, 'He has no hands'?"

Reason to trust

JOHN 6:37—"All that the Father gives Me will come to Me, and the one who comes to Me I will by no means cast out."

TRUTH

Rely on God's truth. Also see Authenticity, Honesty.

Speak only truth

JOB 6:25 "How forceful are right words!"

Liberating truth

JOHN 8:32—"You shall know the truth, and the truth shall make you free."

Epitome of truth

JOHN 14:6—"Jesus said to him, 'I am the way, the truth, and the life. No one comes to the Father except through Me.'"

Guidance into truth

JOHN 16:13—"The Spirit of truth . . . will guide you into all truth."

God cannot lie

TITUS 1:2—"In hope of eternal life which God, who cannot lie, promised before time began."

UNITY

Unity is oneness in faith, fellowship, and effort. Also see Cooperation, Fellowship, Friendship.

One heart, new spirit

EZEKIEL 11:19–20—"I will give them one heart, and I will put a new spirit within them, and take the stony heart out of their flesh, and give them a heart of flesh, that they may walk in My statutes and keep My judgments and do them; and they shall be My people, and I will be their God."

Basis for unity

AMOS 3:3—"Can two walk together, unless they are agreed?"

Quorum for prayer

MATTHEW 18:20—"Where two or three are gathered together in My name, I am there in the midst of them."

Marriage unity

MARK 10:7–9—"'A man shall leave his father and mother and be joined to his wife, and the two shall become one flesh'; so then they are no longer two, but one flesh. Therefore what God has joined together, let not man separate."

Unifying love

JOHN 13:35—"By this all will know that you are My disciples, if you have love for one another."

Meditation: **Unity in Christ,** John 17:20–22: "I do not pray for these alone, but also for those who will believe in Me through their word; that they all may be one, as You, Father, are in Me, and I in You; that they also may be one in Us, that the world may believe that You sent Me. And the glory which You gave Me I have given them, that they may be one just as We are one."

Fellow workers

1 CORINTHIANS 3:9—"We are God's fellow workers; you are God's field, you are God's building."

Meditation: **Being like-minded,** Philippians 2:1–4: "If there is any consolation in Christ, if any comfort of love, if any fellowship of the Spirit, if any affection and mercy, fulfill my joy by being like-minded, having the same love, being of one accord, of one mind. Let nothing be done through selfish ambition or conceit, but in lowliness of mind let each esteem others better than himself. Let each of you look out not only for his own interests, but also for the interests of others."

VICTORY

Although poles apart, defeat and victory encompass opportunity for enrichment.

Claim God's name

PSALM 54:1—"Save me, O God, by Your name, and vindicate me by Your strength."

Overcoming the world

JOHN 16:33—"These things I have spoken to you, that in Me you may have peace. In the world you will have tribulation; but be of good cheer, I have overcome the world."

Meditation: **Victory over sin,** Romans 6:11–18: "Reckon yourselves to be dead indeed to sin, but alive to God in Christ Jesus our Lord. Therefore do not let sin reign in your mortal body, that you should obey it in its lusts. And do not present your members as instruments of unrighteousness to sin, but present yourselves to God as being alive from the dead, and your members as instruments of righteousness to God. For sin shall not have dominion over you, for you are not under law but under grace. What then? Shall we sin because we are not under law but under grace? Certainly not! Do you not know that to whom you present yourselves slaves to obey, you are that one's slaves whom you obey, whether of sin leading to death, or of obedience leading to righteousness? But God be thanked that though you were slaves of sin, yet you obeyed from the heart that form of doctrine to which you were delivered. And having been set free from sin, you became slaves of righteousness."

God on your side

ROMANS 8:31—"If God is for us, who can be against us?"

Victory in Christ

2 CORINTHIANS 2:14—"Thanks be to God who always leads us in triumph in Christ, and through us diffuses the fragrance of His knowledge in every place."

> Prayer is dialogue, not monologue.
>
> —ANDREW MURRAY

Helping another find victory

GALATIANS 6:1–2—"If a man is overtaken in any trespass, you who are spiritual restore such a one in a spirit of gentleness, considering yourself lest you also be tempted. Bear one another's burdens, and so fulfill the law of Christ."

Overcoming faith

1 JOHN 5:4—"Whatever is born of God overcomes the world. And this is the victory that has overcome the world—our faith."

VISION

Vision is point of view provided by faith, realized through prayer and obedience.

A new vision

ISAIAH 43:19—"I will do a new thing, now it shall spring forth; shall

---

STEPS Nugget

INVENTORY

Consistent, earnest prayer should make a difference not only in the people and projects prayed for but also in the life of the person who does the praying.

As you advance in the STEPS prayer method, take frequent inventory of your personal progress. You should find yourself becoming a better person, a more sincere and genuine Christian as a side benefit to your prayer times.

To continue improving, pray for the poise and courage to ask for a trusted friend's help in identifying and correcting habits, traits, and characteristics that may hinder you from relating to others as effectively as you would like to do.

Also, check the topics for reinforcement from the Bible. Make two scriptures particularly relevant— "Whether you eat or drink, or whatever you do, do all to the glory of God" (1 Cor. 10:31); and "The fruit of the Spirit is love, joy, peace, longsuffering, kindness, goodness, faithfulness, gentleness, self-control" (Gal. 5:22–23).

---

you not know it? I will even make a road in the wilderness and rivers in the desert."

Make room for vision

ISAIAH 54:2–3—"Enlarge the place of your tent, and let them stretch out the curtains of your dwellings; do not spare; lengthen your cords, and strengthen your stakes. For you shall expand to the right and to the left."

Visions of youth

JOEL 2:28—"It shall come to pass afterward that I will pour out My Spirit on all flesh; your sons and your daughters shall prophesy, your old men shall dream dreams, your young men shall see visions."

Example of expanded vision

HABAKKUK 1:5—"Look among the nations and watch—be utterly astounded! For I will work a work in your days which you would not believe, though it were told you."

Guidance implements vision

JOHN 14:26—"The Holy Spirit, whom the Father will send in My name, He will teach you all things, and bring to your remembrance all things that I said to you."

Eyes of the heart

EPHESIANS 1:18—"The eyes of your understanding being enlightened; that you may know what is the hope of His calling, what are the riches of the glory of His inheritance in the saints."

WEAKNESS

A sure access to spiritual strength lies in recognizing personal weakness.

Strength in trouble

PSALM 37:39—"The salvation of the righteous is from the LORD; He is their strength in the time of trouble."

Source of strength

PSALM 73:26—"My flesh and my heart fail; but God is the strength of my heart and my portion forever."

Strong tower

PROVERBS 18:10—"The name of the LORD is a strong tower; the righteous run to it and are safe."

Weakness provides strength

2 CORINTHIANS 12:9—"'My grace is sufficient for you, for My strength is made perfect in weakness.' Therefore most gladly I will rather boast in my infirmities, that the power of Christ may rest upon me."

Weakness overcome through Christ

PHILIPPIANS 4:13—"I can do all things through Christ who strengthens me."

WISDOM

Let the Bible become your sure guide to spiritual and practical wisdom.

Come to the fountain

PSALM 36:9—"With You is the fountain of life; in Your light we see light."

Taught by the Lord

PSALM 94:11–12—"The LORD knows the thoughts of man, that they are futile. Blessed is the man whom You instruct, O LORD, and teach out of Your law."

Introduction to wisdom

PSALM 111:10—"The fear of the LORD is the beginning of wisdom; a good understanding have all those who do His commandments. His praise endures forever."

Meditation: **A lamp to your feet,** Psalm 119:103–5: "How sweet are Your words to my taste, sweeter than honey to my mouth! Through Your precepts I get understanding; therefore I hate every false way. Your word is a lamp to my feet and a light to my path."

Meditation: **Wisdom available for you,** Ephesians 3:14–19: "I bow my knees to the Father of our Lord Jesus Christ, from whom the whole family in heaven and earth is named, that He would grant you, according to the riches of His glory, to be strengthened with might through His Spirit in the inner man, that Christ may dwell in your hearts through faith; that you, being rooted and grounded in love, may be able to comprehend with all the saints what is the width and length and depth and height—to know the love of Christ which passes knowledge; that you may be filled with all the fullness of God."

Ask God for wisdom

JAMES 1:5—"If any of you lacks wisdom, let him ask of God, who gives to all liberally and without reproach, and it will be given to him."

Heaven's wisdom described

JAMES 3:17—"The wisdom that is from above is first pure, then peaceable, gentle, willing to yield, full of mercy and good fruits, without partiality and without hypocrisy."

WITNESS

Experience for yourself; share with others.

Tell God's wonders

PSALM 9:1—"I will praise You, O LORD, with my whole heart; I will tell of all Your marvelous works."

Redeemed give witness

PSALM 107:2—"Let the redeemed of the LORD say so, whom He has redeemed from the hand of the enemy."

Caring enough to cry

PSALM 126:5–6—"Those who sow in tears shall reap in joy. He who continually goes forth weeping, bearing seed for sowing, shall doubtless come again with rejoicing, bringing his sheaves with him."

Let your light shine

MATTHEW 5:16—"Let your light so shine before men, that they may see your good works and glorify your Father in heaven."

Meditation: **Last words of Jesus,** Acts 1:6–8: "When they had come together, they asked Him, saying, 'Lord, will You at this time restore the kingdom to Israel?' And He said to them, 'It is not for you to know times or seasons which the Father has put in His own authority. But you shall receive power when the Holy Spirit has come upon you; and you shall be witnesses to Me in Jerusalem, and in all Judea and Samaria, and to the end of the earth.'"

Be proud of the gospel

ROMANS 1:16—"I am not ashamed of the gospel of Christ, for it is the power of God to salvation for everyone who believes, for the Jew first and also for the Greek."

WORRY

Faith is to worry what morning is to midnight.

Give your worry to the Lord

PSALM 55:22—"Cast your burden on the LORD, and He shall sustain you; He shall never permit the righteous to be moved."

No fear of bad news

PSALM 112:7—"He will not be afraid of evil tidings; his heart is stead-fast, trusting in the LORD."

An encouraging word

PROVERBS 12:25—"Anxiety in the heart of man causes depression, but a good word makes it glad."

Meditation: **Not to worry,** Matthew 6:27–29: "Which of you by worrying can add one cubit to his stature? So why do you worry about clothing? Consider the lilies of the field, how they grow: they neither toil nor spin; and yet I say to you that even Solomon in all his glory was not arrayed like one of these."

Your available Lord

ACTS 2:25—"I foresaw the LORD always before my face, for He is at my right hand, that I may not be shaken."

Sure cure for worry

PHILIPPIANS 4:6–7—"Be anxious for nothing, but in everything by prayer and supplication, with thanksgiving, let your requests be made known to God; and the peace of God, which surpasses all understanding, will guard your hearts and minds through Christ Jesus."

> The chief purpose of prayer is that God may be glorified in the answer.
>
> —R. A. TORREY

WORSHIP

Beyond description or definition, worship is life's most meaningful experience. Also see Praise.

Meditation: **David's prayer,** 1 Chronicles 29:10–13: "Blessed are You, LORD God of Israel, our Father, forever and ever. Yours, O LORD, is the greatness, the power and the glory, the victory and the majesty; for all that is in heaven and in earth is Yours; Yours is the kingdom, O LORD, and You are exalted as head over all. Both riches and honor come from You, and You reign over all. In Your hand is power and might; in Your hand it is to make great and to give strength to all. Now therefore, our God, we thank You and praise Your glorious name."

Words of worship

PSALM 19:14—"Let the words of my mouth and the meditation of my heart be acceptable in Your sight, O LORD, my strength and my Redeemer."

Worthy of worship

PSALM 73:24–25—"You will guide me with Your counsel, and afterward receive me to glory. Whom have I in heaven but You? And there is none upon earth that I desire besides You."

Willing learner

PSALM 86:11–12—"Teach me Your way, O LORD; I will walk in Your truth; unite my heart to fear Your name. I will praise You, O Lord my God, with all my heart, and I will glorify Your name forevermore."

Meditation: **Intimate relationship with your Lord,** Psalm 139:1–6: "O LORD, You have searched me and known me. You know my sitting down and my rising up; You understand my thought afar off. You comprehend my path and my lying down, and are acquainted with all my ways. For there is not a word on my tongue, but behold, O LORD, You know it altogether. You have hedged me behind and before, and laid Your hand upon me. Such knowledge is too wonderful for me; it is high, I cannot attain it."

Recognizing God's greatness

PSALM 145:3—"Great is the LORD, and greatly to be praised; and His greatness is unsearchable."

Exclusive glory

ISAIAH 42:8—"I am the LORD, that is My name; and My glory I will not give to another."

Meditation: **Christ as Creator and Redeemer,** Colossians 1:16–18: "By Him all things were created that are in heaven and that are on earth, visible and invisible, whether thrones or dominions or principalities or powers. All things were created through Him and for Him. And He is before all things, and in Him all things consist. And He is the head of the body, the church, who is the beginning, the firstborn from the dead, that in all things He may have the preeminence."

Worship boldly

HEBREWS 4:14–16—"Seeing then that we have a great High Priest who has passed through the heavens, Jesus the Son of God, let us hold fast our confession. For we do not have a High Priest who cannot sympathize with our weaknesses, but was in all points tempted as we are, yet without sin. Let us therefore come boldly to the throne of grace, that we may obtain mercy and find grace to help in time of need."

YOUTH

By eternity's calendar, the oldest among us is young.

Anchored in youth

PSALM 71:5—"You are my hope, O Lord GOD; You are my trust from my youth."

Clean up your act

PSALM 119:9—"How can a young man cleanse his way? By taking heed according to Your word."

Time for decision

ECCLESIASTES 12:1—"Remember now your Creator in the days of your youth, before the difficult days come, and the years draw near when you say, 'I have no pleasure in them.'"

Maturing youth

LAMENTATIONS 3:27—"It is good for a man to bear the yoke in his youth."

Decision time

DANIEL 1:8—"Daniel purposed in his heart that he would not defile himself with the portion of the king's delicacies, nor with the wine which he drank; therefore he requested of the chief of the eunuchs that he might not defile himself."

Never underestimate your potential

1 TIMOTHY 4:12—"Let no one despise your youth, but be an example to the believers in word, in conduct, in love, in spirit, in faith, in purity."

Run from lust

2 TIMOTHY 2:22—"Flee also youthful lusts; but pursue righteousness, faith, love, peace with those who call on the Lord out of a pure heart."

First-class reputation

TITUS 2:6–8—"Exhort the young men to be sober-minded, in all things showing yourself to be a pattern of good works; in doctrine showing integrity, reverence, incorruptibility, sound speech that cannot be condemned, that one who is an opponent may be ashamed, having nothing evil to say of you."

STEPS Nugget

WHAT MAKES A PRAYER WARRIOR?

In 1980, I had the privilege of producing a feature motion picture on the life of Hudson Taylor, the missionary who took the gospel into the interior of China. Spending very little time in England, he had to depend solely on God to provide funds.

We filmed several of the incidents where God supplied his needs entirely by prayer. In one scene, after his wife had told him there was no more food, he clutched the Bible in his hands and said, "No more food, but all of God's promises."

Many think of Hudson Taylor as one of the greatest prayer warriors of all time.

But you and I can commune with God in the same manner Hudson Taylor did. He used the STEPS method, relating the promises in the Bible to the needs of his ministry.

So can we!

ZEAL

Having zeal means having adrenaline of the spirit, motivation for obedience and service. Also see Determination, Vision.

Altar fire

LEVITICUS 6:13—"A fire shall always be burning on the altar; it shall never go out."

Zeal with no envy

PROVERBS 23:17—"Do not let your heart envy sinners, but be zealous for the fear of the LORD all the day."

Meditation: **Zeal based on Scripture,** Acts 18:24–28: "A certain Jew named Apollos, born at Alexandria, an eloquent man and mighty in the Scriptures, came to Ephesus. This man had been instructed in the way of the Lord; and being fervent in spirit, he spoke and taught accurately the things of the Lord, though he knew only the baptism of John. So he began to speak boldly in the synagogue. When Aquila and Priscilla heard him, they took him aside and explained to him the way of God more accurately. And when he desired to cross to Achaia, the brethren wrote, exhorting the disciples to receive him; and when he arrived, he greatly helped those who had believed through grace; for he vigorously refuted the Jews publicly, showing from the Scriptures that Jesus is the Christ."

Zeal without knowledge

ROMANS 10:2—"I bear them witness that they have a zeal for God, but not according to knowledge."

Fervent zeal

ROMANS 12:10–11—"Be kindly affectionate to one another with brotherly love, in honor giving preference to one another; not lagging in diligence, fervent in spirit, serving the Lord."

Appendix A
Proof Positive

> You shall know the truth, and the
> truth shall make you free.

—JOHN 8:32

Do you have faith problems?

Are you open to the potential of a mind-boggling paradigm shift in which you take a new look at Jesus and the Bible?

In Romans 10:17, the Bible overtly states that "faith comes by hearing, and hearing by the word of God."

Are you in the mood for an experiment?

Call it quits anytime you choose.

Find a copy of the gospel of John, which is the fourth book in the New Testament. It's less than forty pages, an easy read.

First, spend a couple of hours browsing the gospel from its opening verse, "In the beginning was the Word," to the concluding phrase, "The world itself could not contain the books that would be written."

Criticize.

Question.

But read every word, each event, the entire gospel of John.

The point is for you to have a preliminary knowledge of the

content, no matter what may be your attitude toward that content.

Second, immediately if possible—otherwise, as soon as you can—read through the gospel of John again.

A bit of orientation, however, before you begin. Thumb ahead to a couple of things that are of special value to your experiment. Invest a few serious moments pondering the context surrounding each of the two quotations: "You shall know the truth, and the truth shall make you free" (8:32); and "Jesus said to him, 'I am the way, the truth, and the life. No one comes to the Father except through Me'" (14:6).

Also, before you begin your reading, I suggest a prayer, for example, "Okay, God, I'm interested. If You're out there someplace and if You can be known, reveal Yourself to me. My mind is open."

Proceed. Read the gospel of John a second time thoughtfully, with a willingness to be convinced, no matter how deep your skepticism may be or has been.

Read about each event in the life of Jesus, including miracles He performed.

Be open to your scrutiny. Your uncertainty. Doubt. But throughout the reading, pledge an open mind, an open heart.

As you near the conclusion of the gospel of John, you come to the last two verses of chapter 20. Please read them several times with an open mind and an open heart: "Jesus did many other signs in the presence of His disciples, which are not written in this book; but these are written that you may believe that Jesus is the Christ, the Son of God, and that believing you may have life in His name."

Will you?

May the Lord do for you what He has done for others with whom I have shared this experiment. For questions or comments, write:

Ken Anderson Ministries
P.O. Box 618
Winona Lake, IN 46590
findit@kconline.com

Appendix B
STEPS Spin-Offs

If you abide in Me, and My words abide in you, you will ask
what you desire, and it shall be done for you.

—JOHN 15:7

As your prayer avocation grows and matures, think of adding
expanded spin-offs to explore and enjoy. Here are some options others have pursued:

1. Develop a notebook prayer list of people and organizations you
wish to consistently remember. You can also use your notebook for
personal items, objectives, and aspirations.

2. Ask the Lord to give you a prayer partner, someone with whom
you can meet on a regular basis, sharing concerns, praying in confidence for each other's deepest needs.

3. Keep an open heart and mind to sharing the STEPS method
with another Christian. This kind of discipleship can be profoundly
fulfilling.

4. Explore the potential of setting up a Web site in which you
share experiences with others.

5. Place a classified ad, offering to pray for people in need. It could
bring some interesting and worthy responses.

6. Consider selecting a specific ministry for which to pray, an out-reach of your church, or perhaps an independent agency. Learn all you can about the ministry you select. Perhaps plan a holiday visit to its primary site.

I met a woman who believed she had received a missionary call to pray for a specific mission field.

"I am convinced my call to prayer," she said, "is as real as the call to service the Lord gave to missionaries who work full-time on that field."

My wife and I helped establish an audiovisual mission for national Christians across the Two-thirds World. We publish a monthly prayer calendar, which many of our friends use as a daily prayer guide.

If you would like to sample an example, write to:

InterComm
P.O. Box 618
Winona Lake, IN 46590

7. Pray continually. In 1 Thessalonians 5:17, the Bible tells you to "pray without ceasing." What does that mean? Could it be touching every event of the day in an attitude of prayer? The telephone rings. Take a silent moment to commit call and caller to the Lord, then pick up the phone. A stranger speaks to you, you go to an appointment, someone speaks to you angrily or critically—whatever happens, encase and undergird each encounter and event with prayer.

If you fear possible overload, select one day of the week for this procedure.

8. Create a photo album of people for whom you pray.

9. Use your church directory as a guide to prayer.

10. Go through the Psalms, Proverbs, or other selected biblical books. Chapter by chapter, verse by verse, extend and enjoy your expanding meditation expertise.

Topics Index

Ability 45

Abortion 45

Abundance 47

Access 48

Accomplishment 48

Accusation 49

Agreement 50

Alcohol 51

Angels 52

Anger 53

Answer 54

Anxiety 55

Argument 57

Asking 59

Assurance 60

Attitude 62

Authenticity 64

Authority 65

Backsliding 66

Bankruptcy 67

Behavior 69

Bible 71

Birthday 73

Blessing 74

Boldness 76

Building 77

Burden 78

Business 78

Carnality 79

Character 80

Children 82

Choice 83

Christmas 84

Church 85

Citizenship 87

Cleansing 87

Comfort 88

Commendation 89

Commitment 90

Communication 93

Compassion 94

Complacency 95

Comprehension 96

Compromise 98

Confession 99

Confidence 101

Conflict 102

Confusion 103

Consolation 104

Contentment 105

Conversion 107

Cooperation 108

Correction 109

Counsel 110

Courage 111

Covet 112

Creation 113

Crisis 115

Criticism 116

Cults 117

Danger 119

Death 119

Debt 121

Deceit 121

Decision 123

Defeat 124

Delay 125

Deliverance 126

Demons 128

Depravity 129

Depression 130

Desire 131

Despair 132

Determination 133

Disagreement 134

Disappointment 134

Discernment 135

Discipleship 137

Discipline 138

Discouragement 139

Discretion 140

Discrimination 141

Disobedience 142

Dissension 143

Divorce 144

Doctrine 146

Doubt 147

Easter 148

Ego 150

Emotions 151

Encouragement 152

Enemy 153

Envy 154

Evaluation 154

Evangelism 155

Evil 156

Example 157

Failure 159

Faith 160

Faithfulness 161

Fame 162

Family 164

Fasting 167

Father 168

Fear 169

Fellowship 170

Financial 171

Forgiveness 173

Friendship 174

Fulfillment 175

Future 176

Generosity 177

Goals 178

God 180

God's Will 181

Golden Rule 182

Gossip 183

Gratitude 184

Greed 185

Growth 185

Guidance 186

Guilt 188

Happiness 189

Hatred 190

Healing 191

Health 192

Heresy 192

Holiness 193

Holy Spirit 194

Home 195

Honesty 196

Hope 197

Hospitality 198
Humility 199
Hypocrisy 201
Immorality 202
Intro 203
Investment 206
Jealousy 206
Jesus 208
Joy 209
Kindness 210
Knowledge 211
Leadership 211
Loneliness 212
Love 213
Marriage 214
Maturity 215
Meditation 217
Mercy 224
Morality 225
Morning 226
Mother 226
Nature 227
Neighbors 228
New Year 230
Obedience 230
Old Age 231
Opposition 232
Oppression 233
Outreach 233
Pain 235
Parents 236
Patience 236
Persecution 237
Praise 238
Pregnancy 240
Pride 240
Priority 242
Prison 244
Promise 245
Protection 245

Provision 247
Purity 248
Questions 249
Rejection 250
Relationship 250
Renewal 251
Repentance 253
Ridicule 254
Romance 254
Second Coming 255
Secrets 256
Shame 257
Sickness 257
Slander 258
Sleep 259
Sorrow 259
Stewardship 260
Strength 261
Stress 262
Struggle 263
Success 264
Suffering 265
Temptation 266
Testing 268
Timidity 269
Trauma 270
Trouble 271
Trust 272
Truth 273
Unity 273
Victory 275
Vision 276
Weakness 278
Wisdom 279
Witness 280
Worry 281
Worship 282
Youth 284
Zeal 286

STEPS Nuggets Index

Computerized Prayer   207

Discover Your Seventh Sense   91

Effective Prayer Requires Hard Work
   267

Extra but Often Ordinary   229

Fasting   165

Fragrant Intercession   63

Getting Serious About Prayer   26

Inside Look at Coveting   114

Inventory   277

Layology   145

Praying Continually 163

Simplicity Is the Key   46

Spiritual Health   189

To Whom Am I Speaking?   243

Unanswered Prayer   75

Understanding the Trinity   172

What Makes a Prayer Warrior? 285

Who Believes in Demons?   127

About the Author

Ken Anderson is the founder of Gospel Films and InterComm. He has produced and directed two hundred motion pictures and videos, including *Pilgrim's Progress* and *Hudson Taylor*.

His audiovisual ministry has taken him to more than one hundred countries, including Pakistan, India, Germany, France, England, Switzerland, Transkei, Zimbabwe, and Honduras. He also served as media lecturer at the Haggai Institute in Singapore for twenty-five years.

Anderson has written more than fifty books, including the best-selling *Where to Find It in the Bible*, and has been named Feature Article Writer of the Year by the Evangelical Press Association. He has also written numerous scripts for the *Unshackled* radio broadcast.

He has been married to his wife, Doris, for sixty-one years. They have four sons and three daughters.

My master takes care of me.
I am not poor in any way.
He provides abundantly for my physical needs
And my spiritual needs as well.
He helps me do what is right
Because He keeps His promises.
Although I go through the worst trial I can imagine,
Even dying
There is nothing to be afraid of.
You are with me.
Guiding every step I take.
You treat me with honor
In front of those who want to see me dishonored.
Your blessings overwhelm me.
I know that everything that happens or will happen in my
life is an expression of your love and mercy toward me.
I am so glad I will be with you forever!

A paraphrase of the Twenty-third Psalm by Carol Wheeler Clark